TOM ROSS
THE GAME'S GONE

TOM ROSS
THE GAME'S GONE

WITH **KEITH DIXON** AND **DAVID SALT**

FOREWORDS by JASPER CARROTT and DAVID GOLD

First Publishied in Great Britain in 2016 by DB Publishing, an imprint of JMD Media Ltd

ISBN 978-1-78091-529-6

Printed and bound in the UK by Copytech (UK) Ltd Peterborough

CONTENTS

THE GAME'S GONE!
INTRODUCTION

Confucius said, 'choose a job you love and you will never have to work a day in your life,' well I have never worked a day in my 35-year radio career because I have always loved what I was doing and showed I had a passion for it. I was told by Richard Park that I was a radio practitioner and that was the best compliment I could ever receive.

Without doubt I've got the best job on the planet by a million miles. It's brilliant broadcasting to the city I love, was born in and grew up in. Every single day I can't wait to get to the studios and that is what keeps me going and of course my competitive and overwhelming desire to be the number one radio station for sport in the West Midlands. I have told my bosses at Free Radio that the first day I wake up and don't want to come to work then he won't need to get rid of me because I will pack it in. In my commentaries and phone in's I sell passion, excitement, desire, liberally laced with humour and understanding, as I take the listener on an emotional roller coaster ride.

This book is called *THE GAME'S GONE!* Why? Because I've not only said it repeatedly since 1993 and now it has sort of stuck and become one of the 'catchphrases' associated with me, along with 'You Nugget' and 'You Doughnut' – and crazy things like 'you'll do for me'. However it's also because I do believe that the game that has given me and millions of others so much pleasure and also given me a fantastic living and career 'has gone'. The game is now all about money with the needs of the fans coming way down the list. It's so far up its own backside with its insular and paranoid attitude to anyone not in it that, in my opinion, the game as a sport of the people really has gone, hence 'The Game's Gone'.

The start of 'the game's gone' began in the column I used to write for the Birmingham Sports Argus. It was at the time SKY TV got into football and what I actually wrote was, 'the game's in mortal danger from SKY TV' – not the way that they do it, because they do it brilliantly but it's the way they control the game through money, kick-off times and other things that distance the clubs from their traditional and loyal fans. And it attracts too many foreign players to the detriment of the English game and the English national team.

The phrase 'the game's gone' which I'm not sure is grammatically correct, was first said by me on the Friday night phone in on BRMB around 1993-94. That Friday night 'phone in' by the way is the longest running football 'phone in' on the dial.

Up to now I have rejected a few approaches to write my autobiography – to be honest because I wondered who the hell would want to read it? However people I respect who have written books assured me I have a story to tell. So now the time seems right. Why? Well recently I had one of my family get-togethers and I was looking at my grandkids and I thought, 'If I die tomorrow they won't know much about their granddad' and what he did in his lifetime. I know it sounds morbid but that's how you think when you get older.

So at the tail end of my career and with the Independent Radio News (I.R.N.) Gold award for '30 years outstanding service to radio' sitting proudly on a shelf at home I decided to speak with Keith Dixon, my initial ghostwriter, to see if we could work on the book together – and here we are!

Being on the radio was something I had always wanted to do; I had been a presenter on BHBN the hospital Radio station and was the man on the microphone at St Andrews and to be fair got the broadcasting bug. So when the opportunity to break into radio came I grabbed it with both hands. It wasn't long before I was offered a full-time job and to be fair, despite taking a huge drop in salary, I jumped at the chance.

It was definitely a light bulb moment for me and thankfully 39-years later the light is still on and shining just as brightly.

So after talking with Gary Newbon and Jasper Carrott I quit my job as National Sales Manager at Dun and Bradstreet where I was based in London, but lived in Birmingham. It meant me taking a 66% salary drop, handing back the company car, vacating the office in London and the responsibility for over £200m worth of business for a microphone!

But I was buzzin', at last I was where I wanted to be and I have loved every single minute even though there were some dark times which I talk frankly about.

Enjoy my story; I hope you find it a good read. It's full of stories, memories and laughs and a few tears.

I have made good decisions and bad decisions but they have always been my decisions.

I have written this book in the same way I have led my life – never short of belief in myself, striving to be number one but more concerned about living life by my own standards and not anyone else's and also doing the best I can every single day of my life. I have done most of this from memory and have done my best to ensure the dates etc are correct but if there are any errors I apologise.

And you know what, my life's been brilliant!

Read on…

ACKNOWLEDGEMENTS

Regarding the production of *THE GAME'S GONE* I would like to acknowledge the contribution of the following people:

My wife Anne, sons Thomas and Jon and daughters Tracy and Amy, for their love support and gentle criticism throughout this process, which began in January 2015.

Thanks to my grandchildren Jessica, Thomas, Laura, Mia, Freddie, Zachary, Joanna, Sophia, Amelia and Jackson, who are all very special to me and make me feel blessed and full of love for them every single day. They are one of the major motivations for the book. Also not forgetting my two grandchildren no longer with us, Izabela and Ellie Grace.

To my friends, professional colleagues, directors, managers and players for their 'kind' endorsements within the book, for them to find the time to write something on my behalf is truly humbling —seeing what people think of you is like being in the pews at your own funeral. I can only thank you all from the bottom of my heart.

Special thanks to the men who wrote The Forewords to my book – it does not often happen, having two forewords, but I like to do things differently – Jasper and David are great friends and are also an inspiration to me, guys I owe you one!

To David Salt (Salty) for his brilliant help at the toughest of times and for proof-reading and having the balls to tell me what should be in and what should not be in. And also for his structural advice to complete and polish the finished manuscript and also at times restoring my confidence about it. I couldn't have done it without your input pal.

To my initial co-writer, Keith Dixon, without whom I am sure I would never have had the discipline to sit down and put it all together in the first place and also for spending hours listening to my ramblings at Moxhull Hall Hotel. Keith is a prolific author and I can honestly say without his initial effort the book would never have happened. I can't thank you enough Keith.

Thanks also to the Moxhull Hall owner Andreas Kalavanas and his senior men Tony Sendur and Gary Kaas for the space and endless tea and coffee.

A big thank you to Free Radio for the occasional use of the boardroom.

To Roy Smilijanic, Birmingham City's official photographer for the many pictures he has made available for the book. Even though I have not been able to use them all I want to say a big thank you to one of the business's nice guys. Cheers Roy

To my great pal Colin Tattum for his fantastic and professional help in getting all the words of the draft in some sort of order.

Massive thanks to photographer Emma Smith for the cover photograph, and for including me in the 'Mr Birmingham' exhibition, which made me so proud.

But special thanks goes to the hundreds of thousands of listeners who have grown up tuning into my football programmes and Breakfast shows on BRMB, Xtra am, Capital Gold, and now Free radio in my home town of Birmingham. To me you are all friends and are what make this job so special; so thank you for letting me into your homes and lives via the airwaves. Respect to all those that I have argued and debated with over the last 35 years. I have loved every minute. It was never about being right but always about having different opinions.

And finally thanks to the publishers, DB, for getting the book out on the shelves, especially Steve Caron who despite me being a nightmare to deal with, has always been confident about the book.

DEDICATION
TOMMY ROSS – MY DAD

I have been privileged during my life and in particular my career to meet many rich and famous people. However no one has ever managed to get anywhere near my dad Tommy who is, was and always will be my only hero, and inspiration. He was what we call in Birmingham 'a proper bloke'. A man who I always admired. A man whom I always wanted to emulate but sadly failed.

My dad was a football mad tough Glaswegian who never had the proverbial pot to p*** in, never owned a car or a house and yet was rich beyond belief with love and affection for his family and with a wise head.

He was a man who had buckets of love to give and never ever short changed us kids and his grandchildren when it came to love and affection, even if we lost out in the early days with material things.

With no TV to distract us he would sit down on a Sunday afternoon and do a quiz that he had taken out of the *Scottish Sunday Post* with us kids. Or he would play Ludo, Draughts, Snakes and Ladders or Housey Housey (Bingo) to keep us amused. I remember him getting his hands on a second hand horse racing game called Escalado. We would play as a family even though some of the horses were broken. I loved my mom to bits but my dad was just the most loveable, likeable man you could ever meet. No one ever had a bad word to say about him.

I have spent my life trying to walk in his footsteps and have failed miserably.

I know he was proud of me being on the radio doing the Xtra Am breakfast show and of course doing all the football commentaries on BRMB but that would never stop him bringing me down to earth if needed.

The hardest thing I have ever had to do was speak at his funeral service. I am not ashamed to admit I broke down, as I realised I would not have my dad, my hero, my advisor, my mentor, my pal around anymore.

He did his bit in World War Two where he met my mom who was also in the army. I and each of my brothers and sisters have one of his medals and it's something I will treasure till the day I die.

Dad never stole a thing in his life, never hurt anyone, and I never heard him utter a bad word about anybody else either.

He was a truly remarkable man who taught me three things about how to live my life that still stand me in good stead to this day.

- To live my life by my standards and not anyone else's.
- Never be ashamed to pick up my wages, in other words work hard.
- Never let anyone take the piss.

I miss him every single day and when I have tough decisions to make and need advice I think to myself 'what would Dad have said or done'?

The end of his life was a misery in Heartlands Hospital and I will never forgive them for what they put him through for six weeks. I would have given every single penny and thing I own just to have him stay with me for a few years longer, however I genuinely believe he guides me by how he taught me to live my life.

FOREWORD
JASPER CARROTT

FORWARD is a word that means a great deal to me and Tom.

Firstly, it is the motto of our beloved City of Birmingham, a city that has been our home for some six or seven decades. It is where we both grew up and where our lives, attitudes and careers were forged to a background of post-war austerity and dramatic social change.

Our childhood was one of ration books, Co-op numbers, Prudential reps, Saturday mornings at the cinema, lying to the rent collectors, football on the Recs and many more aspects of living in sparse but innocent times that are so foreign to the generation of today.

Forward is also descriptive of our attitude to life in general. We look to the future more so than the past although never forgetting where we came from. Our feet are firmly on the ground without a doubt, but never still.

Tom is another Brummie that's done good. From humble beginnings he has achieved through hard work and perseverance a success that has been recognised in many ways with awards and accolades from both public and peers.

When I first knew him he was a bustling, enthusiastic electrician who was in charge of a company that dealt in mysterious, technical activities that were beyond my comprehension. He came to my house and re-wired and re-fitted all the ancient electrics that were a danger to anyone who lived there. When he had finished it all looked great, but was even more lethal than it was before!

It did not surprise me therefore when he told me he had decided to change direction and go into radio presenting and commentating. It was a dream that he had fostered for many years, but it was a major change to make, considering he had family and financial commitments to consider. We talked long and hard and I left him to make the final decision in his own time, the result of which you are now reading.

Surprisingly, like me, Tom was not a natural to the business in the early days. He had to learn from the ground up, how to deal with all the complexities and pitfalls, to suffer the ups and downs without getting disheartened and to keep his nose to the grindstone. I have said many times that there are more talented comedians than me, but I don't know many who work harder. Tom is the same, he works harder than any other presenter I know, but it has paid off.

Not all the payments have been beneficial mind; when you spend as much time as he does travelling, writing, reporting, well something has to give. Only the Pope has spent more time at the altar than Tom. At his last wedding his ex-wives arrived on a double decker bus with another behind carrying his offspring.

In the book you are about to read you will come face-to-face with a very honest man. He will tell you all about his life and career, the many stories and tales of the characters he has met, the frustrations, the glories, the sad times and the good times, a few of which I have had the privilege of sharing.

Tom has been important in my life, a loyal friend and trusted companion for nearly forty years. I am not the only one. You will know why after the last page.

FOREWORD
DAVID GOLD

From the moment we joined up with David Sullivan to take a 50% share of Birmingham City Football Club Tom's name kept on being mentioned as someone in the media you could trust.

So my brother Ralph and I started to listen to Tom's very popular post match phone in. After one game we were stuck in traffic listening to Tom when one of the Blues callers said, 'Tom can you thank David Sullivan and those other two geezers for all they have done since they bought Blues'. Ralph and I knew then we would have to improve our profile or risk always being known as 'the other two geezers' even though we owned half of the football club.

Over the years Tom and I became great friends and still are to this day. We were friends both professionally and personally and I was delighted to attend his wedding to Anne in the summer of 2015. We have had some fantastic times at the Blues including the Worthington Cup Final, The Play-off Final, the promotion game at Reading to name but a few.

Listening to Tom after every game became essential listening for us and helped us get to know and understand the Blues culture. I also did a number of BRMB Q & A forums with Tom and Karren Brady and found those extremely helpful and a great way to get our message out to the supporters.

During the time I was at Birmingham, Tom was extremely fair in his dealings with the club and one thing that most impressed us was that he would always get the facts before speaking on the radio whether it was a criticism or praise.

Tom is a well-known Bluenose, however we found when talking to directors of other clubs in the Birmingham area that he had the same reputation with them for being professional, fair and honest.

Socially we have had some brilliant times, some of which I am sure will be written about in this book. We have had many laughs and also shed some tears over the 20 plus years we have known each other, yet he has remained a stalwart throughout.

I will always be grateful for the wonderful words he spoke at my mom Rose's memorial service in Birmingham. He is a true man of the people and has great integrity. Tom always says it as it is and will not compromise on his core values. He will never tell you what you want to hear but he will tell you the truth.

He was always welcome in the Birmingham boardroom and will always be welcome in my home as I am delighted and honoured to call him my great pal.

CHAPTER ONE
TIN BATHS AND OUTSIDE LOOS

In 1947 I was born to Tommy and Mary Ross at 2/437 New John Street West in Birmingham B19. You went up the entry at the side of number 437, which was Millman's shop and you came into a yard with five houses we were number two.

It was in between Summer Lane and Newtown Row, which was part of the Birmingham inner city slums, where Hockley met Aston, so it was real Villa territory.

Back-to-Back dwellings (you couldn't call them houses) were built around an entry and everyone in the area was known to 'live up the entry'. Our entry, which was down the side of Millman's, the general store where Mom used to get what she needed, 'on the strap' or 'on the tick' during the week with full payment expected on pay day (Friday). Outside Millman's was a chewing gum vending machine, which had Wrigley's and Beech Nut chewing gum to buy, however I'd worked it out that if you put your money in and hit the front of the machine in a certain way then two packs would come out!

Another memory of Millman's was frozen Jubbly orange drinks, which were never designed to be frozen, but were a real alternative to an ice-lolly but if the Jubbly popped out of its carton then it was impossible to get it back in. So my mates and I would find it hilarious if you managed to 'pop' someone else's Jubbly.

I am sure people thought we were Japanese because when the rent man called and knocked the door it was my job to shout 'shin't in'.

The Ross family was a big 'un, eight of us survived from a potential family of ten; alongside Mom and Dad there was Frank, who was from Dad's first marriage, me, John and Danny together with Cathy and Lesley. We lost two babies at birth, one of which was a twin sister to Lesley. As kids so often do Cathy and I fought like crazy but we grew out of that. We are a close family without living in each other's pockets.

My sister Lesley-Ann has been a rock to the family. She looked after Mom and Dad as they got into their old age and suffered from Dementia. Lesley has been brilliant and has taken on the role as matriarch of the Ross family. She is a female Don

Corleone. You would be ill advised to mess with her. As one mugger found out when he tried to steal her handbag in Erdington – I think he might still be unconscious.

I was born into abject poverty and by poverty I don't mean we didn't have an iPhone 6. I am saying we had less than nothing and in those post war years there were no benefits. You had to make do. Often I had holes in my socks, pumps (plimsolls) and trousers.

There were five homes down our entry, the one on the right which backed onto Millman's was occupied by the Millman's, and on the left were the Hodgetts, in the bottom left-hand corner was Mrs Tandy, an older lady who used to get fed up with me and my elder brother Frank playing football in the yard in the 60s, so much so that when she could get her hands on our red plastic Frido football she would burst it before returning it – we didn't like her for that but it only stopped us for a little time as you could repair a Frido with a hot knife!

I can't remember who lived in the middle, but we lived in the right-hand corner 'house' – when you went through the door you were in – in the left-hand corner was a cupboard with the gas meter, there was a fireplace, a cooker and in the right-hand corner a door, which led to the pantry, which was really the top of the cellar with a sink with running cold water.

The front had a bay sash window, which had a settee in front of it, there was a drop-leaf table and some chairs and that was it! The only bedroom was occupied by Mom and Dad and we slept in the attic – all six of us with Dad's Army coat draped over us to keep us warm. The attic always doubled as a play area and I had the habit of hanging out the attic window. I was always doing daft things.

In those early days we had no electricity only gas, which meant gas mantle lighting. That was only downstairs so you needed a candle in the bedroom or attic.

Bath nights were once a week usually on a Sunday. The kettle and saucepan would be on the stove heating the water for the tin bath that would be sat in front of the fire. I would be first (thank God).

The gas lighter would come round every night to illuminate the yard by lighting the lamppost. I was nine years of age before we got electricity! And then only downstairs.

We had a cellar and it was my job to go down and get the coal. It was pitch black and as a young boy I was petrified about what might be down there.

However I absolutely adored my childhood – I had free hobnail boots courtesy of the *Mail* newspaper! I'd get up at 7 o'clock, wash in bitterly cold water, fetch the paper and then get back home to share in a massive pan of porridge – Scottish style i.e. salt instead of sugar – all washed down with sterilized milk (it kept better) – we had no luxuries but occasionally we would get a bar of Lifebuoy soap to replace the carbolic. What a treat?

There was no peer pressure as a kid, as none of my mates had anything either and were as poor as us. Not like today when parents are always under pressure to get the latest gizmo so there kids can be like their pals.

Me and my sister Catherine circa 1950- see I told you we were poor.

Christmas was something of a non-event in those early days; the idea of wanting a new bike for Christmas never entered your head. Mom would save what she could throughout the year with the local Christmas club at The House That Jack Built store on Newtown Row and then buy us clothes,

She always thought if we were to have an accident then Christmas was the best time because our underwear would be new and clean! Perish the thought we were knocked down in August?

If we did have any toys they were usually games and jigsaws that we could all play with.

It was the same with holidays – we never went on holiday ever. Instead we went to stay with our relatives in Scotland, usually Aunt Peggy and Uncle Sammy in Glasgow at 3 up 61 Rumford St, Bridgeton. It was in the East End of Glasgow and a staunch Rangers area, which was a problem as my Dad was Celtic daft. Dad took me to many Celtic – Rangers derbies at Celtic Park where we would stand in 'The Jungle'.

We would always spend a day at Saltcoats, a seaside town that has more jellyfish on the beach than anywhere I know.

Sometimes I would travel to Belfast with my Granny Sullivan and end up staying with my scary Aunt Lizzie in Carrickfergus, which was a lovely town on the Loch not far from Belfast. Aunt Lizzie scared the life out of me. She was a staunch Catholic who said decades of the rosary every single night and was always saying 'Jesus Mary and Joseph' to anything and everything or 'Holy Mary Mother Of God' what did you do that for.

Clothes were never a consideration in those days, I wore short grey trousers held up with a stripy 'S' belt (the clasp was shaped like a snake) but mine was so old the elasticity had gone so I had to tie the two halves together, grey socks and black pumps. Not exactly the height of fashion but I didn't care because all my mates were dressed the same. No one was any different. There was no pressure on us like there is on the kids of today who want to wear better brands than their classmates, have the best telephone and be dropped off to school in a top of the range car. Although the Jones' existed no one was trying to keep up with them! In fact they were probably poorer than the Rosses if that was possible.

Having said that if you owned a football, not that I ever did, you were always first picked at playtime.

Mom and Dad had met in Belgium whilst both serving in their respective sections of the Army. Dad was always reluctant to talk about his wartime experiences but each of his children got one of his medals when he died so he must have done his bit. Jobs were few and far between in those immediate post-war years – Mom worked part-time as a bar maid at The Britannia Inn on the corner of New John Street West and Summer Lane whilst Dad got a few hours there as a pot man.

But things eased as we moved into the late 50s and I can remember both Mom and Dad working hard. Mom used to go off to work in Hatchett Street along with her sister Pauline wearing her hair in a turban with an apron over her pinafore dress and when she came home she would spend hours removing the swarf (little slivers of brass) out of her fingers using Swarfega – these were really tough times.

Things really started to improve for us when Dad got a great job at Fisher & Ludlow on the Chester Road. He went to work in overalls with his 'pieces' wrapped in paper and he loved it and went on to eventually be promoted to a 'gang leader', which I suppose is something like a foreman for a small team of men who had to reach a daily quota to earn their money. If one man slacked they didn't earn so it was the gang leaders job to ensure they did. Sometimes he would wear a cow-gown just like the one Ronnie Barker wore in the TV programme *Open All Hours*.

Dad was 'sexist' before the phrase became commonplace – but not in a nasty way. Let me explain! He would never let me wash the dishes and would say that was my sister Cathy's job, but likewise she would never go down the cellar for the coal or light the fire because that was man's work according to my Dad.

It was also my job to go and get the coal from the coal-merchants yard in Moorsom Street off Summer Lane. They would give you a barrow and you would leave a deposit to ensure you brought it back. Loaded up with coal and with its heavy metal wheels made it murder to get home. Once home the coal was put in the cellar, which is where it stayed until we needed a fire – then it was down to me to go down the steps to the cellar, complete with rats and mice, in the pitch black with a piece of lighted paper instead of a candle. How I didn't break my neck or set the house on fire heaven only knows. Health and Safety did not exist. Then I had to light the fire using a metal draw tin and a piece of paper to create a vacuum so that it 'caught' and then we would all sit around the fire and only move when the front of our legs were red, mottled and sore – but we were warm. Dad never owned a car or a house but he provided a safe and protected life for his family.

I remember vividly four aspects of our diet in those days:

- Mom, because we were Catholic would have the edict that 'we never eat meat on a Friday' the fact that we never ate meat any other day was immaterial to her unless of course it was a tin of luncheon meat (Spam) – so that meant Friday was, when we could afford it, Fish 'n Chips night – Dad would buy a 'six of chips' (6d equivalent to two and a half pence today) and a piece of fish for a shilling (equivalent to five pence today) and then split it equally between the eight of us – no mean feat.

- Occasionally on a Sunday we would get a Swiss Roll for tea and Dad would cut it into about 200 slices – they were so thin you could see through 'em.

- Dad could feed us all on one egg – using a combination of scrambled egg and eggy bread, which we called 'switched' egg.

- To keep us fit and healthy the council provided Castor Oil and Malt by the spoonful but it could not keep away chest problems (we all had it due to the smog – a combination of smoke and fog) and the nits (every kid had nits – on a Sunday night after a tin bath Mom would have me and my sister Cathy kneeling in front of her so she could run the metal 'nit' comb through our hair. Bad enough for me but you could hear my sister's screams from Summer Lane as she had long curly hair.
- Any health problems we had to go to Gem Street clinic for anything we had to have done – the dentist – the nit nurse and the doctor. I suffered with my chest and still do to this day – I had to have X-rays every six months and the treatment I had was to sit under sun lamps which improved things, as I was a TB suspect as a kid – that's why I always feel better when I am in the Spanish sun. I had chronic bronchitis due to the damp conditions we lived in, plus that smog – no wonder.

The 60s were an improvement on the 50s as Dad had got a job as a gang leader at Fisher & Ludlow in Castle Bromwich (it's the Jaguar plant now). Things were so good we acquired a third or fourth hand old stereogram. On a Sunday Mom would play her 78s which included Little Richard, Buddy Holly, Johnny Ray, she loved to rock & roll but she also loved ballads and one of her favourites was Malcolm Vaughan's *St Theresa of the Roses* – She also loved her Irish songs while my Dad loved his Scottish songs so my introduction to music was varied to say the least.

My Dad would be playing his Jimmy Shand music and Andy Stewart songs while my Mom would be singing *If your Irish Come into the Parlour* or *I'll Tell Me Ma* and in my mind I can still hear her now singing at the top of her voice *My Name is McNamara I'm The Leader of the Band*.

On Sunday night we would listen to Radio Luxembourg on frequency 208 or *Journey into Space* – that's when I became a radio nut – no television then as only the posh people had a TV. The definition of posh to me was those who had an inside toilet, a bathroom and a privet hedge. I didn't see grass until I was 11!

My Mom and Gran would tell me about the racism they suffered in Brum when they first moved here from Northern Ireland. There was real hatred, she would see signs saying 'NO BLACKS NO IRISH' in fact she was expelled from The Rosary for hitting a man who called her an 'Irish Tinker'.

I went to St Chad's RC School from infants through to seniors and I loved it, although I didn't love getting the slipper off Mr Conklin or the cane from the feared Headmistress Sister Etna. My great mates in those days were Micky Allsop, whose daughter Joanne is part of the senior management of Birmingham City, Leo Sharpe (whose son is Lee Sharpe, the footballer), George Gifford, Foxy, Charlie Ford, William Burke, John Williams, Michael McMahon, Micky Price, Gerrard Clark, Gerry Keogh, Joseph Bibby, Hugie Halpin, and many more whose names escape me.

In the playground with my mates at St Chads RC School around 1962

Something happened when I was 11 years old, which still affects me today – it was Christmas and after visiting the Lewis's department store to see Father Christmas and Uncle Holly arrive. Me and some of my mates were playing on the St Chad's Cathedral steps when John Williams threw a bottle which smashed and cut the back of my leg.

The ambulance was called and they took me to the General Hospital where they treated me and sent me home, but I was in pain for days and had to go back. They finally diagnosed that I had ripped my Achilles muscle, which they had not initially noticed. To this day I cannot full extend my left foot, which is my kicking foot – I sometimes wonder if that stopped me developing my football to the maximum – mind you then it was considered to be 'one of those things' an accident. However today it would probably result in a multi-million pound lawsuit.

My biggest and hardest challenge came when I had an accident at nine years old that left me blind in my left eye. I don't ever talk about it and never make it an excuse for anything either. Despite it, I managed to play football to a good non-league standard and become a respected football commentator for one of the biggest local radio stations in the country. I made a decision at a young age that I would forget about it and never let it stand in the way of anything I wanted to do. To be honest the fact that it happened at so young an age was the best thing because it meant my right eye compensated for it and adjusted to maximise my peripheral vision. I have never ever talked to anyone, family or friends about it because had I done so, it would mean I accepted it was a problem and I just didn't. By refusing to accept it as a problem meant that I could never use it as an excuse for anything from playing football to commentating on the world cup.

I had a spate of bad luck because around the same time I got bitten by the Midland Counties' milkman's horse, which has resulted in me, still to this day having a genuine fear of horses.

My Mom had some great phrases based on her inherited Irish wisdom. She would say, 'I am going to whitewash this ceiling yellow' or 'whose coat is this jacket'? Or 'you three are a fine pair'.

When I played up she would say, 'You wait until your father gets home!' but Dad never did anything unless he was pushed, it was always my Mom that disciplined us and sometimes with my Dads webbed army belt.

She was quicker on the draw than John Wayne! If I was cheeky and ran she could get her shoe off and hit me with it before I reached the door. My dad was rarely more than an interested bystander.

And I remember my Mom ironing – we had a metal iron, which she would put on the gas to get it hot, spit on it and then iron with it. That's how they did it. No secret about it, but when I was young my Dad had a suit and it went to the pawnshop on a Monday and he picked it up on Friday. Mom used a bit of brown paper to iron the creases into his suit; you know water on the brown paper and iron your creases in.

One of my jobs was to go and get 'the messages' a Scottish phrase for shopping. The Co-op (I should be able to remember my Mom's dividend 'Divi' number) in Summer Lane was where she liked to get her shopping as it was cheaper than Millman's the small shop at the top of our entry.

She would send me for the messages and say to me 'get a handy carrier' which was a brown paper bag with string handles. Sometimes I was sent to a greengrocers in Farm Street because they sold 'peeled' potatoes. This was because with both Mom and Dad working it was easier. The ready peeled potatoes were kept in water in a bucket. So after buying them I'd be halfway home up Summer Lane when the water soaked into the handy carrier and the spuds would be falling out the bottom of it and I have to run all over the place to pick 'em up. Happy Days?

I remember my surroundings really well, if you walked up New John Street West to Summer Lane on the left-hand corner was a cake/pie shop, next to that Baines the fishing tackle shop. I became great friends with Colin Baines who tried to get me into fishing, but I wasn't having any of that. On the opposite of the road was the Brittannia Inn.

On the right hand corner was a sweet shop, which sold hot Vimto while on the opposite corner was the Post Office.

To the right of the sweet shop heading down Summer Lane was an outdoor called The Vine. Next was the Co-op, After the Post Office on the opposite side of the road was Allens the chip shop, the newsagents and the Police Station a bit further down on the corner of Bridge Street.

Further down Summer Lane was Doctor Hamilton's our GP. He only seemed to prescribe Gee's linctus for anything that was wrong with you.

The Britannia pub was known as 'the Brit' where occasionally I would go round the back nick some beer bottles take 'em back into the pub's outdoor to return them and get the deposit back on the bottles. This often paid for me to go swimming with my mates at Woodcock Street swimming baths. However eventually the gaffer worked it and started marking the bottles – so I was rumbled and had to do a runner. Not a nice thing for a good Catholic boy.

All that just to get threepence so I could go swimming. My mom got me a second hand pair of swimming trunks that looked good until you went into the water. They were made of a fabric that when wet would hang around my knees when I got out of the water. Nevertheless it was a big treat for me to visit to the swimming baths because at St Chad's we had nothing other than a playground, so there was the added bonus of getting clean, as we only had a once a week bath in the tin bath at home.

At St Chad's in Brearley Street upstairs housed the seniors while the infants were downstairs. The junior school was in Shadwell Street just behind St Chad's Cathedral. The lovely Mr Wells was the Headmaster.

There we had a playground upstairs and two on the ground floor because the building was horseshoe style.

Because the school was so small we would have to leave the building for PE, swimming, metalwork and woodwork. It was on a corporation bus to Burford Road

St Chads RC -my Infant and Senior school

playing fields for PE but we had to walk to Woodcock Street for swimming. It was the same for metalwork and woodwork that meant a walk to Alma Street School.

What did I learn from those early days of poverty? A very valuable lesson. If you can't afford it don't have it and I apply that philosophy to this day. I learnt early in my life the value of money.

I am not tight by any means, but I always want enough money to cover for every eventuality. I owe no one a single penny. I have a credit card of course which is paid off in full every month on the dot. That is not me being smug and boasting, but it's the philosophy instilled in me by my upbringing and seeing my Mom and Dad worrying about the rent and paying off the 'provident man'. Even when I got married at a young age and had a baby boy and was broke most of the time I would rather not have whatever it was than be in debt. I think it's right that if you want something bad enough then you should work hard and save for it.

One of the reasons I have never moved to a really big house, even when I could afford it was that I never wanted that financial millstone around my neck. I never wanted to be in a position where I needed the boss more than he needed me. So if I ever lost my job I would be able to cope. That was my take on life and money. And of course it shows my insecurities. I have always worried about losing my job. Call it old fashioned and sexist, but I wanted to provide for my family and to do that I had to work. That is why I have always worked harder than, or as hard as, anyone because I wanted to be the last one out the door.

I never had the pressures young people have today, well I did have pressure, but of a different sort. My pressures were about feeding and clothing my family. Today the pressures seem to be owning the latest iPhone or iPad or flat screen TV. Today's kids think they are poor if they don't have the latest iphone 6. When Anne started on about getting the latest ipad or iphone for her birthday I went crazy and got her an iRon (only joking). So today young people are under different pressures and to be honest, in my opinion some people equate happiness and contentment with having the latest expensive gadgets and or other material things

When I was a young man I remember talking to my Granny Sullivan about my ambitions and what I wanted to be when I left School, I said to her that one day I wanted own a Rolex watch and a Jaguar E-Type car, I've got the watch but I haven't got the E-Type – yet!

When she heard this my Gran said, 'People like us don't own cars son'. That stuck with me and made me even more determined to work hard and escape poverty. So yes I am proud of my achievements – a kid with limited education – no Grammar school, no College, no University got to do the best job in the world in my opinion.

To use a football analogy, life hits you with lots of tackles and kicks – well in life just like on the football field I never shirked a tackle and although I have never been the best at anything I have always done my best. That meant I could sleep at night and look my kids in the face.

Like lots of people I came to a crossroads in my life, let me explain!

At School, as I was just in my teenage years I wanted and needed to belong so I, like others, ended up in a gang.

My life changed suddenly as it was a bad crowd to be with, but no one forced me it was my decision and I could have walked away at any time but didn't, so I blame no one but myself. When I say they were bad they were not muggers, burglars, or criminals but were naughty and trying to act big time when we were anything but, in fact we were pathetic, however, as I now realise, we were on a path that could have so easily led to worse things,

I was desperate to be accepted so I went along with them, nicking sweets from shops – nothing serious but it was wrong. Then we decided we would run away to Sutton Coldfield – imagine that fleeing to Sutton Coldfield, which we chose on the basis that we believed 'they will never find us there!' We kept our escape provisions (the sweets and food we had nicked) on top of a concrete building in Aston Park. Anyway the time came and four or five of us left home and walked to Sutton Coldfield where we just wandered around the streets. (I was supposed to be staying the night at my Grans) It got later and later until around 2 am we were picked up by a Copper on a push bike in Sutton who threatened us with his big black torch.

He called for a Black Maria to take us back to Bridge Street Police Station and they put us in the cells – for no reason other than to teach us a lesson I guess. They contacted our parents and they came to the station to collect us. All my mates' parents were in tears and hugging and kissing their sons. However not mine! I remember my Mom's face it was thunderous and I thought, 'I am in for it'. No hugging or kissing just my Mom saying in front of the policemen, 'Wait till I get you home'. But she couldn't wait. Every ten yards or so on the walk back down New John Street West she'd whack me round the back of my head. I think it would be fair to say that whilst Mom was doing the whacking Dad was an active supporter of her actions. I got a good hiding from Mom when we were home and I was sobbing and saying stuff like, 'it wasn't me it was the others', in other words lying through my teeth. There was none of the bravado that I had showed with the gang.

The last thing Mom said to me before she went to bed, was, 'You can talk to a thief but you can't talk to a liar because you never know if he's telling you the truth'.

That left me and Dad downstairs – he was a stocky, hard-drinking, non-swearing Glaswegian and like most men of his era was reluctant to show his emotions but on that night we had our first Father and Son real conversation. It wasn't easy for either of us, as in those days it was the norm for children to be seen but not heard.

It wasn't a lecture but he opened up to me by telling me things about himself. He told me how he had been stabbed with a bayonet in Glasgow by a rival football fan while wearing his Celtic scarf. I realised later in my life that he was trying to get me to talk and through talking help me shape my life for a better future.

That talk was the greatest thing to happen to me in my life because we were not a family to have in depth conversations or make outward shows of affection, and even to this day I am not a tactile person.

As I was blaming the others for me bringing trouble to the family door my Dad suddenly said, 'son you have to live your life by your standards and not by other peoples standards', this was his wise head putting me straight as I said in my introduction.

However I was also grounded and was told that I had to give up my Saturday job, which was helping one of the Mothers Pride bakers to deliver bread and cakes to the shops. I loved that job and Dad by stopping me doing it taught me another valuable lesson. Do wrong and there is a punishment and that punishment must hurt and it did. But I went to bed and could not get out of my head how much I had let my Mom and Dad down.

We had nothing and lived in poverty but my Mom was a proud woman who would never take a penny that didn't belong to her and would rather go without. We were always warned not to being trouble to her door. I did and I am still ashamed to this day that I let them down, as they did not deserve it.

That moment changed my outlook completely and it has subsequently taught me that the relationship you have with your parents has a lot to do with how successful you become. I cherished my parents because they gave me the basics: character and discipline.

It was after this incident that I decided I wanted to make them proud of me and so wanted to stay on at school and get my GCEs and a decent job. I spoke to my teachers and have to say they were surprised that I wanted to stay on and buckle down and study. I did though and achieved over 25 external exam results in many subjects, but mainly Commerce, Accounts, Maths and English. I had a lot of catching up to do but the teachers at St Chad's were brilliant and helped me enormously. I ended up as Head Boy and Head Altar Boy at St Chad's Cathedral. Boy had I changed.

I never swore or raised my voice to my Mom. However on one occasion, when I was about 40, and had popped into Mom and Dad's to have a cup of tea and chat after working at a match that Blues had lost. As she usually did Mom started talking about the game, Trevor Francis this and Trevor Francis that, so that in the end I just said, 'Oh, for God's sake Mom', and a voice from behind the newspaper said, 'That's your Mother your talking to!' and that was that, I shut up quick.

They had some difficult times and on one occasion Mom walked out on Dad when I was around 10 and to this day I can remember hearing him sobbing and begging her to stay. Mom, who was a good-looking woman had met someone else and left. She later realised she had made a mistake but she did not move straight back in, as she stayed with Mrs Phillips in a house right by our entry for a while for reasons I never understood. She moved back in a few days later and all was back to normal. And that is the way it stayed until they both passed away.

However because of this my elder brother Frank had a real problem with Mom and it had a long-lasting effect on his relationship with her.

I am sure that this experience has also had an effect on me and my relationship with women.

Whether Dad's chat with me worked or not is for other people to judge but I have been teetotal all my life and have never smoked, not even tried a cigarette.

Shortly after the running away from home incident I became an altar boy at St. Chad's Cathedral before eventually becoming a head altar boy serving mass in Latin virtually every day. I think Mom thought I might end up as a priest as I used to go away on retreats and it was a really important part of my life at the time.

I became a Pioneer, which is a Catholic organisation that vows to abstain from alcohol for life.

From that day forward I led my life based on Dad's mantra which to reiterate was:
- Live your life by your standards and not anyone else's.
- Never be ashamed to pick up your wages (in other words work hard and earn every penny).
- Never do anyone any harm but never let anyone take the piss.

Shortly after the incident with the police I was told I was going to live with my Granny Sullivan. I protested saying 'What about school?' but I was told I would have to get up even earlier and catch the bus into town – so no help there then. So there it was another chapter opening up in my life moving out of the slums to live at 30 Yockleton Road, Lea Village. It was a different world –

My Grans house had an inside bathroom with hot and cold water and a toilet – how posh was that and by the way it had a privet hedge? As well as front and back gardens. This was brilliant for a kid from the slums. Let me point out It really wasn't posh at all but compared to the inner city back to back slums it was.

There was so much countryside with real woods such as Chelmsley, Yorkswood and Bluebell, while we played football over Donkeys Hollow by the railway line – I loved it!

I loved my Grandad John Sullivan to bits – he was a man who worked hard and when the work was finished loved a drink. It was the drink that eventually killed him. He was a tough Belfast navvy and ex Royal Navy man, but was also a man with a heart of gold and lots of love for his grandchildren even though he gave my Gran a hard time. I just loved living there. Also living there was my Aunt Pauline, her husband Roy and my cousin Eddie, who was only a toddler.

Grandad always had dogs and in particular Staffordshire Bull Terriers and they were brilliant. I had great fun taking them for walks over the fields with my Grandad.

Times were still tough, so I had to earn some money to pay for bus fares etc. and to help Gran with the bills, so I got myself not one but two paper rounds. One was at Scrivens in Lea Village. My round included Hurstcroft Road, Gressel Lane, and

Moodyscroft Road and one of my customers turned out to be Fred Atkinson the father of Ron Atkinson, who is still a big pal of mine to this day.

After I finished my round at Scrivens I would eat breakfast and get the 14E bus to town where I did a second paper round at WH Smiths. This was delivering the Birmingham Post and the Financial Times to the offices in Newhall Street. That done I would run to St. Chad's in Brearley Street in time to play football with my pals before the bell rang for lessons to start at 9 am

This wasn't to earn money for holidays or gadgets but to help my Gran and pay for my keep.

I was not naturally gifted at school and had to work hard to pass exams but I always did my best after my light bulb moment with my Dad. You might find this hard to believe but even to this day, all 69 years, I wake up every morning and say to myself that 'I am going to do the best I can today and if that's not good enough then tough'.

Growing up at St. Chad's was great for me, particularly when I was in years five and six and in what they called the Commercial class. I had decided not to leave at the age of 15 and that was a big decision because the family needed the money I would earn from working.

I was determined to stay on at school and cram as much in as I could to catch up on those wasted years. I knew this was a massive opportunity and probably the last for me to get a career. David Begley, the Deputy Headmaster kept asking me 'Are you sure?' because he knew the financial implications of a boy from my circumstances staying on at school would bring. Also I had not been the best at school until after the police incident, so he probably thought that I was wasting my time. However I was determined to stay on and get my GCE's etc. as I knew it would help me get a good job.

I am forever grateful to my Mom and Dad for supporting me in that decision particularly as it worked out well, I got over 25 external certificates including O Levels and found I had a real bent for mathematics. I guess I got that from my Dad who loved a bet and could always work out the odds and potential payouts in his head. Sometimes in the early days I would 'run his bet' (no betting shops or on-line betting sites in those days) – just a man shiftily standing on the corner of Moorsom Street. Dad had wrapped the money in his betting slip and I handed it over, no receipt it was all done on trust.

At School I just loved commerce and principles of accounts and because I was good at it I made up my mind I wanted to be an accountant.

At that time I spent a good part of my day looking after other classes, the rest of the time I was in David Begley's bookkeeping and commerce classes because of my desire to be an Accountant.

I became Head Boy of St Chad's in my final year when I was 16 which was a great honour and privilege for a scruff like me. It meant I had the authority to dish out lines to pupils who broke the rules. This was my first taste of leadership.

Making Head Boys speech at St Chads 1964

I remember just before I left at 17 as head-boy I had to deliver the awards night speech to the whole school. Father Nightingale wrote it I just had to read it, so I guess that was my first public speaking gig. That was just days before I left. I was a gregarious outgoing laugh a minute boy in my final two years.

I left St Chad's in July 1964 and decided I would take a gap weekend. I left school on the Friday and started work on the Monday. However deep down I didn't want to leave school as I felt secure but it was time to go out and earn a living. The school got me an interview at Gothic Electrical in Hospital Street for a job in the Accounts department. I must have done well enough in the interview because I left school on the Friday and on Monday turned up at Gothic Electrical Supplies Limited.

I was due to meet a guy called Fred Dawson who was the general manager and who would introduce me to the accounts department, however he said they had a problem in the buying department and would I help out there until they filled it and then I could move to the accounts department.

So I started there and was earning the princely sum of £3.10s per week and of course most of that went to Mom, although she did have a rule which was no matter how much I earned she would only take £3 off me, which was fine but at the start of my working life I was left with ten bob. I really enjoyed the Buying Department and working for Bill Cheadle who was ex-RAF. I stayed there and never did get to Accounts. By the time I was 18 I had bought myself an Austin A35 van in blue, registration 817 GVP, funny how you always remember the registration number of your first car.

31

It was around 1967–68 that I started teaching myself to play the guitar after buying a second-hand jumbo guitar I saw in a shop window for five quid. I bought second-hand books such as Bert Weedon's *Play In A Day* and would sit for hours annoying neighbours and family alike with continual renditions of *My Bonnie Lies Over The Ocean* and other such ditties including lots of Irish songs such as *I'll Tell My Ma*, I found it very therapeutic and stress relieving and it became very useful at family get togethers.

It was at Gothic Electrical that I got my first taste of entertaining. They would hold free and easy nights for the staff where members of the staff would perform. I suppose it was like an early *Britain's Got Talent*, but more like Birmingham's Got Talent. I was one of the shows organisers and they were great fun. I and a colleague and friend John Stott, who was from Bolton teamed up, John and I played guitars performing as Sonny and Cher in the full outfits. Don't ask who was Cher? We did *I Got You Babe* we also did stuff like *If I Had a Hammer*. I remember Fred Dawson calling us into his office and presenting us with a 'pen' each and saying you too could have a future in show business; little did he know. John and I also went around a few pubs performing our small repertoire of songs and handing round a pint glass to earn a few pennies. But it soon petered out as I left Gothic because I was getting married.

However my taste for performing in front of people was then limited to family parties especially New Year's Eve when the Ross clan came down from Glasgow. It was my job, as the only non-drinker, to play the guitar and get everyone singing along to Scottish and Irish songs. These do's sometimes lasted two days. I played till my fingers bled, now where have I heard that before? Bryan Adams of course and later you can hear about my bizarre meeting with the rock legend.

One of the ways I made extra money was at weekends when I would help Bobby Bent the milkman, so whilst he was enjoying a bacon sandwich with his female customers I was delivering the milk, I'm sure many of his customers thought I was the milkman.

My best pal at this time was Derek Lum and we were inseparable and boy did we have some fun in our white T-shirts and ice blue skin-tight jeans with Cuban heeled boots. His Dad was the caretaker at St George's School in what is now Newtown. His bedroom was on the front of the bungalow. We used to regularly climb out of the window and take the short walk into town to meet up with a couple of girls. We would come back at all hours and get in the same way we had got out. One day we climbed out only to meet his Dad, so that was the end of that. We had no cares and enjoyed life to the full.

I also worked at the Surfside Stop coffee and burger bar at the bottom of Constitution Hill. I started downstairs washing the plates and coffee cups. I gradually made my way up and was looking after the downstairs for a year or so. However I was also in work at Gothic Electrical at 8.30am yet was not leaving the Surfside Stop until 3am.

To be fair it was later if I went up to the Penthouse Suite nightclub, which was above the coffee bar.

Eventually I gave all that up because I decided I wanted to get into sales, mainly because you controlled how much you earned based on how hard you worked and because I had the gift of the gab. Another important factor was that I was getting married to Maureen and knew that I had to grow up and provide for her and our family.

So I moved to City Electrical Factors as a sales rep with a company car. I quickly progressed through to be their Wolverhampton Branch Manager before I was given the job of taking the CEF Brand to Scotland. The only CEF they knew in Scotland in those days was Central and East Fife Co-op.

I lived in Scotland during the week and came home on Friday nights and returned early Monday mornings. I lived in digs in a house behind Barshaw Park Golf Club.

My initial responsibility was to find a property for the first CEF branch in Scotland, which ultimately was in Paisley. Maureen didn't really want to move to Scotland because she was close to her family while I was travelling back each weekend to play football. So I moved back to Birmingham and the owners of CEF, Tom Mackie and Ray Priestly were brilliant with me.

I left to join another electrical wholesalers called Superlamp Metallic as Birmingham Branch Manager and before long I was appointed Regional Manager responsible for the Midlands and North East.

I fell out with the company because they wanted me to do some stock transfers between branches that would be counted in both. It was to make the figures look good and was illegal. I refused and made my point at a board meeting and was quickly shown the door. I was not prepared to jeopardise my integrity.

When I left I knew that; a) if I wanted to make the decisions and b) earn some real money I would have to own my own company. So along with a former Superlamp colleague Bob Ravenhall we set about making it happen. A guy I had known and dealt with for years Bert Eales, he said he would come in with us but it would be his daughter Janice who would officially be on our board of directors. We worked our 'you know what's' off and quickly had the turnover in the millions. However disaster struck when Bert Eales company, Eales Electrical, went bust due to the building crisis and took us down for a load of money.

Bob and I stayed on working to pay off creditors until we had paid them all off.

I did a little firefighting for Paddy and Tommy Lynch's Lyndon Electrical wholesalers who had been badly advised by people who should have known better. There was a lot to put right due to some horrific buying. This was also at the time of my split up and subsequent divorce from Maureen and that took its toll and my focus. I was not doing as well as I wanted so left. Thankfully Paddy Lynch is still one of my best pals.

I decided then I wanted out of the electrical wholesaler business and wanted to try something new and equally challenging.

I joined business credit rating company Dun and Bradstreet, as Birmingham Branch Manager where I was very successful, mainly due to having a brilliant team working with me. I was fortunate to win Branch Manager of the Year. The result of that was a promotion to National Sales Manager responsible for £200m of business and employing a team of salespeople both field and telephone all over the country. However it meant I would have to move to London, which I refused to do. The compromise was a first class rail ticket.

I was totally committed to work, catching the 06.18am train to my office in the City, the financial district of London and not returning home until around 9.00pm.

If I was not in the office I was out all over the place, driven by the fact that in my world men provide for their families. I was always fearful of losing my job so worked hard and was fortunate to never have had a day off sick in my life. This mentality clearly had a negative impact on my marriages.

If you asked any of my employers or employees what I was like to work with they might not like me but I am sure they would undoubtedly say, 'We respected him, we trusted him and he was honest and worked hard'. That was enough for me. The hard work definitely came from an insecurity in my mind about losing my job. I had the philosophy that if you were the hardest worker you would more than likely be the last out of the door.

I remember when Orion took over BRMB Phil Riley the CEO asked me what I thought of the place. My reply was, 'A lot of people work here but not enough love it!' and I can honestly say I have loved everywhere I worked and gave everything I could. Good bad or indifferent I could not have worked harder. I could have been better at my job but I could never have worked harder. I could only do my best if that was not good enough then so be it.

CHAPTER TWO
RADIO DAZE

A few words from RICHARD PARK

Richard is Executive Director of Global Radio who own Capital Radio and Heart FM. He was voted the most influential man in Radio in 2001. He pioneered live kick by kick football in Glasgow at Clyde FM, and at Capital Radio. He was also the Headmaster in the TV Show *Fame Academy*. He appointed Tom as BRMB's Head of Sport in 1993 just after Capital Radio had bought the Birmingham Radio station BRMB.

Richard had this to say about Tom in October 2015.

> *'Tom Ross is one of the greatest broadcasters on British commercial Radio. His knowledge of Midland's football is second to none. His passion and enthusiasm for broadcasting is unsurpassed. One of the best sports broadcasters the UK has ever produced!'*

When I was working for Superlamp Mettalic we sponsored a game on 18 October 1975 at St Andrew's, Blues v Leeds United, which ended 2–2. Part of the deal was to pick a man of the match and present them with an award. As a massive Bluenose it was no contest, irrespective of performance, I was always going to choose Trevor Francis. He came into the sponsors lounge with Jasper Carrott and Gary Newbon. That was my first meeting with any of them and I am glad to say I got on very well with them and they are all close friends to this very day.

A few weeks later I answered the phone at my Streetly home and a voice said, 'Hi Its Trevor Francis', to which I replied 'piss off', as I thought one of my mates was winding me up. However it was TF and we had a chat. He had been told that I was a music nut and wanted to know if we could get together to talk music and swap albums etc. By the way he still has my John Otway and Wild Willy Barrett LP?

I went to his home in Knowle and we had a great chat about music and discovered that we were both massive ELO fans. TF then passed my name onto Blues commercial

Behind the decks as Blues match day announcer in late 70s

manager Geoff Greaves who called me and asked me if I would like to be the man on the microphone at Blues home games? Did I? You bet your boots I did.

I started doing all the games and it was tough to say the least, because of the very poor Tannoy system. There were only three speakers in the corner (where the tunnel is now) so if you sat close to that you were deafened but if you were in the Tilton etc. you couldn't hear it. But I just got on with it because there was no money to improve it.

I loved doing this, but at the start couldn't face sitting in the commentary box above the old tunnel in the old Main Stand and missing the atmosphere and mates on the Tilton. So I would do my thing playing songs and reading out the team news and then at five to three I would run round to stand with my pals on the Tilton. At half time I would run back and do the half-time scores etc. before returning to the Tilton to watch the second half. It was the same at full-time.

This was not feasible so I gave up my place on the Tilton and sat in the box making all the match-day announcements. When I started at BRMB covering games I asked BRMB to put the line into the box which they did allowing me to do both.

I had got the broadcasting bug and wanted to do more so I contacted BHBN the Hospital Radio station which was based in the County Ground at Edgbaston. I went for an audition and was chuffed to pass it.

They wanted presenters and not DJs and that was brilliant for me because I wanted to learn the presenting business properly. I had to go to the local hospitals visiting patients and getting requests to play for them on my show. I absolutely loved doing this. It was a proper grounding in radio technique but more importantly taught me that there were not listeners but real people with real day-to-day issues, who not only relied on me to be their friend but to be aware of their issues and concerns. This helped prepare me for when I eventually did get a job at BRMB.

The crew at BHBN were brilliant and very helpful Alan Jolly, Alan Dedicoat (now the voice of the lottery), Roger Cunningham, Chris Tickle and Paul Franks. I eventually did a midweek show with Paul called *Nightline* and also a Saturday morning show with him and he was, and still is, an excellent radio broadcaster.

I remember Jasper coming into the BHBN studios and doing an interview with me and that earned me lots of brownie points at the station.

In fact Jasper also donated some seats to his Birmingham Hippodrome gig so that BHBN could raise some much-needed funds and talked about them on stage. A proper caring Brummie legend

After a year or so I contacted Tim Russon the Sports Editor at BBC Radio Birmingham and he gave me a freelance job covering Blues games all over the country. My very first one was a pre-season friendly at St Andrew's against Dutch giants Ajax.

At BHBN hospital radio where it all started around 1976/7

A few words from TONY BUTLER

Tony was one of the first stars of local radio in Britain, known for a distinctive local accent and sometimes controversial style. In 2007 he was honoured by the Radio Academy with a Lifetime Achievement Award. He began his journalistic career in local papers in Birmingham before beginning to contribute to BBC national and regional radio in the 1960s. His strong regional accent caused problems at the staid BBC and he later recalled how he was encouraged to soften his natural accent. At one point the BBC even provided elocution lessons. He gave Tom his start at BRMB in 1981. And over 30 years later Tom repaid the favour by employing Tony to co-host the Friday night football phone in.

'I have never met a man who works as hard as Tom Ross on his sport. He lives, eats and sleeps football, and he is the most competitive man I have ever met.

'Ross must be the first with the transfer news, goals, manager comings and goings, the coaches' tactics and player's injuries. He will not share information, not even with his team.

Whilst working on the Friday "phone in" with Tom, he had a list of transfers over the past five years involving Midlands clubs. "That's interesting," I said" I'll have a copy."

"'No way," Tom refused to give me a copy, "you do your own research," he said. When I pointed out I was on the same team, he curtly told me to get my own. I didn't get a copy; such was Tom's competitive nature.

'He has built up a following second to none. He relies on trust and never breaks a confidence.

'All his competitors hate him – TV, Radio, Newspaper reporters and commentators. They hate him because he's first 99% of the time. They hate him because he says things they are afraid to say and print. They hate him because he does things they wish they could do but don't have the guts to.

'Will there be another Tom Ross? I doubt it.

'A rare talent, and an honest man, he had the best base in Midland football for years and you don't better that.

Why I even liked him, some of the time!'

In 1981 I got a call from Tony Butler who asked me if I would like to cover the Blues games for him on BRMB. I was absolutely thrilled to be involved with BRMB and working for Tony Butler because everyone listened to him. He asked me to meet him at the D Club at St Andrew's one lunchtime to discuss the details.

I bought him a beer and he said, 'right my boy Saturday away at Stoke are you up for it?'

'Of course,' I said, 'no problem,' and that was that. That was my interview!

I thought I had done a decent job for him but sadly he was not as pleased as I was. The following day, a Sunday, I was making my debut for the BRMB charity football team that Tony ran. It was at the Tally Ho police ground. I walked into the dressing room and in front of everyone Tony said, 'If that's the best you can do you can sod off back to the BBC.'

To say I was gobsmacked was an understatement.

However I was on the list for next week and he used me non-stop. But Tony was tough, he wanted reports short and sharp around 25 seconds and woe betide if you went over because he would just cut you off while you were in mid-flow. But you learned and learned quickly or did not last; it was as simple as that.

I now realise that on that first day Tony was probably testing me. Because I had two choices crumble or stick two fingers up to him and show him. Well I have never shirked a tackle in my life and wasn't about to start then. It was without doubt the best thing that ever happened to me in my career. I will never be able to thank Tony Butler enough and when I got the chance to help him I didn't hesitate but more about that later.

I continued to cover the Blues games on a freelance contract basis for BRMB and also played football and cricket for the stations charity teams. In 1984 I had a phone call that told me Tony had been sacked following an altercation with Brian Savin over extending cricket coverage of a very important match involving Warwickshire into Brian's show. It all got a bit heated and physical which resulted in Tony being suspended and ultimately sacked.

Tony's number two George Gavin immediately took over the reins and the running of the sports department and presenting the sports shows and phone in. George grabbed the opportunity and was in my opinion a fantastic operator.

I got on brilliantly with George at that time, both professionally and personally and George got me to join him on the Friday night phone in. I have to say in my opinion and I think that of the listener to, the chemistry worked. We would argue and row about football matters usually Blues, Albion, and Villa it certainly got the listeners taking sides. It was a formula that worked. The beauty was that it was not put on, because we disagreed about a lot of things football wise.

When there was a strike by the BRMB journalists the head of news Brian Sheppard asked me to do the breakfast sports bulletins into the Les Ross show. I was not a member of the NUJ so I was cool about doing it. The journalists did not agree and it was tough driving through their picket lines and some not very nice things were said.

When it was confirmed that Tony had indeed left BRMB it seemed pretty obvious that George Gavin would get the job. He was, without doubt, the overwhelmingly obvious choice and in my opinion was a shoo-in. However I was sitting with George one day when he said that he had heard that John Inverdale was to be announced as Tony Butler's replacement. Apparently it was John Inverdale who had called the station and said to George that he was taking over and wanted to know details about the place. If this was true then it was very unprofessional of Inverdale, who had been offered the job but should have waited until BRMB announced it officially.

George was rightly devastated and a little angry. BRMB were not happy with John Inverdale and as I understand it withdrew the offer and George quite rightly got the gig.

It was at this time that the hugely popular and famous Sports Forums started with George as the host. That first series were co-funded with Ansell's and were live with the first ever guest being Brian Clough. Other guests included Ron Atkinson, Tessa Sanderson and Lyn Davies, Eric Bristow, Graham Turner, Freddie Trueman, Ron Saunders, David Moorcroft and Geoff Capes, Henry Cooper and Pat Cowdell, Terry Griffiths, Jack Charlton, Tommy Docherty, and the West Bromwich Albion management team of John Giles, Norman Hunter, and Nobby Styles.

I became a 'gun mic' near the end of the series, which meant I went round the audience soliciting questions and sometimes if it was quiet giving them questions to ask. That first series was I believe the first ever co-funded outside broadcast done after the IBA (Independent Radio Authority) relaxed their rules on co-funding.

Little did I know then that a few years later I would be hosting the famous sports forums all over the West Midlands.

One of the 80s Sports Forums with George Gavin and the team.

I knew they were going to appoint a number two to work with George in the Sports department and as a freelancer who had done bulletins and was doing a phone in with George I believed I had a great chance of getting the gig. However, despite applying, I was never really considered and the job went to Grant Coleman a lovely lad who came up from the south coast. He was a recognised journalist and that gave him a massive advantage over me and my enthusiasm.

I was at that time National Sales Manager for Dun & Bradstreet one of the top ten biggest companies in the world. I ran a sales force with a turnover of £200 million.

Grant did not last too long because he wanted to get back to the south coast and when I heard he was leaving to join BBC Radio Solent, I once again applied for the job and this time I was determined to get it.

A few words from BRIAN SHEPPARD
Brian was the long-serving Head of News and Sport at BRMB and gave Tom his big chance on radio

'Tom got his big break in radio – Birmingham's much-loved BRMB Radio – because of a strike. The two-month walkout over staffing cuts began in May 1985. Up until then Tom had been a freelance, holding down a day job. He'd been recruited by the legendary Tony Butler whose team of butchers, bakers and candlestick makers phoned in weekend football reports. We relied on them. We couldn't afford to match the staffing levels of the BBC but the audience didn't mind. They loved the occasional cock-ups and irreverence that inevitably occurred.

'Butler had been succeeded by George Gavin who, as an NUJ man, joined the walkout, but Tom was not a member of the union. And, always his own man, he was not about to be coerced into turning his back on the audience or the Newsroom, which I ran single-handedly for several weeks.

'At the crack of dawn every morning Tom crossed the token picket line outside the station, then at Aston Cross, ignoring the mild abuse of his colleagues and joined me in the Newsroom to compile the sports bulletins. He'd always struck me as easy to get along with but single-minded and without his output during the strike we would have had no credible sports coverage in a region that lives for its football. And no Friday night sports phone in either – unthinkable! So, the strike eventually over, I offered Tom a job on staff as a sports reporter. He'd earned it. Less generous colleagues said he made sure he was in the right place at the right time. One could argue that's a good sports reporter's job. The rest as they say is history. A senior colleague of mine remembers, "he had something of an ego," but given we couldn't match the BBC's bigger staff or greater facilities; we had built the sports department up on personality, views and comment. Tom was in his element with that format.

'However now came the difficult bit. We had to teach Tom to read and write. Put him front of a microphone and he was in his element but writing tightly-worded sports scripts was an art that evaded him for some time. Ask for 100 words and you got War and Peace. No, that's unfair. You just got the first chapter. Teaching him to read scripts in the style of the newsreader was also headache-inducing. But then we realised it didn't really matter. Brummies were interested in what he had to say, not how he said it.

'So my memories of Tom. A grafter, always prepared to take constructive criticism – from me at any rate – and totally consumed by football. And he had a cheerful, matey manner, which got the best out of the people he interviewed. He didn't put himself on another level.

'A story remembered by a senior colleague illustrates that. Tom was covering a Birmingham city match at Tottenham where the Blues fans were being the usual boisterous selves. Suddenly a broad north London voice rent the air "Shut up you northern c----." Tom turned to one of his colleagues in the press box and said in an aggrieved tone: "I'm not a northern c---. I'm a Midlands c---".

'Tom wouldn't mind if you agreed or not.'

I met with Brian Sheppard who was Head of News and Sport and he really tried to talk me out of it, not because he didn't think I could do the job, but because of the drop in salary etc. I would be taking. It amounted to a 66% drop, which was massive and I would lose my company car and unlimited expense account.

I had already had a chat with Gary Newbon and Jasper Carrott who both told me to follow my dream because I would end up regretting it if I didn't

Tony Bushill, my boss at Dun & Bradstreet was brilliant and did not stand in my way so there I was in radio in the 80s on a salary of £9,000. Avrill my wife at the time was understandably not happy to say the least. But I always had confidence in my ability to succeed and always felt that if I worked hard the rest would follow.

So I was appointed assistant to George Gavin who had just been appointed Sports Editor, as I said George was a terrific operator from whom I learned a hell of a lot about sports journalism including how to write sports news items in the correct way, that was short, pithy and that suited the independent radio style.

I remember the Head of News Brian Sheppard once saying to me after I had left him a sports story on the news readers desk – 'Ross is English your native language?'

I also recall 'Shep' explaining to me about how to write stories short and concisely. This was after I had left a sports story that would have taken up half the bulletin. He said he could tell the story of the Bible in a single sentence – I said disbelievingly how and he replied, 'In the beginning God made Heaven and Earth, that's the story the rest is just the detail'.

He must have cost the company a fortune in plastic rulers because he used to put it in his back trouser pocket and then sit down!

The BRMB newsroom at that time was famous for developing radio talent and at that time included Nicole Pullman, Winifred Robinson, Kim Sabido, June Kelly, Adrian Britton, James Coghill, Roger Walker and later the wonderfully talented Victoria Derbyshire. Many of that newsroom talent went into TV.

We also had David Icke in the newsroom in the early days, who had been a professional footballer with Coventry City and Hereford United. He was another great operator before he left and went into TV where he announced he was 'The Son Of God' although I am certain he never meant exactly that. From being a talented journalist he sadly went to being ridiculed everywhere.

I had to spend the first two weeks working in the newsroom to get a feel for the business. My first story was to go to Stourbridge and cover a story about Stourbridge sausages – ah the romance of radio.

I was providing sports material for the major news bulletins which lasted fifteen minutes and were aired four times during the day: at 8am 11 am 1pm and 11pm. I had to learn quickly or I would not have lasted. (No Human Resource departments in those days) it was all about getting to the location, recording the story, returning to the studio, listen to the recording and decide what's important, edit the tape, write the story and submit to the News Editor.

Interviewing the legend that is George Best with the Birmingham Mail's Peter White

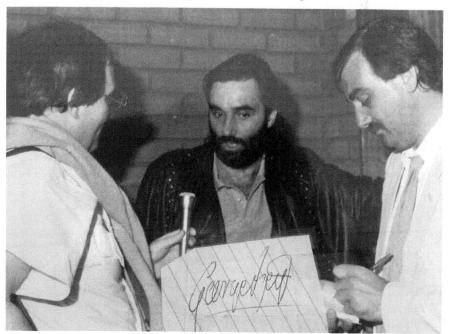

I also had to learn quickly how to type, as we did all stories and bulletins on Remington typewriters. Needless to say I had a huge supply of Tippex in my desk draw.

We got our stories from personal relationships at the clubs by checking in with the managers and players at all the clubs we covered which in those days were Aston Villa, Birmingham City, West Bromwich Albion, Wolverhampton Wanderers, Walsall and Coventry City. We would call them most days or just go to the training ground and chat to the manager or player concerned. No press officers putting hurdles in your way in those days.

We also used Ceefax and Oracle teletext systems and of course read through the newspapers on a daily basis to ensure we were always on top of the news in our patch.

We had the horse racing results on the back of every single news bulletin throughout the afternoon.

At first it was George Reeves and latterly Don Clarke who read the racing results. Either George or I would pick a Horse of the Day and a Greyhound of the Night tip for the listeners.

I remember almost choking when I heard George Reeves say while reading the racing results one afternoon, 'The Horse of the Day collapsed and died'.

However even though I was on sport I had to do my bit for the news room when needed; I recall covering a story about Prince Charles' visit to the Bus and Tram Museum in Witton Lane, It was the closest I had ever been to royalty and enjoyed doing live reports into the new bulletins. I was called into the newsroom a few weeks afterwards and shown a letter from Buckingham Palace by deputy news editor Howard Bennett saying what a great job Mr Ross had done and Prince Charles wanted to convey his thanks. I was chuffed to bits until I found out it was a wind up by the News Room. What a doughnut I was.

I absolutely loved General Election nights, which were hectic with all hands to the pump. We would all be given a "count" to go to and could be anywhere from Solihull to Dudley. I remember doing the count at Dudley and would be required to ring in with updates for the news bulletins. When the counting was finished and announced I would have to do a considered 'voicer' piece announcing who had won and what it meant. Then I had to interview the winner and the loser as well as the Mayor. Remember I was not and never had been a journalist and this stretched me, but I loved it.

Every Christmas we did a charity carol concert at The back of the Town Hall in the centre of Brum where thousands turned up to sing along with us and raise much needed money for local charities.

And in line with BRMB's philosophy of getting out and about in the community we always did a pantomime around the same time.

However sport was my main thing and under George I was allowed to set my own agenda within limits as long as he was kept in the loop. I wanted to be different,

The BRMB Carol Concert held every year in Chamberlain Square to raise money for charity.

A BRMB pantomime at a Birmingham Theatre in the 80s when me and Phil Holden played the "Ugly Sisters". No surprise there!!

unique and build a relationship not only with the listeners but also the football people that would ultimately provide the content. At that time I was helped because my pal Garry Pendrey was assistant to Alan Buckley at Walsall and so paved the way for me to get exclusive interviews. Because of my relationship at Blues it was no problem getting interviews with the manager and players. Playing for the West Bromwich Albion All Stars Charity team gave me an 'in' into the baggies and again allowed me to build my relationships. I had fantastic relationships with Ron Atkinson, Billy McNeill, John Gregory, Brian Little, Ron Saunders, Garry Pendrey, Alan Buckley, Tommy Coakley, Ray Graydon, Ray Harford, Denis Smith, Graham Turner, Tommy Docherty, Jim Smith, John Sillett. Terry Cooper, Dave McKay, Lou Macari, and many more. Lots of those professional relationships also developed into friendships that last to this day.

Since I was appointed head of Sport in 1993 I have also had fantastic relationships with Steve Bruce, Alex McLeish, Graham Taylor, Gary Megson, Tony Mowbray, Roberto Di Matteo, and Gordon Strachan to name a few.

These relationships enabled me to get my 'own' stories about the players and the club, sometimes I would just turn up at the ground or the training facility and asked to see the manager and most times it was a case of 'Hang on and he will see you!'

I would be able to go to Bodymoor Heath and sit with players, chatting to Gareth Southgate, Neil Cox, Paul Merson or anyone else. I would go to Hall Green Greyhound track with Ray Harford on a Friday night and be enthralled with his tactical know how; he was first to say that one day we will play with no forwards and let us see what the defenders do? I would be interviewing Ron Atkinson when he was in the bath or listening to John Gregory play the guitar while chatting all things Bruce Springsteen (we are both massive Boss fans).

Brian Little was a really nice guy and very accommodating to the media and would let me sit in the canteen chatting to the players while I waited for him. A lovely man although sometimes I thought he was too nice.

When Gary Megson was staying in a local hotel when he was appointed manager of the Baggies I would go and have a meal with him and keep him company and he never forgot it. I was always welcome in his room before games where I would get the latest team news etc.

At the Blues training ground wherever it was at that time I would be welcome to have a cup of tea with the players and manager before doing an interview.

Terry Cooper was absolutely brilliant, a diamond. We would train together at Paddy Lynch's boxing Gym and regularly go out on Saturday nights after the game usually to Umberto's Italian restaurant on the Stratford Road in Shirley. Those nights were legendary and rarely ended until four or five am.

At Wolves Graham Turner would call me into the dressing room area for a cup of team with him and Garry Pendrey after games and the banter was terrific which is not unusual when Garry is in the room.

A few words from BARRY FRY

Barry is one of the most charismatic men in football and a former manager of Birmingham City. He has also managed Southend, Peterborough United and Barnett – he played for Manchester United, Bolton Wanderers, Luton and Leyton Orient.

'I first met Tom Ross when I became manager of Birmingham City Football Club and since then we have formed a great professional relationship as well as a personal friendship. Tom was very helpful to me when I first went into Birmingham, he took me to all the local pubs and clubs, doing fans forums in around the city, meeting thousands of like-minded Bluenoses. They were as mad as me so we got on great!

'As a broadcaster, I have never known such a popular guy as Tom. The owners, directors, the staff, the management team and the players of not only Birmingham City, but other clubs across the Midlands, had such great respect for Tom because of the professional way he went about his business.

'Even when he criticised people, it was always done constructively. He was also great company when he wasn't broadcasting. He spent many hours in my company and made me piss myself laughing on so many occasions! He had some great stories!

'Although I got the sack at Birmingham over 20 years ago, Tom and I have remained friends ever since and he always welcomes me back with open arms whenever I return to St Andrew's.

Tom is a top man and different class.

Barry Fry was brilliant and could not have been more helpful when he took over at Blues and was always ready to go out for a meal and a chat or spend time having a cup of tea and that helped me get established as the BRMB Head of Sport when I took over from George.

All this helped to build trust between the players, managers and I, which was vital for me because my whole professional life has been built on building relationships and friendships that would not only help me on the radio but socially as well. Here I was a football nutcase and enjoying life with the managers and players of our local clubs.

It was the same with all the other media men such as Ray Matts, Peter White, Martin Swain, Ian Johnson, Denis Sunley, Leon Hickman, David Harrison, Neil Harman, Michael Ward, Barry Flatman, and Colin Tattum. The banter would fly around the place especially with the Atkinsons, Megsons and Gregorys around the training grounds. It was a pleasure to go to the training grounds in those days, sadly it's not quite so friendly and pleasant these days. Those journalists would always be prepared to help me with advice etc.

What a difference to the way things are done today, you have no direct access with the players, in fact often you are given the impression that the club is doing you a favour by making a player available at a press conference. All the journalists, both local and national have to attend a weekly press conference with the manager at a pre-determined time organised by the Media and Communications team, who act as a barrier between the club and the media. We all sit there as a collective with our tape recorders on the table and all get the same response from the same question. It has made the whole process sterile and everyone gets the same story – so it's letting the fans/readers/listeners down in my opinion.

We are also forced to sit in training ground car parks waiting for the green light to go down to the offices. In fact I am sure it's easier to get into Syria than it is Villa's training ground.

Over a period of time my relationship with George soured. To this day I don't really know why.

In the late 1980s things were starting to happen for me In terms of a profile and this was only down to George giving me the opportunity to be a part of the Friday night football phone in. I was getting a following and for the first time Blues' fans had a voice on local radio. I am not sure George liked this

Things were not right and one time I was angry and locked the Sport office door and said we needed to sort it out. From around that time it was uneasy but it got much worse around 91–92.

I suppose that when two people are working in close proximity there is always the chance of disagreements, which I had no problem with. However, it was not just that, George eventually ostracised me and left me out of things – like when he had to put a team out to play at Villa Park in a charity match and he excluded me.

I remember when a Blues story about David Rennie was in the *Evening Mail* and not on BRMB. George rightly tackled me about it and wanted to know why I had not got the story. I wrongly snapped at him, probably because I was angry with myself and embarrassed that I had missed the story. No ifs or buts, George was right and I was wrong. I did apologise to George as he was my line manager and as the Sports Editor was right to ask why we didn't have the story.

However two weeks before that George had totally lost it in the office when I passed on a message from Terry Cooper that he would not be able to do some video work with George. George went berserk and was abusive to me even though all I did was pass on a message. George said as far as he was concerned everyone could f**k off. You know what they say about shooting the messenger?

He did say later that he had calmed down although he never apologised for the abuse he gave me. I did forget about it, as life is too short. However after the Rennie incident two weeks later the relationship was never the same.

I wrote to George explaining how it was affecting my home life and listing everything that had happened. It summed up exactly how I was feeling. I am not a quitter and was prepared to live with the atmosphere.

On the Friday night after he received my letter all he said was, 'I got your letter'.

Did things improve? Only slightly if I am honest and the stress and upset must have shown in my face because I was approached on a couple of occasions by the then News Editor Colin Palmer who had seen what was happening and asked me if I wanted him to intervene. I said no, as I had to the previous News Editor Brian Sheppard. I was determined one way or another I would sort it out myself. I did not need anyone to sort it for me and I did not want to make matters worse. I was not totally surprised when, after West Bromwich Albion had reached the Play-off Final against Port Vale at Wembley in May 1993, he put me down as touchline reporter and used a freelance as his co-commentator.

As it happened I enjoyed myself pitch side talking to Baggies goalkeeper Tony Lange during the game as I forged yet another relationship.

I was producing the BRMB Sports Forums, which George hosted and I have to say he was absolutely brilliant at it. I even acted as his comedy warm-up man for ten minutes before each forum began. I would tell football related gags such as they have so many injuries their team picture is an X-ray or they are sponsored by BUPA. Or I explained that when Robert Hopkins saw "Mark One" on the front of his Blues team shirt he thought it was an instruction. Mark One were the shirt sponsors.

My work ethic meant I would go anywhere to any game in midweek and still be in the following day and never bothered to take a day off. I worked hard for George, BRMB and myself as per my dad's words to me.

Some things George did really hurt rather than make me angry, like the time he went on holiday to Greece for two weeks despite knowing I was in the West Bromwich Albion All Stars team that were playing in a Cup Final at Wembley. The game was to be played in front of 80,000 fans as a warm up game before the League Cup Final. It would have seen me realising a boyhood dream to play at Wembley. All football supporters would know how disappointing that would be! The game was on a Saturday and George went on holiday the same day. I was devastated, as I had played in every single round. But the job came first and that was that and one has to learn how to deal with and accept disappointment. George had a right to go on holiday and not worry about my personal needs.

However I hosted the Saturday programme and even had the Baggies players on live after they won the Wembley final against a Nottingham team – Garry Pendrey scoring the winner.

Eventually as I said earlier things came to a head and one day I locked the office door and said let's sort this out, I was so angry I was ready to fight, even though I knew that would mean I would lose my job, which meant so much to me. But even that fizzled out without anything really being sorted.

We never came to blows but things were never the same again.

One of the worst things that happened and upset me most came about as Blues were looking to be sold after the Kumar Brothers clothing empire collapsed. My pal Paddy

Lynch and John White along with a mega rich American were negotiating to buy it. I was asked if I would be interested in joining as Commercial Director. I said in principal I would be interested in talking to them but get the club first and we would talk further. It was all to be confidential as I was employed by BRMB radio.

One Friday night on the phone in George and I and the listeners were discussing the possible buyers of the club and Paddy's consortium came up. George suddenly mentioned on air that I could be joining Birmingham City if the consortium got the club. I was gobsmacked and batted it away. But George could have spoken to me about it at any time before the show started, but didn't, preferring to embarrass me on air and put my job at risk.

I have to admit that my confidence took a blow at that time and I was feeling low, but I was determined not to be beaten. Remember up to the time this started I had looked up to, respected and admired George. Afterwards I still admired him as a great broadcaster but lost all respect for him.

If I see him on the circuit we don't speak and to be honest I try to avoid him whenever possible. I have to say, that despite our difficulties professionally I respected George and still do, but personally he ended up being an arse to me and I lost all respect for him.

Having said that he was and is still a great operator and I learned a lot and of course can never thank him enough for giving me the opportunity on the phone in, because without that I may never have had the career I have. I was in awe of his journalistic and writing ability.

In 1993 Capital Radio bought the BRMB radio group and Richard Park, the head honcho called George and I into the office of Ian Rufus (Managing Director). Richard Park announced his plans for the station, very simply he wanted live football on the airwaves, however, he also said that he wanted to turn BRMB into Aston Villa FM. You can guess my reaction! I told him I didn't agree with what he was planning and that he would alienate half of the football audience in Birmingham. I advised him to talk to the *Evening Mail* and take advice from them.

I knew of Richard's reputation as a no nonsense tough boss and I have to be honest it did cross my mind that I might be shown the door. Fortunately he listened, even if he didn't say so at the time, and we did not become Aston Villa FM. I know from later conversations with others in his management team that he recognised I was not a 'Yes Man', which ultimately earned me a place in 'Park's Posse'.

Richard said he wanted us to do commentaries the Capital Way full of passion and excitement and that suited me down to the ground because that was what I was all about. He asked Paul Cooney to come down from Scotland to produce the Saturday Sport and I got on with him brilliantly. George would be at the main game with Ian Crocker who was drafted in from Capital in London to do the commentary with George as pundit while I would be at another game. I am not sure George liked this and it was not too long after that he left for the BBC.

Richard negotiated exclusive commentary deals with the local clubs and a new chapter in BRMB sport broadcasting was about to take off.

Richard became my mentor and meant that I was able to re-focus myself away from the difficulties with George who left later that year to work at BBC Radio 5 live. Since then George has forged a brilliant career at SKY TV covering the Football League.

Shortly after George left, Richard Park said he wanted to talk to me, so we went to the local pub, just 100 yards from the BRMB studios. He said he wanted me to be his Head of Sport and I had a Brokeback Mountain moment and could have kissed him. All those years of working hard and enduring that horrible atmosphere with George faded away as I realised I was going to be Head of Sport at BRMB in my own town I could have jumped for joy. It could not get better than that for me. I would be following two fantastic operators in Tony Butler and George Gavin and running the sport on the greatest radio station on the planet BRMB and in the greatest town in the world Birmingham, for Brummies' how lucky was I?

So there I was doing the greatest job in the world and more importantly I could do it my way. I did not want to be the new Tony Butler or George Gavin. I wanted to do it my way and had my own ideas and plans. I decided right away that I would give it my best shot and give everything to getting BRMB to the number one position in the audience ratings.

All this happened in 1993, which had turned out to be some year. The audience figures were soon on the up and although Villa fans were worried when I was promoted to Head of Sport that the station's coverage might become biased to Blues, they soon recognised that I was fair to all teams in the region. It is a fact that the majority of my radio awards are for my coverage of Villa games!

I was a journalist by experience rather than training not having gone to university like most journalists, but I believe that the audience is the only relevant judge in deciding whether I was and still am doing a good job or not. In the 90s I started to write a column for the *Sports Argus* and latterly the *Evening Mail* and more recently the *Birmingham Mail*. I still write for the *Mail* and am proud and privileged to do so.

I hope I have brought to my writing what has been my mantra whatever job I have had and wherever I have worked and that is full of passion and enthusiasm.

Although I am very confident and self-opinionated, I am also extremely self-critical due to what I have always believed is a healthy level of insecurity, i.e. I never want to be sacked! So my philosophy was if you work harder than anyone else you will be the last out of the door.

Although I know I am not the best broadcaster in the business I believe my style of presenting and commentating pleased most of the listeners. I make no apologies for being all about passion, excitement and enthusiasm, if I can't be passionate, enthusiastic and excited about the game I am at how can I expect the listener to be. My job for 90 minutes is to take them on an emotional roller coaster ride.

I told those working for and with me that the BRMB philosophy from the day I was appointed was that we would no longer be presenting a radio sport programme but a unique sporting event.

Let me explain it from my perspective! From the very first football match ever in eighteen hundred and frozen to death, no two games have ever been the same. No two goals, free kicks, fouls, throw ins, nothing has ever been the same and experienced before. So every time I turned up to a game I was buzzing because it was a unique sporting event that had never happened before and would never happen again and so it was a privilege to be there.

Even if the game was not the best there was always something to hook and keep the listener with you. For example, 'can they hang on to a point, there's seven minutes to go can they hang on? Count it down with me'. I would then say, 'six minutes to go can they do it,' or two minutes away from a brilliant point. That kept the audience on the edge of their seats and they stayed with me to the final whistle.

We quickly took the station to number one in the audience ratings and we stayed top of the tree through to 2004!

I was devastated when Capital Radio said in 2004 that because of financial restraints they would be dropping live football commentaries as part of a cost-cutting exercise. I made it quite clear that if there was no football coverage then the audience would drop like a stone and that's what happened over the time when there was no live kick by kick football coverage. I was still going to games doing live programmes with reports from other games.

However regional MD Mark Lee had been doing some research and found that not doing football commentaries affected the other programmes particularly the breakfast show. He had a meeting with Local Programme Director Adam Bridge and they decided it was a no brainer so I was asked to go to the clubs and do some commentary deals and start doing live commentaries again.

Once again despite that short interruption we took the sport back to number one in the ratings.

In 2009 BRMB along with Merica, Wyvern, Beacon and Heart 106 (Nottingham), as well as the respective Gold Stations were sold to ORION Media giving me the opportunity to link up with the CEO Phil Riley whom I had worked with at BRMB in the 80s.

I remember saying at the time: 'It's the best thing that has happened to BRMB and the other stations since the early 90s. They have revitalised the station, the staff and the listeners. It's absolutely brilliant just watch the stations go from strength to strength'. Little did I know what was in store a few years later particularly for me but more about that later?

In 1996 I was asked to be acting programme manager of BRMB's sister station Xtra Am by Clive Dickens while a colleague Mark Sadler was asked to do the same job on

BRMB. This was while Richard Park recruited a full time Programme Controller for BRMB and Xtra-AM, which, as well as being the home of live kick by kick football commentaries also played 60s 70s and 80s music.

I loved being the acting programme controller because of my love of music, at this time little did I know that I would be the Breakfast Presenter a few years later.

One day the staff were called to a meeting where we were introduced to Paul Jackson who was to be the new programme director of both BRMB and XTRA am. I was gobsmacked because no one had told me what was happening or that I would now not be looking after the Xtra AM station.

I received a nice letter from Richard and one from the BRMB/Xtra am Managing Director David Bagley apologising for not telling me and also thanking me for my efforts and saying they viewed me in a new light.

Therein lies the secret of my lasting 35- years – my work ethic.

I found the new PD Paul Jackson a dream to work with. As well as being a chip off the old block being Richard Parks's son, he was focused on taking BRMB to greater heights. Having said that as well as working hard he partied hard and we had some fantastic times until he left to join Virgin Radio in London.

Paul bought into me and was great at making me feel wanted and important to the radio station.

When Paul eventually left I rang Richard Park and suggested that he should appoint Adam Bridge as Programme Controller of BRMB and Xtra Am. Richard thought it was a conspiracy because the BRMB MD at the time Jane Turnbull had also been on the phone backing Adam. Richard, hands up it was!

Adam cared about BRMB passionately and was in my opinion great for the station and for me personally. He had worked for BRMB on production when he arrived from Invicta Radio along with Paul Jackson. I employed Adam on the Sports team as a commentator after Jim Proudfoot left.

In 2009 when Global Radio were looking to sell BRMB, Mercia, Beacon, Wyvern and Heart in Nottingham, Adam, who was then regional Programme Director, set about looking for someone to finance a management buyout. He contacted LDC (Lloyds Development Capital) who were interested but as I understood at the time they wanted a CEO with experience so Adam suggested Phil Riley who had done a fantastic job setting up Heart FM. Phil came in with David Lloyd and yet surprisingly didn't keep Adam who had been instrumental in bringing them to the negotiating table. I think Adam could have stayed and taken over as MD of Mercia but he was BRMB through and through and felt let down and eventually left and ended up at BBC Radio WM

Adam was one of the best and most knowledgeable FM programme controllers around in my opinion and had a lot to offer ORION Media but sadly, and to their loss, he moved on.

In my opinion many presenters forget who they are broadcasting to and are more DJ's than presenters. My personal rules and disciplines for myself for presenting either sport or music shows are:

- To be at my best I can only be myself at all times.
- I try to get the right balance between preparation and spontaneity.
- Focus on the listener.
- I always treat people as I would want to be treated myself.
- I am a friend to the listener not a presenter.
- For me a great song is a great song regardless of what era it's from.
- I always try to bring humour into any show.
- I remind myself that it has to be entertaining.
- On football commentaries I set the scene by always remembering that the listeners are blind so need to paint a picture that their minds can turn into live pictures. By always telling the listener where the ball is. A left wing corner at the Holte End. A penalty at the Tilton End. Attacking the Brummie Road end etc. Never say, 'they are kicking left to right,' because that depends on where the commentator is sitting
- Repeat the score as often as possible because most listeners 'drop in' on the programme, very few are there from start to finish.
- Preparation for match days.
- Get the best producer you can – someone who gets it and gets what you are trying to achieve.
- Go to all the pre-match press conferences to question the manager and get his feel for the game;
- Prepare scripts.
- Decide the running order.
- Get exclusive team news.
- I always drive the pundit to all away games, but home or away I always aim to get to the ground three hours before kick-off. This is so I can confirm teams and do last minute preparations and of course in case there is a problem with the 'line' and we need to get a BT engineer to sort it.
- I try hard to get plenty of banter, humour and entertainment into the football programme as I can, be it in the pre-match build up, the live commentary or post-match phone in. so I am always looking for things that can contribute to this. Very often that involves the pundit.

Typical example was with Villa pundit Pat Heard who bored the pants off me and Ian Taylor on the way to a Newcastle game. He was rattling on about only seeing one daffodil yet? And also unbelievably about the working intricacies of an 'average speed camera'.

I nicknamed him Uncle Albert on air (a reference to Only Fools and Horses Uncle Albert who bored everyone with 'during the war' stories.) It stuck and the listeners also joined in.

I loved working with Tony 'Bomber' Brown. Bomber would bring a flask of soup to every single game for us to have at half time, very welcome in the coldest winter days. I used to say on air that Mrs Brown had made it specially and gave the soup names such as Shrewsbury mint pea. I said it was Mrs Brown's finest and made from scratch with fresh vegetables etc. Bomber would be out and about in Walsall or at the Merry Hill Shopping centre andpeople would ask for recipes for Mrs Brown's finest. His lovely wife Irene was also frequently asked for the recipe. Little did they know it was really Heinz finest?

One day Jon McCarthy, Colin Tattum and I on our way to Sunderland where Birmingham City were playing and had stopped at a Little Chef, as we often did for a cup of team and some toast etc. We had only been in there a few minutes when in walked the Birmingham City owner Carson Yeung, and directors Vico Hui, Sammy Yu, etc. They had not long taken over the club and here was this self-styled multi-millionaire sitting in a Little Chef. I should have realised that day that they would eventually have financial problems.

Every year the Blues All Stars charity fund-raising team that Kevan Broadhurst and I started in 1992 has a Christmas meal and booze up to say thank you to the players. I always leave early after the meal because I don't drink and there is always a game the following day. Two years ago the boozing session went on most of the night and started again on the Saturday morning with champagne etc.

Blues were playing that day but I was at another game while Kevan was due to be at Blues as our pundit doing live kick by kick commentary with Chris Coles.

I crossed to Kevan for the first link only to be greeted with an 'eehhhh Rossi'. I knew straight away that he was still pissed from the ex-player's night out. I said nothing on air but said, 'thanks Kev we'll talk again shortly' and quickly went to an ad break.

I knew I could not speak to Kevan on air or allow him on air and told him this down the line during the break. He said that he was fine and if I did not put him on we were finished. This was a problem for me because Kevan has been a friend since the 70s, I knew this was just the hangover and drink talking, but I could not put him on air. I did not hear from him for a few days so decided to call him. Kev was brilliant and apologised and that was that. We continued where we left off. I would have been devastated to lose him because not only was he a good friend but was also a brilliant pundit who brought an insight about the game to the listener. And he was great at the banter, usually at my expense – but that was always OK with me.

How Kevan is not in the game as a coach or manager is beyond me. He has so much to give the game and in my opinion has a natural way of coaching so that people fully understand what's expected. It's crazy when you see some of the Muppets who are taking fortunes out of the game just because they have the regulatory badges or more importantly are part of a management clique.

A few words from KASH GILL

Kash became a world champion in kickboxing at the age of 21. In 1991, he won the WKA light middleweight and super welterweight full contact titles. The following year he won the WKA middleweight championship. He was the International Sport Karate Association freestyle champion of 1993. Standing tall at 6ft 3in, Kash has an impressive line-up of British, European and World titles. He is the first UK Asian to be a world champion in a contact sport and became four times World Kickboxing Champion, an achievement that has never been beaten.

> *'I first met Tom Ross in 1991 when he was covering my fight for the world title against Alex Tui of Australia where we had a war and I knocked him out in round six. Tom became a friend and mentor a bit like Harry Carpenter was to Henry Cooper.*
>
> *'He also covered my world middleweight boxing title contest against Mike "Cobra" Cole of the United States of America, which was beamed on Sky Sports and Transworld International.*
>
> *'Often he would get me into the studio to promote me or my fights and we always had plenty of banter as I am a Villa fan!*
>
> *'I have had 101 fights in my career and my first fight was at the Aston Villa Leisure Centre because Birmingham is my home. Tom was there on that occasion and has supported me throughout my career and we have developed a lot of mutual respect for each other. He wrote the Foreword for my book My Life in a Flash, which was published in 2012 and we are soon to do something to celebrate my 35 years in Martial Arts.*
>
> *'Tom is a great guy and a good friend to me'.*

People often ask why I didn't do more TV, well I do have a mirror in my house if I ever needed reminding that I have the perfect 'face for radio'. However I have done some TV and had my moments – literally just a few moments:

I had been covering kick boxing for a few years when In 1993 Paul Ingram who ran the Kickboxing Association WKA and also Stuart Promotions contacted me and asked if I would like to host a kickboxing programme on SKY TV doing six two hour events a year for three years. Trans World International would produce the programmes, which would be aired on SKY TV.

Despite having no TV experience I jumped at the chance because it meant not only doing commentary on World Championship Kickboxing bouts all over Britain, but I would also get the chance to host the programme from the venue. It was also out of my comfort zone and would challenge me.

Now this should have shot me to TV stardom but sadly it didn't? Although the programme was well received by kickboxing fans across the country and Europe.

I would go to various venues and commentate on the bouts working with a brilliant Trans World team who to be honest made it easy for me.

On the Tuesday after the event I would go to Trans World in London and top and tail the show and voice into and out of break links.

Trans World told Paul that they were pleased with the commentary, which was my usual banter style and they were also delighted with the narration and that meant a lot to me.

I loved doing these and my pundit was former World Champion Howard 'The Hawk' Brown

However for one show on 27 February at the Aston Villa Leisure Centre my co-commentator was none other than the gorgeous Cynthia Rothrock better known as China O'Brien a brilliant martial arts movie star who was the female Steven Segal. She was also a former martial arts World champion.

I had watched Cynthia many times playing the female detective China O'Brien and here I was at the Villa Leisure Centre with her doing live commentary with me – It don't get much better than that.

The Kickboxing world had many characters including the phenomenal Kash 'the flash' Gill, Gary Sandland, Kirkwood Walker, Eval Denton, Howard Brown, Lawrence White,

However my very first television appearance was in a Jasper Carrott sketch, which was shot at the Blues training ground in Damson Lane in the late 70s. Jasper asked if I would play the part of the referee in a short sketch he was doing for ATV's Gary Newbon, which would be shown on TV as part of the Midland Soccer Writers awards night. I loved it and had nothing to do but blow a whistle. I remember John Richards was in the sketch as well as a number of other local players.

I get asked reasonably often to comment on major West Midlands football issues for SKY TV, while I have also locked horns on Central with Gary Newbon over my opinion that TV is ruining football.

Central TV used Ian Taylor and me on a few Monday nights to look back at the weekend's action while just a few months ago I was talking football for an hour on the new local TV station Big Centre TV. If you want me to talk football – no problem if it's anything else, forget it.

AWARDS

Tom has won a number of Radio Academy awards for his passionate style of broadcasting and love of the Midlands teams. Tom though is quite philosophical about it. 'I have always believed that you don't have to go chasing awards they will come to you if you are producing what the listener wants'. The academy awards are the radio industry's OSCARS.

1985 – Best Sports Coverage.
1997 – Sports Broadcaster.
2003 – Keep Right On To the Premiership.
2009 – The Sports Forum with Aston Villa boss Martin O'Neill.
Tom was the first Brummie to win a coveted New York Radio Gold Medal for his coverage of the 1997 Coca Cola Cup Final beating 2,500 other countries to lift the award. He has also been a New York radio award finalist.
In 1997 he was runner-up in the BT Sports Journalist of the Year Awards.
In 2011 he received the IRN GOLD award in London for 30 years outstanding contribution to radio.
In 2012 his coverage/commentary of the Carling Cup Final won the IRN Sports story of the year award.
In 2012 he was named Sports Journalist of the Year at the Midlands Press awards.

What matters more to me than the award itself is what the judges had to say about the programme and myself that made them decide I was worthy of the award.

Let me explain! When I was appointed Head of Sport I sat and thought long and hard about what I wanted to achieve personally and also what I thought the majority of listeners wanted from their radio presenter and their radio station.

I did not want to be the next Tony Butler or George Gavin, both of whom I respected as broadcasters. I just wanted to put my own stamp on the sport output of BRMB and wanted to do it my way.

I know that the only real judges of radio are the listeners but generally those you meet and also your family and friends tell you how brilliant everything is. However those faceless people who judge the Radio Academy entries don't know you and have no reason to say anything good or bad so you would always get the truth.

They are not local people so judge every entry on its merits. Twice they said things about me and/or my programme that confirmed to me that what I had set out to do in 1993 I had achieved. I can honestly remember saying to myself 'that'll do for me'.

One of those Radio Oscars was in 2003 for 'Keep Right On To The Premiership' the story of Bimingham City winning promotion to the Premier League for the first time.

SPORTS AWARD

Keep Right On To The Premiership

Here's what the judges had to say. . .

"You 'lived the experience' with this programme! Unabashed bias toward the home team, Birmingham. This was an emotional roller coaster, where at times you didn't know whether to laugh or cry. Rock stars and comedians, past and present players, combined with the people on the terraces, all fans, and what fans, in a collective outpouring of passion, warmth and affection for their club.

This was compelling radio, bringing you the drama, excitement, fun and above all the love of life which surrounds great sporting occasions."

What the judges said about my 2002 "Keep Right On To The Premiership" programme.

The second was for the Martin O'Neil Football Forum. This is where we take the manager of a club out to a social club to meet the fans. The fans get to ask him questions.

What the Judges said about my 2009 Martin O'Neil Sports Forum.

2009

THE SPORTS AWARD

The Football Forum

Here's what the judges had to say. . .

"Tom Ross brilliantly hosts a celebration of one of the finest UK soccer managers of his generation. From Ross's heart warming intro onwards, there are none of the clichés that undermine similar programmes. Audience and listener are super-served with the knowledge and charm of both of the central characters, O'Neil and Ross. And the mutual respect is tangible."

GRADUATES OF THE ROSS ACADEMY

A few words from IAN DANTER

Ian is a Talksport presenter who was given his start in radio by Tom. Ian is also a talented musician and recording artist and is one half of the Bluenose Brothers with Tom.

'Sometime in the late 2000's I was sent by TalkSPORT to cover a Blues game at St Andrew's on a Sunday morning (I'm fairly sure it was a Blues/ Baggies derby game). As I looked around at the broadcast colleagues sat alongside me in the press box, something became alarmingly clear.

'Mike Taylor, Ian Crocker, Jim Proudfoot, Mark Bolton, Mark Regan, Nigel Pearson, myself... all of us there shared a common broadcasting bond as we'd learnt our trade down the years. And that 'common bond' was sat in the far top left of the press area, looking down on us all like the protégés we once were. More like Tom Soprano or Tom Corleone than Tom Ross.

'Tom is the man who got me into broadcasting in 1998, and as he still delights in telling me regularly, "I can f****** get you out of broadcasting as well!" You always knew what he wanted from you as a radio commentator and his words resonated very early on; "How long's gone, which way are they kicking, where's the ball, if there's a corner, which two stands is it being taken between, what's the score, KEEP mentioning the score...!"

'Fail to do any of that from moment one, and you were essentially no good to him and the high standards he set as Sports Editor. Those good habits drummed into me led – some 13 years later – to me getting a chance to commentate on a World Cup semi-final on UK national radio live from Cape Town. That's all down to what Tom taught me to do, and for that I shall forever be in his debt. To be fair, he would never let me forget it anyway.

'I also have many happy memories of his "unplanned" moments in broadcasting...

- The fight with a reporter at Stockport during a Friday phone in I was producing which led to me having to play the longest commercial break in Capital Gold history (eight minutes in total) as Tom had a blazing row (complete with fisticuffs that I heard down the ISDN line) over the claim he was sat in the bloke's regular seat... Tom stayed put in the end of course...

- The grand announcement prior to a game that "Coming up now we've got a minute's silence for the Queen Mother... who passed away several days ago... and rightly so as well..."

- *The numerous times he intended to give out the phone number for the post match football phone in, only to mistakenly start giving out his own mobile number... and stop himself just in time...*
- *The passing of a former manager in the Midlands, whose death Tom described on air as "a problem for him..."*
- *But let's be honest, if I last 35 years at the top of the business like Tom has, I bet I'd have more than my fair share of "Colemanballs" to endure.*

'Next time you're in Birmingham and you find yourself a few floors up somewhere, look out the window and ask yourself what you're staring at. The answer, to paraphrase the man himself, is "It's Tom's town..." Yes, we've had Butler and Gavin, but no one has dominated this city and its insatiable thirst for football like Tom Ross has.

We shall not see his like again.'

Having always played football I am always conscious of how important the team is although I am also aware of how important it is for the team to have one leader. The man who makes the decisions and whose neck is on the block if it all goes wrong.

I have always worked harder and longer than anyone in my team because for me that is leading by example. Whether I was at BRMB or Dun & Bradstreet, or City Electrical Factors I realised that you are only as good as your team.

I have always felt that hard work wins in the end, however if you are part of a team where you work hard but others don't, you will fail. So it is vital that the team is all onside and prepared to work as hard as the leader.

This was a serious management weakness of mine. I expected everyone to work as hard as me and put in the long hours to get the job done whether that meant 60 hours a week or 80.I didn't realise or probably didn't accept that they had lives to lead and relationships to take into consideration.

I had a winning mentality where rotas and clock watching were not welcome. This I suspect comes from my poverty stricken working class background. I wanted to get out of that environment so decided to work hard in whatever job I had.

I know I pushed my staff too hard and I don't and won't apologise for that. I was just driven to be number one in my chosen field because as the Americans say 'second is first placed loser'.

I am sure some of my team over the years have felt they were good enough to be the number one, the boss, the main presenter and I would agree that some were definitely knowledgeable enough however there can only be one 'gaffer' and I was the man in the job so it would be done my way.

However if you do your best for me and work hard and are loyal I would not complain. It might not be good enough, but if it is your best you can't do anymore.

What I really hated with a passion was those team members with great ability who didn't try to do their best but just did enough. I would have no hesitation in showing them the door but would work hard trying to improve those who gave everything and tried their best.

I have always been honest to everyone in my team because I have a philosophy that says, 'If you don't like the answer – don't ask the question'.

During my time in radio I have been helped enormously by many people whose advice and friendship have contributed in no small way to whatever success I have had in local radio broadcasting. That is why I am pleased to see some of those who I have helped along the way doing so well in the business.

Ian Danter always called it the 'Ross Academy' well if that is true then some of the candidates would include:

IAN DANTER – One day I got a letter (remember them) from a man called Keith Laurent who told me about his mate who worked at Musical Exchanges selling guitars etc. Apparently this mate Ian Danter was brilliant at impressions and did a mean Trevor Francis, Barry Fry and also of me which he often did when I was not around and brought the office to tears of laughter.

I got them to send me a tape and he was excellent at a wide range of sporting impressions. So I got Ian in and asked him to provide a four-minute sketch involving various sporting personalities for my *Saturday Goalzone* programme. They were brilliant.

It wasn't long before our programming people had given him his own show *The Barmy Brummies* and of course I started him out on the sport covering Walsall games. He found it hard to deal with Ray Graydon, the Saddlers boss who always wanted journalists to turn up in a tie and with neat short hair – neither were Dant's trademark.

Ian and I formed the Bluenose Brothers and you can read more about that elsewhere. He has developed as a talented broadcaster and is now a recognised presenter on TalkSPORT and has also released two brilliant solo albums.

JIM PROUDFOOT – who is now working for TalkSPORT and Absolute Radio and is an excellent commentator– I recall that I tried to 'de-posh' Jim's vocabulary as he would use words like perspicacity, which I had never heard of and I was sure the listeners wouldn't know it – ironically it means 'easily understood, lucid'.

NIGEL PEARSON – top man (not him his clothes), who is now presenting/commentating on Darts and Speedway on television and working with TALK SPORT. And is also chairman of the Cradley Heathens Speedway Team. A great operator who has worked hard at his profession.

JACK WOODWARD – who currently works for Aston Villa TV – Jack is a lovely man who would not say boo to the proverbial goose however he was a bit like Jim in terms of using big words that no listener would understand. So I told him, 'Jack use words that ordinary people will know'. He replied 'I don't know any ordinary people as I went to public school,'. We had to part company. He is still doing a fantastic job at Aston Villa.

IAN 'CROCK' CROCKER – Crock left Capital Radio in London as a radio nobody who was one of Jonathan Pearce's team. Crock quickly became a broadcasting somebody in the West Midlands. He was a brilliant commentator for me and despite us not always seeing eye to eye we worked well as a commentary team. It was no surprise to me when he was given the opportunity by SKY TV in 1997 to commentate on TV football games. He covers the games in Scotland and I personally think that is a waste of his talent because he is a top operator and should be presenting the big Premier League games.

I spent a lot of time on the road with Ian Crocker travelling to games all over the country and of course sampling all the fare that the catering vans around the grounds could provide. This was long before clubs provided food and drink for the media. Although he used to drive me mad about the musical *Les Miserable*, as he had been to see it millions of times. He definitely didn't appreciate my constant Bruce Springsteen CDs.

I remember getting locked in at Norwich with Crock and having to walk across the pitch and climb over the wall to get out after 7pm. My phone in in those days on Xtra Am was 90 minutes plus extra time. We had the same situation at Southend, the grounds-man was the only one left at Roots Hall apart from us and he had a wedding do to go to. So we arranged that we would shut the door behind us.

One other eventful trip saw us at Elland Road for a Leeds v Villa clash. We returned to my car only to see the police around it and two Villa supporters blowing up the tyres with a foot pump. The policemen told me that they had caught the lads letting down my tyres for a joke? I was not happy and the policemen shipped them off to the local nick and I followed behind. When we got to the police station I persuade police not to charge them. They agreed saying they would give them a right good rollicking. As Crock and I were walking to my car the two Villa fans walked out of the station and shouted after me. Not to apologise but to ask for a 'Bronx Hat'. To be honest I laughed my head off at their cheek and sent them one in the post.

A 'Bronx hat' is a woolly hat similar to what Sylvester Stallone wore in the Rocky movies. Marketing told me they wanted to do some sport marketing and could I come up with any ideas. I suggested the woolly hats, which were also known as Beanie hats. I thought it would be cooler and sportier to call them 'Bronx hats'. They were in our team's colours and would have the station logo on the front and a saying that identified the teams on the back such as Boing Boing, or Keep Right On. I tried to make them special, so on air sold it as something you couldn't buy only win. It was brilliant and to this day listeners still ask for a 'Bronx hat', I even persuaded some of the coaches to wear them and quite often you would see them on TV or in newspaper pictures. An inexpensive but effective idea.

MARK BOLTON – who up until 2011 was SKY's Spanish football man. I gave Mark an opportunity to commentate for BRMB and to be fair he was a quick learner and quickly became an important member of the team. One day I got a call from Gary Newbon who asked me to tear up Marks contract, as he wanted him to join Central TV's Sports team. He left with my blessing and he went on to join SKY TV. I didn't have to let him go but I took the approach, which I had always had and that was, 'I will not stand in people's way' and 'If they don't want to be here then they are best gone'.

MARK 'REGO' REGAN – It was the same with Mark who was another good operator who was with me at BRMB when in 2003 he asked if I would release him from his contract so he could take up an appointment at Sports Editor at BBC WM. I liked Mark and believe I had done him a favour in tearing up his contract at BRMB so he could develop his career.

However I was disappointed to find out that he had been bad-mouthing me at the BBC. So one day I pulled him aside at a West Bromwich Albion press conference and made it clear that I would not stand for that. (Although not exactly in those words). We didn't speak for some considerable time mainly because I cannot be two faced. However I am delighted that we now get on very well again, something I am really delighted about.

I have won many awards and plaudits for my radio presenting and commentaries. However while I take all the credit being in the front line, or the sharp end so to speak, I have to make it clear that I could not have done it without working with some brilliant producers. I have been fortunate to work with some top class producers, some good ones and some not so good. It is a vital role.

You know you have a good producer when you develop that sixth sense where he knows what you need and you feel confident because he is at the other end of the line when you are out at football grounds.

We presenters can get caught up in things and forget what is important.

My first producer was **Anthony Gay** who went on to be MD at Hallam FM. He helped me to get to grips with a lot of things and I was devastated when he left.

Ian Powell and I got on famously and like me he had come into the business late in his career and we worked together superbly. He had that wonderful sixth sense, when he knew what I wanted and when I wanted it. He left to go back into the building trade and was sadly missed by me.

In 2006 I gave a young snotty nosed kid from Walsall a chance in the backroom on sport and without doubt it was the best thing I ever did. **David Salt** just settled into the job and we clicked immediately. We argued at times and that is healthy but he added a new dimension to what we did despite my reluctance to change.

He eventually became my producer and was my producer at the time of the record figures and he should take some credit for those. He also produced the Football Forum with Martin O'Neill that won me a Sony Academy award. He knew what I was thinking and would inspire me to do better. That is some feat when you are dealing with someone who thinks he knows it all.

Sadly, as is often the case, he was so good of course he was promoted to other things and could no longer produce the *Goalzone*. He was promoted to deputy brand director for Free Radio and is now Content Director for Free Radio's new owners Bauer Media. He is always available to discuss things with me. He has always championed Sport and lifted me when I have been down after a show. I am pleased to say he has become a great friend both professionally and personally.

The academy would certainly teach the following lessons:
When doing live kick by kick commentary we have to remember that it's all about selling passion, enthusiasm, and excitement by taking the listener on an emotional roller coaster ride where they will experience every known emotion to man. From happy to sad, hope to despair, nervous to confident, anticipation to disappointment, anger to calmness, and yes at times hate to love as well as shedding tears of joy or hurt.

As a commentator you are obliged to create an atmosphere to engage the listener. However you can't say a game is good when it isn't. What you can do though is find something to hook the listener so that he will stay with you until the end. There is always something, even in a 0–0 draw to be positive enthusiastic about. Otherwise you are effectively telling your audience to switch off and for me that is a cardinal sin in the world of radio.

For example in a game that was not the best he can say things like, 'can they hang on to what would be a great point?' Or, 'can they create one last chance to win the game?'

A common mistake by commentators is that they believe listeners are hanging on to their every word for the entire 90 minutes when that is just not the case. True some do, but lots are out and about shopping or whatever and getting in and out of the car, or if they are home answering the door or making tea or whatever. So it is important to keep on giving the latest score so that the listener knows how his team are doing. I also count down the game to increase the drama and tension.

Every listener who calls a phone in is paying the presenter and the radio station a massive compliment and that should never be forgotten. I treat them all as friends even if we disagree because that's how friends are. That's how they view me and that's how I do it. Unless, of course, they are abusive, aggressive, racist or homophobic – and then the gloves are off.

When I used to go to pubs and social clubs after playing non-league football we would sit and shoot the breeze about all things football. The banter flowed between Villa, Blues and Albion fans and yes sometimes it got heated, but we always ended up still pals because that's what we were. So when I took over as the host of the famous Friday night phone in on BRMB I decided to try and re-create that pub environment on the radio, talking, arguing and debating the big local football issues but still staying mates. There is no rule that says phone in's cannot be fun, full of banter, and be humorous, engaging, and entertaining as well as seriously debating the big issues.

That's why I never use big words on the radio apart from the fact I don't know any. I remember once hearing a local commentator talking about a 'coruscating performance?' I remember thinking what the hell was he talking about? So I looked it up and found it meant sparkling! – Well why not say sparkling? Talk the language of your listener because the minute he feels you're talking down to him or being educationally superior he will be off.

The way the world communicates is so different these days and that has meant that the phone in has had to change even more.

Years ago if your team lost a midweek game you would have to wait until the Friday night BRMB football phone in to air your anger, or you would send a letter to your local newspaper.

Now you can do it instantly 24/7 with the advent of social media sites Facebook and Twitter as well as texting and emailing, while there are various supporters forums, official club websites etc and of coursed local and national phone ins that allow you to get it off your chest quickly and make your views comments and opinions heard.

Over the last couple of years this has forced me to re-evaluate my approach to phone ins. I decided to make my programmes a banter chat and phone in show with a pundit working alongside me to not only add expertise, but also as a foil for my banter and I have to say in my opinion it works. And to be honest it's a phone in if you want it to be but there is no pressure to fill the show with calls. Having said that the lines are often red-hot if there is a big debate about things like the appointment of a new manager or if a team has lost a few games on the spin.

I started this new approach on Monday nights with former Aston Villa midfielder and Holte End Hero Ian Taylor and with Wolves legend and England U21 goalkeeper Matt Murray on a Friday. It proved successful with great banter that I hope the listeners enjoyed as much as we did. The comments on social media suggested they did. However we treated the serious issues as seriously as any fan would.

This means treating each text message, Facebook post, and Tweet as a call and discussing them as if they were on the phone. If you ignore social media in the modern world you are asking for trouble. A lot of people are not comfortable speaking live on the radio, but are quite happy to enter into a social media or text debate.

The world has moved on and in our business, whatever your age, you either embrace it or get left behind.

As of Aug 2016 the Goalzone has around 90,000 social media followers, which is a lot locally and far outshines any other local media social media totals.

However as much as it's a fantastic way to communicate and a brilliant way of keeping in touch with friends and family, the loony tunes very often hijack it and can cause great offence and hurt with their personal abuse. They are known as social media trolls.

I know what I call them, however In the interest of good taste I will just call them keyboard cowards. At one time it needed drink to turn cowards into brave men, sadly now all it takes is a computer.

I have been personally abused on a number of occasions and I have to say I am pretty thick skinned but when it affects your family and hurts them it's time to take action.

Someone would ask me a question on Facebook at one am and I would wake up in the morning to abuse because I have not responded immediately and accusing me of not caring about my followers.

I made a decision early on that I would control social media and not let it control me. Part of the problem with having so many friends/followers on social media is that they all expect an answer immediately. I just don't have the time to do it. There is no sport social media manager whose sole job it is, is to post every few minutes. I am not sitting on social media all day. Many presenters do not interact, but I like to argue the toss and debate issues and try my best to answer as many as I can and enjoy it.

I have no problem with anyone not liking me, or not rating me as a sports presenter or commentator but why should I allow them to hate me in my own backyard? Just so they can feel big by abusing me and more often than not without putting their real name. If they are abusive I block or delete them. Thankfully it's only a handful.

One great example happened when Blues were trying to sign Charles N'Zogbia from Wigan. Alex McLeish rang me and said the N'Zogbia deal is done and dusted, all agreed and he will put pen to paper tomorrow. He said go ahead and use it! So I put it out on BRMB sports bulletins and on our social media sites Facebook and Twitter.

Late that night Charles N'Zogbia or his agent said they wanted more money or the deal was off. He was told there was no more money and that a deal had been agreed. The upshot is that the deal was off. I still to this day cannot believe the personal abuse I took over that. My family were extremely upset. It wasn't Charles N'Zogbia that got abused for reneging on a deal but me – work that one out.

With the man I owe so much to, the legend Tony Butler

That persuaded me to delete all my family and friends and set up a private Facebook page for family and close friends, which I love and is great fun.

Quite a few years ago around about 2005 I was contacted by the BBC about my Friday night football phone in. They wanted it to be the focal point of a Radio 4 documentary about football phone in's. They said they wanted to use the legendary BRMB 'phone in', which in my opinion had more to do with Tony Butler than me.

They interviewed both of us, me because I was the longest serving host of the programme and Tony because he was the man who brought the football phone in to the airwaves. Not surprisingly we both had the same idea and feelings about 'phone ins'. However it was an honour that the BBC used an independent radio station as the main focus in a documentary, particularly when they have their own football phone in's.

Interestingly the broadcaster Clive Tildsley who also did a column in the *Daily Telegraph* used the BRMB phone in as the subject for one of his columns – saying it was essential listening?

Mind you I never get too carried away by any success perceived by me or others because I often walk into a press room anywhere in the country and some ex player or journalist will say, 'Are you still doing the radio – haven't they found you out yet?'

I always say this to fellow presenters and it is something that has served me well over the years, 'You are never as good as everyone tells you, you are – but you are never as bad as you think you are'.

I just love the banter with the listeners after the game. There was a Villa fan who came on after every match and was called Ashok and spoke with an Asian accent but was not Asian. He was hilarious and something the listeners looked forward to, although I am sure it is something that would be frowned on today. He used to take the micky out of Blues in such a way as even the Blues fans loved it. Sadly he died at the age of 35 rather suddenly and I went to his funeral and was amazed at how many people turned up.

Another was Acker whom I inherited from Tony Butler. Acker was a staunch Villa fan and would not call Birmingham City by its name preferring to just call the club 'Small Heath'. Acker left and went to live in Spain and one day he sent me a couple of photographs. One was him standing by the sea with his thumbs up and said this is for the Villa fans. The other showed him mooning – guess who that was for.

A more recent one was Lee the Baggies fan. Lee would come on and speak for five minutes plus and not come up for breath and then say, 'Up the Baggies ta-ra'. He became legendary and at times made some brilliant points but would then ruin it by saying he would be the best player Albion had if they would let him go to the training ground. Or he would say he would take the training and show them how to do whatever.

One listener who was a musician did a Rap song called *Lee the Baggie* and it was brilliant and you can still find it on YouTube. Lee even impressed Jasper Carrott who said to me that when he came out of St Andrew's he could not wait to put the post-match 'phone in' on to hear Lee and that all the people in his car would try and guess how many times Lee would say 'Tom' during his rant on the radio. I don't remember ever actually having a debate with Lee and it would have been a waste of time because he never ever went to the games. One day he called my pundit Tony Brown a prat, I immediately banned him and he is the only person I can remember banning from the airwaves. Bomber is a Baggies legend and deserved more respect than that. However Lee was radio gold and I loved his calls.

But one thing that cannot be denied is that the callers, texters, Facebookers and Tweeters are the real stars of the show.

There have been some crazy moments when commentating on football matches, here are just a few:

BRISTOL CITY – ASHTON GATE

Tommy Mooney was my pundit on the day and we were located in an enclosed press box within the stand so therefore surrounded by Bristol City supporters. Also next to us was former Villa player Scott Murray who was a pundit for BBC Radio Bristol.

Now the local BBC were texting and apologising for the noise of BRMB because we are loud. Well I am.

Anyway this guy outside the window suddenly turns round and starts accusing us of talking rubbish and being biased etc (remember Blues were winning so I am not sure what being biased meant). I was on air and said, 'excuse me we are working and on air so would he mind not shouting and swearing etc'.

As the half-time whistle blew he stood up and started shouting and gesticulating at us and telling us how we were cheating Brummies. Again I spoke to him and said he should not be doing that and he continued even more aggressively saying all sorts of things and he started pointing at us and that riled Tommy who made it clear to him in no uncertain terms that he should stop pointing and being aggressive. I quickly went to a break.

During the second half and at the end of the game he continued moaning at us while we were live on air and as he walked off all I could think of saying was, 'Have a safe journey home-thanks for the points'.

MIDDLESBROUGH – AYRESOME PARK

Covering a game between any of our clubs and Middlesbrough at the old Ayersome Park was a nightmare. You would be put in a row and every two minutes someone would be asking you to stand up so they could get past as kick-off approached. This is normally all right but you have to move when people want to get past and on this occasion a lot of people had interrupted me and I was on air when yet another person started tapping me on the shoulder. Now remember I am speaking on the radio so can't say anything but this man kept on tapping me on the shoulder. I eventually lost it and took of my headphones and let him have it both barrels and ended with telling him to f*** off. He went past to take his seat with the Radio Tees sports guys and I sat back down when the guy next to me said do you know who you have just told to f*** off? I said no to which he replied it was Chubby Brown. He was doing some work on the radio during the game? When I calmed down I apologised to him and it suddenly struck me that I am probably the only person to ever tell Chubby Brown to F*** off while he has made a living out of telling everyone else to f*** off.

MR BIRMINGHAM

I am quite happy being the Master of Ceremonies at sporting and or business dinners and interviewing sports stars or businessmen. Also doing auctions to raise money for charity is no problem and to be fair in these situations I am at my best.

Where I am not so comfortable is when I am the guest of honour. I do not like in anyway shape or form the focus being on me. That is why I have turned down numerous opportunities to accept an award or be introduced on the pitch at either St Andrew's, The Hawthorns or Villa Park.

In 2014 I received a telephone call from Emma Smith asking me if I would be photographed for a 'Mr Birmingham' exhibition of photographs. She ran through the list of those that were also being asked to participate and my first question to her was why on earth me?

However I was delighted to have the pictures taken – no problem there, especially with the way they can photo-shop and airbrush pictures these days. I was allowed to choose where I would be photographed and I chose St Andrew's. Well why not?

However what was difficult was turning up at the exhibition at Millennium Point in Birmingham and standing with all the other 'Mr Birmingham' participants while people looked at the pictures. That I found excruciatingly painful. Having said that I was absolutely proud and privileged to be included in my hometown.

After the exhibition the framed photographs were going to be auctioned for charity but in November I got another call from Emma saying that the photographs were going to be exhibited once again. This time at Grand Central in the John Lewis store.

I was delighted when she gave me permission to use one of the pictures as the cover for *The Game's Gone.*

CHAPTER THREE
THE BEAUTIFUL BUT CRUEL GAME

A few words from ROBERTO DI MATTEO

Roberto managed West Bromwich Albion between 2009 and 2011. He previously played for Lazio and Chelsea. He won 34 caps for Italy. He also managed MK Dons and Chelsea where he won the FA Cup and Champions League.

'I met Tom during my time at West Bromwich Albion. He has a great understanding of the game and therefore is able to communicate and share his comments with his public in an uncomplicated way. What distinguishes him from the rest of his peers is his passion for his job and football. He is a humble and easy-going person.

'It was very pleasant to speak to Tom about football during my time at West Bromwich Albion'.

When my dad came down from Scotland he was a fanatical football fan and wanted a local club to follow. We lived in New John Street West, Aston and I have to say it was a massive Villa area. So why did my dad choose Blues over Villa? Well it was quite simple a fellow Scotsman Alex Govan played for Blues and that was enough for my Dad who adored the goal-scoring winger.

Later in life I got to know Alex Govan through a video I narrated and helped to make called *The History of the Blues*. It was a wonderful day when Alex was at Blues to see a game and I got the chance to introduce him to my Dad who was absolutely thrilled. Alex had a long chat with him and my mom and I was so grateful and told Alex so. From that day Alex sent my Dad a Christmas card every year and always signed it Alex, *Keep Right On*. He did this until my Dad passed away. I have to say I also got a card every single year from Alex and they always took pride of place – Sadly Alex passed away in 2016. What a man. Can you imagine that happening with today's players?

One of my favourite football pics-with Blues legends Gil Merrick, Alex Govan, and Eddie Brown my Dads favourite players.

My Dad taught me to sing *Keep Right On* when I was a young boy. As a Scotsman he knew the Harry Lauder song so that when Alex brought it to Blues and they adopted it he couldn't wait to teach me it. It became the clubs battle hymn in 1956 after Alex sang it as they left the coach at the quarter-final.

Every other Saturday, oh how simple it was in those days pre SKY TV, we would walk down New John Street West to the bus stop and get the last number 19 bus that went passed St Andrew's. However we had to walk back.

The 19 was the lesser known City Circle Corporation bus route. There were three circle bus routes in those days. The number eight Inner Circle, number 19 City Circle and the number 11 Outer Circle. Only the number 11 is still operational today.

I can remember sitting on the 19 with my bobble hat on and my rattle in my hand. My hat had a few star badges on that had pictures of the players on them. Whenever Dad could afford it he would buy me one – but that wasn't often.

He rarely if ever paid for me to get into the ground as he would lift me over the turnstile and give the operator 'a drink' to turn a blind eye. We always went in the Emelline Street entrance to the Kop. I would then make my way down to the wall at the front and get my place. This was of course unless my Mom came with us and then we would be in the family lower Paddock at the Railway End.

Many times I used to take my football boots (solid toe capped with nailed in studs) to the game in case Blues were short, ah the innocence of youth. Mom knitted me a blue and white scarf with the names of the players sewed in blue on the white panels, which went well with my second-hand rattle, which she painted blue. These along with my star badges meant I was ready for action.

My first game was in 1956 at home to West Bromwich Albion and I remember vividly Trevor Smith being in the team. He along with Ken Green the left-back became my heroes. Blues won that 2–1 to go sixth in the league and by the way, were already in the FA Cup Final. I thought this is the team for me. Again… the innocence of youth!

My elder brother Frank managed to get two tickets for the FA Cup Final, but I was too young to go so he went with a pal. I was devastated but Dad pacified me by saying he would take me next time – I'm still waiting!

There were only two Blues fans in our School, St Chad's, me and Cornelius Walsh. We regularly got beat up by Villa fans. Con and I used to go to the games when in our teens. He lived on Aston Road North with his Granddad who came from Cork. I must have had many conversations with him over the years but never understood a word he said.

Con was with me in 1963 when we saw Blues win the first leg of the Football League Cup Final 3–1 against Aston Villa thanks to two goals from Ken Leek and one from the brilliant Jimmy Bloomfield. I was on the Holte End for the second leg, which ended 0–0 and Blues lifted the trophy. In those days it was not considered a major trophy as it was not at Wembley, There was no European qualification for winning and a few of the bigger teams did not take part. However even if it was not the FA Cup it was magnificent for me to watch the players lifting the cup and at Villa Park. Con and I talked about it for ages.

Watching Blues compete in two European Finals was also special for me. They lost both over two legs one to Barcelona and the other to Roma. The competition was the Inter-Cities Fairs Cup. They drew 0–0 with the Spaniards in 1960 in the first leg of the final, but lost 4–1 in the second leg in the Nou Camp.

The following season in 1961 we saw the famous Italian side Inter Milan at St Andrew's with Blues winning 2–1. Blues also won the second leg 2–1 to set up a two-legged final against Roma. The first leg under floodlights ended 2–2 with Mike Hellawell and Bryan Orritt scoring. However Blues lost the second leg 2–0 with the game ending in a brawl. Great times for a young kid from the back-to-back slums of inner Birmingham to see these fantastic foreign teams in the flesh.

I am often asked who is my all-time favourite Blues player and I have to say it's a difficult thing to answer because as a very young boy my hero would change dependant on the era. However without any fear of argument Trevor Francis was the greatest player to ever play for the club.

with pals Trevor Francis and Jasper at the announcement of Trevor getting a Star on Broad Street.

Anyway my all-time list of favourite Blues players include the following in no particular order

- Alex Govan
- Trevor Smith
- Ken Green
- Dick Neal
- Freddie Pickering
- Johnny Vincent
- Bob Latchford
- Trevor Francis
- Bob Hatton
- Kevan Broadhurst
- Mark Dennis
- Julian Dicks
- Garry Pendrey
- Barry Bridges
- Roger Hynd
- Bertie Auld

- Gil Merrick
- Alan Campbell
- Harry Hooper
- Ken Leeke
- Ray Martin
- Eddie Brown
- Peter Murphy
- Barry Bridges
- Ray Martin
- Martin Grainger
- Paul Peschisolido
- Geoff Horsfield
- Martin O'Connor
- Mark Ward
- Maik Taylor
- Stephen Carr
- Barry Ferguson

A few words from COLIN TATTUM

Colin was the *Birmingham Mail's* chief sportswriter covering Birmingham City games and is now the Head of Communications at Birmingham City.

I'm not sure we will see the like of Tom Ross again. I know that sets up the obvious retort of 'thank goodness' – and Rossi wouldn't expect anything less of me to suggest that and answer my own gag at his expense.

But no, we won't.

In short, he is synonymous with the Birmingham and West Midlands football and broadcasting scene. They won't make 'em like him again.

Everywhere you go around the country and you bump into someone who has played, managed or even just passed through our patch, he is well known.

No, let's change that (and he won't like me saying it, the phrase is banded about too much, but he is), Tom is more: he is a Birmingham legend.

It's not just a case of familiarity, or association, why so many know him and know of him, it's a case of respect.

I don't think any of the countless people I have come across connected with football in the region, or sports people in general, have a bad word to say about him. And that is a testament to his character, his probity, his standards and the fact that people can trust him.

The industry Tom made his name and reputation in has changed. There is more wariness, there is not that connection nor openness between journalist and manager/player/owner. As Tom indeed might say – and I love parodying him lamenting – 'the game's gone'.

It has. However, Tom has been a constant. He has gone about his job in a steadfast, professional way throughout those changes over the years and he has never, ever tried to stitch anyone up. Some people – those who have never had to walk in his shoes or understand the role – find it a cheap kick to be critical of his style. Especially via social media behind a keyboard.

But let me say this: if there was no Tom Ross doing what he does and what he has done, our understanding and reporting of the Birmingham and West Midlands scene would be all the poorer, and lacking colour, personality and authoritative fact.

I came into Tom's professional life later than others and, I admit, as a youngster you did feel a little intimidated of him. I used to listen to him on the radio and before I knew it, we were watching and reporting on Birmingham City games in the same press box.

As the new lad on the Birmingham Evening Mail, and still learning as I went, at first Tom was very territorial and protective of his domain and I sensed a certain amount of standoffishness. But that's Tom; he is very competitive, proud of his work and wants to be the best and first to the punch.

Eventually I'd like to think he saw that we had the same kind of standards, views and enthusiasm for the game and Blues. And for the past 25 years or so, we have travelled together – Tom driving and, no, we have not had a prang (somehow) – to games.

And he probably won't realise this, but those journeys to all points of the country were some of the most enjoyable times I have ever had. We would simply talk football, talk shop, recount anecdotes, argue about the team, players (it always seemed to be Cameron Jerome) and although we might often disagree, we never fell out.

Over the years ex-Blues players like Kevan Broadhurst, Jon McCarthy, Darren Carter and Gary Rowett would be with us, as Tom's radio pundit.

It was like being in a dressing room. Any player – from Sunday league to Premier League – will tell you that the chat, the stories, the camaraderie of a dressing room is something that is very special.

Tom is a very private man as well as a public personality and I knew never to pry. We are similar in that respect: if there is a problem we just got on with it. Again, when I was going through a difficult period in my life, those trips, the good times we had at games, the mickey taking and laughs helped me through immensely and he simply said that if I needed anything he was there.

That's a measure of the man. He was brought up the right way (even if he does claim to be Scottish?) and has never lost that work ethic instilled into him by his parents. In fact, I often told him he did too much. He does charity functions, forums, dinners, all sorts and also ran the GOLD radio station, in its various guises, effectively as a one man army.

In 2011, when Blues won the Carling Cup, beating Arsenal at Wembley, it was momentous. Being so close to the highs and travails of the club for so long, such an achievement gets to you that little bit extra. Tom's commentary that evening has to be heard to be believed. The passion, the raw emotion in the voice. It meant so much. For me, that was a magical moment in itself. And when the final whistle went I turned round and it was fitting that Tom was right behind me, in the row and seat above.

We didn't really have to say anything; our wide-eyed, stupid smiles were enough. Jon McCarthy was just giggling and laughing at us. Somehow it seemed appropriate.

Like many, I have been fortunate to come across and then get to know Tom Ross. I'd like to count him not just as an institution in his field, someone you would always listen to and generate debate, but I'd be proud to be considered a friend.

Apart from the infamous Anglo Italian tournament (more about that later) I had to wait until 2011–12 season to see Blues in Europe again. This came as a result of them winning the Carling Cup.

For the record Blues drew 0–0 with Nacional on 18 August winning the home leg on 25 August 3–0. A month later at St Andrew's on 15 September we lost 1–3 to Braga. On 29 September Blues won 2–1 away at Maribor in Slovenia, a second away win was secured at Club Brugge 1–2 on 20 October in Belgium. This was followed by two games in November, against Club Brugge at home on the third, which was drawn 2–2 and then a defeat on the thirtieth away to Braga. Blues involvement in the competition ended on 15 December with a 1–0 win at St Andrew's over Maribor

First up was a trip to the Island of Madeira, which is Portuguese. I had heard a lot about the problems landing at their Funchal Airport so decided to Google it (get me). I found it was known as Europe's most dangerous airport and watched some videos, which as departure date neared I wished I hadn't.

The airport is built on the side of the island with the runway having the sea on one side and homes on a rising hill on the other. Part of the runway is on stilts in the sea. It suffers from dreadful cross winds that makes landing difficult and I have to say different, to say the least and it needs pilots who are experienced in landing there.

I didn't really believe it to be fair, however to say Colin Tattum was nervous was an understatement as we had to stop at Lisbon in our old Belgian Air Force plane to change pilots as we needed one who knew how to land at the Funchal airport. As the plane comes in to land it has to bank steeply as it turns right so all you can see out of the windows on one side is the sea and the other the sky. But we landed with no problems whatsoever, thankfully stopping just feet from the end of the runway –never a problem.

We stayed in a beautiful hotel with glorious sunshine and yet when we got in our taxi and went up to Estadio da Madeira, the stadium, it was cold freezing and foggy but it was a great game and the Euro adventure had begun.

Me, Colin Tattum, Mark Regan and John Wragg went out for a beautiful meal in the centre of Madeira. I could not believe it when Colin and Mark had a hot piece of slate put in front of them and a chunk of raw beef. The Idea being to cut off a piece of raw meat and cook it yourself on the slate? 'For God's sake,' I said to them,' we were doing that 2,000 years ago.' Colin overdid the red wine on his beef and from that moment on he was on another planet.

We left the restaurant and got into a cab because Mark and Colin wanted to go to this pub where the Blues fans were. We told the Taxi driver the name but he wouldn't move. I speak Spanish and although it was in Portugal the taxi driver also spoke Spanish. He told me we were already here and I relayed that to the two lads Mark and Colin who, rather worse for wear thanks to the red wine, insisted they knew the way to it and would direct the taxi driver. Despite my protestations they were adamant. So off we went with them directing the driver. After 20 minutes and 70 Euros the driver pulled up outside the pub, which was next door to the restaurant we had left 20 minutes earlier. To make matters worse John Wragg and I stopped in the cab to go back to the hotel and ended up paying the bill because of those two nuggets.

For the commentary Free Radio (formerly BRMB) and Radio WM (Mark Regan) had booked ISDN lines and I arrived before Mark and inadvertently plugged into the BBC line. Mark arrived and said don't worry they are next to each other anyway. However the one that I had plugged into (the BBC one) did not work. The Portuguese equivalent of BT sent out an engineer who was more like Basil Fawlty when it came to technical issues.

He was less that useless and all he could do was hit it with a hammer, which along with a screwdriver was all he had in his toolbox. I got more irritated as kick off and programme start time drew closer. I almost came to blows with him as I tried to explain what we needed.

In the end Basil couldn't fix it and I might as well have asked Manuel to do it Que? Because that is all he kept on saying.

Next up was Slovenia. Which was a beautiful country and so clean. One thing that's stands in my mind was the absence of customs at the airport. We arrived, got off plane, walked into this building at the end was a door, we walked through it and we were out in the street with all our luggage on trolleys and it was a case of help yourself.

Once our work was finished we went down to the side of the Drava River in Maribor and sat at a pub where the world's oldest Vine was growing on the wall and still had grapes growing. It was over 400 years old and had tourists from all over the world taking photos of it. I was sitting outside the pub having a drink with Colin and the lads when my phone rang and it was Darryl Eales who was the main man at Free Radio's owners LDC. He asked me what I was doing drinking when I should be working. I looked to my left and he was at the next table laughing his head off. He was a massive Blues fan and eventually tried to buy it from Carson Yeung. He offered me a lift back to Brum on the LDC private jet – to this day I do not know why I said no? Preferring instead to travel back on Buddy Holly Airlines with the Blues.

It was on the plane on the way to Slovenia that Blues fans told the Captain/Pilot that it was my birthday. He announced it to everyone and immediately player's, fans and press started singing *Happy Birthday*. A lovely touching emotional moment spoilt by one small thing! It wasn't my birthday?

We went out in the city at night for something to eat and found it very difficult to find somewhere open. Walking down a street with Rob Gurney and Colin Tattum we came across Blues fans outside a bar having more than a few sherbets. As soon as they saw me it was Happy Birthday all over again and despite me asking for mercy they gave me the bumps while I was holding a pint of diet coke – to mine and their amazement I didn't spill a drop.

However as Gary Newbon once said to me as long as they know your name?

Then came Bruges and what can you say. It is without doubt one of the most beautiful of cities in Europe. Although it's fair to say it does love a church and chocolate shop. The people of Bruges were expecting a load of thugs and idiots who were going to smash up the town. They expected this because of irresponsible journalism in one of their local newspapers that talked about 'the invading Zulus'. As it happened a lifetime bond of friendship developed between the people of Bruges and Birmingham. The atmosphere in the big square by the cathedral was truly amazing and in fact is one of the best I have ever experienced with plenty of warm-hearted banter and friendliness in abundance. The local police joined in an impromptu game of football. Just amazing. To this day I don't know how a Blues fan managed to get a Blues flag and hang it out of the top window in the cathedral.

The final game was in Portugal in Braga, which is a city not far from Porto on the west coast. The stadium was carved out of a quarry and built as a Euro 2004 venue. It is bizarre because despite a capacity of 30,000 one end is just a rock face.

We were walking around the square watching the Blues fans enjoying themselves when a funny moment occurred. A local teacher accompanied his class of boys and girls marched into the square and lined up facing the Blues fans and began to sing,

'We are the Champions'. The Blues fans gave them a loud round of applause – one amazing trip.

I met up with some friends, Phil and Jill Teague who lived in Spain and had driven to meet me in Braga. Both fanatical Blues fans and in fact Phil was the Blues electrician for some time before leaving for Spain. I took them to a restaurant highly recommended by John Wragg of the Daily Express and it was a disaster. I have to tell you without any fear of argument it was the worst place and the worst food I have ever experienced anywhere in the world. Obviously no one had told them poisoning is illegal. The fish was only a skeleton and the bread was rock hard!

That Europa League experience proved to me if I needed it to be proved just how fantastic the Blues fans are. It was a massive disappointment for everyone that we did not qualify for the later stages as previously ten points would have got them through.

However it was an amazing journey and one I shall never forget. Sadly I don't think it will ever happen again in my lifetime. However the glass half full side of me says you can never say never, so here's hoping.

To sum up that tournament: Blues had no expectation of getting into a European competition and so were determined to enjoy every moment because they knew that it would be a long time before the club did it again.

I also covered Villa in Europe in the 1990–91 season when firstly I went to Ostrava in Czechoslovakia where Villa faced Banik Ostrava. Ostrava was close to the border with Poland and I have to say it was the poorest country I have ever been in. it was just as the Soviet Union was breaking up. I remember going with George Gavin and two other journo's for a meal and it cost around £3 all-inclusive. It was difficult to spend all the money we had with us things were that cheap.

Walking through the city centre it was just like watching one of those Eastern Bloc spy films with trolley buses and trams and deserted streets.

The four of us got into a cab to go back to our hotel. The cab was a very old yellow car that looked like it was from the 50s or before.

Now just to remind you I don't drink, however the other lads had had a good night and a little worse for wear having sampled the local sherbets etc. The cab driver didn't speak English, but then why should he, and he wore NHS style spectacles where the lens was at least half an inch thick.

Within a few minutes we are going the wrong way down a major road with a massive central reservation full of rocks and debris, which went the length of the road. I am screaming while the others are laughing! I shout at the driver who has no idea what's happening because he cannot see while I could see only too well cars coming toward us. Thankfully he suddenly swerved across the reservation over rocks etc. and bumped down on the other side and we continued with me having had my constipation cured.

The next UEFA Cup game for Villa was against Inter Milan in Italy and what a trip that was! It is one of the beautiful cities and I enjoyed visiting the Duomo Cathedral

Some of the media in Czechoslovakia for Villa's UEFA Cup game v Banik Ostrava.

and going to see Leonardo Da Vinci's painting of the Last Supper. Truly amazing when I could get close enough, due to the numbers of tourists.

Me, George, Rob Beasley and others were leaving our hotel to go and find a restaurant to have dinner when we walked down a street by the station with lots of gorgeous girls standing on one side. Well to be honest we all looked because they were stunning and when one opened the top of her fur coat to show a she had nothing on underneath what could you do? However when she then undid the bottom of the fur coat to show it was Arthur and not Martha and started to cross the road towards us we did the 100 metres in a time that would have put Usain Bolt to shame.

From an early age I only ever wanted to be a footballer. Never wanted to drive a train or fly a plane just play the greatest game at the highest-level possible.

In the early days when I was living with my Gran and Granddad in Lea Village I used to play in the Park, which was between the Tavern pub and Folliot Road, If not there we would play over at Donkey's Hollow by the railway line.

I played with a guy in the park called John Duce who later became my best pal. He was known as pudding and to this day I don't know why, but what a great footballer he was an eight out of 10 every game.

I was at this time training and playing with Hinckley Athletics youth team under the manager ship of Dudley Kernick. Dudley later became the Commercial manager of Stoke City and also helped produce the TV series about a football team called United. Bobby Gould says he was training with Hinckley on Tuesdays and Thursdays at that time but I don't recollect him or perhaps just did not realise.

I was never good enough for a club that was heading into the Southern League and Dudley knew it even if I didn't. However I was such a good trainer, and would run through a wall for him and kick anyone, he did not have the heart to tell me I was not wanted, so what did he do? He left me standing at the clock garage in Castle Bromwich where he used to pick me up with his son Robin. That was his way of telling me I was not good enough. I wrote about it in Dudley's book, which was called *Who the Hell was Dudley Kernick*. I have seen him a couple of times since when he has come back to England from Florida where he now lives and we laugh about it.

At this time I was also invited to go to Barrow for a trial. They were in the Third Division North. I remember travelling alone on the train and the journey seemed to take forever – I played and I remember them saying that they would write to me and to this day I haven't had a letter. I might have been the next Beckham? Somehow I don't think so and probably more Victoria than David.

These knock-backs knocked me sideways and left me disillusioned so I did nothing for a while. One day I saw an advert in *The Argus* for players for a Sunday team playing in the Selly Oak league. I replied to it and was invited by the manager Charlie Newman to turn up for trials. When I got there to my surprise John Duce was also there.

We played in that team together on Sundays for over 20 years and had the time of our lives. It was great fun. The team at the time was called Ladywood Swifts and was due to play in the Selly Oak and District League. Also in the team was George Clamp who went on to have a distinguished non-league career but he also played with us for

My Sunday team –Rosander FC in the Sunday Alliance Premier League.

years. Within a year Charlie changed the name to Rosander with Charlie telling us it was the name of a famous foreign footballer, but we have never been able to verify that.

We were very successful in the Selly Oak League, then we progressed into the North Birmingham League, winning everything before moving into the Sunday Alliance Premier where we didn't win everything although we did reach a cup final. I must have played over 1,300 competitive non-league games and I scored 5 goals – a veritable machine.

The highlight for me was being selected for the League Representative XI to play in a national cup competition.

The pitches in those early days were incredibly bad: Sennelleys Park where you played uphill both halves in three foot of mud or Billesley Common when you needed a taxi if you were playing on pitch 19, which was in a different postcode. I hated matches being called off, so it was always up to me to persuade the referee that the pitch was playable even when it most obviously wasn't!

I recollect when we reached our second cup final, which was to be played at Alvechurch FC against Bournville Tigers.

It was just a great day as all my family were there and for us, who were not really used to anyone watching and for the first time we wore an all-white strip.

The day got better as we won 3–2 and I scored the winner from left-back. It was described in the *Sports Argus* as a 'rasping volley'. Although I think that was journalistic licence. It was one of five goals I scored in over 1,300 games – Pele eat your heart out?

One of the other Rosander players I played with in later years was Chris Allman and coincidentally I caught up with him recently when I found out he was uncle to my great pal Mark Hunt, who owns Fort Used Car Centre in Birmingham and who sponsors my car at Free Radio. What a small world it is?

Mark along with Paddy Lynch and Bomber Fewtrell have been close friends for a long time and we are always out socially. Mark and his lovely wife Jo provided the cars for my wedding to Anne in June 2015. What a coincidence to find Chris was driving the best man and me to the church 35 years after we played together.

I became very friendly with John Westmancoat, who was secretary at the Birmingham County Football Association in Victoria Road in Aston. This was due to being sent off, primarily for fighting a lot. It's a wonder I was not invited to the FA staff parties. I have had so many personal appeals/hearings that John would laugh when I turned up with a 'not you again' smile. Little did he know that I still played when suspended but under someone else's name. Wrong, but I could not stand not playing at the weekend, it was what I looked forward to.

However, little did I know that that friendship would help me when I got into broadcasting with BRMB because he was then the secretary at Walsall under the chairmanship of Ken Weldon and he also ended up at Birmingham City when Ken bought it?

Vic Callow, who eventually became a top Premier League referee once sent me off. Now remember while he was officiating in the PL he also sent off Eric Cantona and Paul Gascoigne. What great company I kept?

When I was playing I always got picked, sometimes to the annoyance of better players in the squad. I was picked I am sure because the manager could trust me and rely on me and I would give everything to the team over the 90 minutes.

I couldn't pass water, but could tackle and run all day and defend with an over my dead body attitude that was in my view, and thankfully the view of managers I played for, a necessity when it came to balance and the makeup of a team.

I have never underestimated the power of desire over ability. The Americans have got it right 'second place is first placed loser' – a player's character is as important as his skill – he has to play the same way whether is being paid £100k a week or £50 a week.

One of my managers said, 'For every concert pianist there has to be someone who carries the piano onto the stage,' well that was me – a piano carrier. The reason I was sent off so many times was because the manager would give me a job to do on the opposition's best player. I would get sent off while their best player was either sent off with me or carried off. So a good swap as far as my managers were concerned. I am definitely ashamed of some of the things I did on the pitch, although I meet up with the guys I played against and they bear no grudges.

One I regret was with a lovely guy called Brian Kenning. He was a tremendous midfielder who had it all. He was the orchestra leader that made their team tick. My manager at the time Phil said you have got to stop him anyway you can. So I nailed him, a couple of times and eventually he had had enough and we started fighting and we both had red cards. The manager just said what a good trade that was?

Anyway back to my dreams with Hinckley Athletic. I was doing my paper round, going to school as I had stayed on and I was training like a lunatic. I ran everywhere and was genuinely as fit as anyone.

At that time I was convinced I was good enough to be in with a chance! But now I know I wasn't anywhere near good enough. Dudley loved my attitude but was spot on; I was just not good enough for that level but to leave me standing at the Clock Garage??

I knew then that desire and commitment were vital but would only get you so far and I also realised that ability without it was just a waste of time, as I had confirmed much later in life. It disappointed me so much that I just concentrated on playing on Sundays with my mates.

Eventually in the 70s I got the chance to join Boldmere St Michael's in the Midland Combination and enjoyed a few fantastic and enjoyable years at Church Road – They were a truly friendly club with an amazing bunch of people.

I remember my first pre-season with the then manager Alan Hampton. Now I was fit but had never trained so hard in my life and will admit to throwing up before we finished. I had a great time I loved it both playing and the social side, which was amazing.

I recollect one time when I was in the second team playing under Robin Whetnall and not having the best of times. I clearly remember one day when we were playing Wolves A team at the Wolves training ground Castlecroft, Robin asked me to play in midfield probably because he felt he needed someone to get into their talented professional midfielders.

On reflection I may have been one of the first defensive sitting midfielders. We drew 0–0 and I probably played the best game I've ever played in my life. I nailed a few of their midfielders and they just did not like it and that Billy Big Time attitude just wound me right up. After the game Robin said he was pleased with my performance and admitted it had surprised him and reminded me that some of those we were playing against would become Wolves first team players. From not being sure I could contribute Robin gave me a huge lift by saying, 'play like that and you will always be in my team'. Yet all I did was run around and get stuck in and to be fair kicked anything that moved and if it didn't I kicked it until it did. It was how most played in those days especially the defensive players.

I remember my brother Frank who was a much more talented player being invited to go to Blues for trials. I was amazed that he didn't go. He said he wouldn't go because he knew he wasn't good enough. I have to be honest it annoyed me that he never went to find out if he was or wasn't good enough. I would have loved that opportunity. I would rather someone tell me I am not good enough instead of me making that decision for them.

However being friends with players I remember in the 80s being invited by Ron Saunders to do a day's pre-season training with Blues at Damson Lane – now that was hard. At various times in 70s and 80s I have trained with Blues injured players running up and down the Kop terraces and boy did I find that tough.

Like most other amateur players I would get a call to play for some team or other when I was not playing myself. Old Nortonians in the Birmingham AFA was one I really enjoyed helping out now and again as it gave me a chance to play with my brother Frank.

Just as I was in my teens I played for St Joseph's in the Catholic Sunday League in the mornings before playing for Rosander in the afternoons. I loved it because again it gave me a chance to play with my Brother Frank. The team was useless to be fair but it was all mates and run by a brilliant guy called Tommy Powell. All this was great grounding for a young teenager in how to deal with situations when the odds are stacked against you.

I have to say I became a better player once I started playing with the WBA All Stars and then the Blues All Stars but more about that later.

Playing on the St Andrews pitch for the first time was a joy I will never forget until the day I die. I have since played on all the other big local grounds but St Andrews was just so special especially with my Dad watching.

My first appearance on my beloved St Andrews in a charity match. One of the biggest thrills of my life.

Although everyone knows I am a Bluenose, most, I am sure, also realise that I love Midland's football and certainly I try in every way to be fair and even-handed in the way I deal with all the clubs in our region. I have some great memories to share with you:

WALSALL

My favourite time with The Saddlers were the days at Fellows Park when Ken Wheldon was the Chairman and Alan Buckley was the manager with my pal Garry Pendrey as his assistant.

I persuaded Alan to take part in the BRMB feature 'Mystery Singing Sports Star', which involved a sports personality singing a song and the listeners winning a prize if they could guess the identity of the mystery guest. Now most of our guests just ran into the microphone but not Alan – his choice of song was *What Can I Say* by Boz Scaggs which was OK, but he could only do it if he came running through as if he was coming on to a stage! Amazing and laugh a minute.

Walsall was a great place for me to go for interviews with no press officer to hold up an imaginary barrier. There was always a cup of tea from the big metal teapot that most clubs had.

I got on great with the players and formed some great friendships that are still strong today. But I have to say they were a nightmare.

87

Whenever I went to interview either Alan or the chairman Ken Weldon, by the time I returned to the car park something would have happened to my BRMB car: On one occasion they had nicked the wheels off it and left it on bricks. Another time I just could not find it as they had moved it down the road. It was bloody annoying but also great banter and fun something I have always loved about the game. Players love it when you join in with the banter. Sadly today journalists or radio broadcasters don't get the opportunity.

Games that stick in my memory about Walsall include the 1984 Milk Cup (League Cup) semi-final against Liverpool who were going for the treble. Remember Walsall had beaten Arsenal at Highbury in the previous round while Liverpool had knocked out Birmingham City.

The first leg of the semi-final at Anfield had ended in a 2–2 draw in which Alan Buckley made a brilliant tactical change by bringing on Kevin Summerfield when the Saddlers were losing 2–1. Kevin equalised. Then Mark Rees, who was one of the 'looney tunes' who messed about with my car, missed a great chance to win the game for the Saddlers.

In the second leg there were 19,951 spectators crammed into Fellows Park and when Ronnie Whelan made the score 2–0 a surge of Liverpool fans caused a perimeter wall to collapse and 24 people were hurt. Liverpool ran out 4–2 winners on aggregate.

Another match I covered was the 2001 Football League Division Two Play-Off Final, which was held at The Millennium Stadium, Cardiff – it was the first season that the arena had been used because Wembley was being re-built. Walsall beat Reading 3–2 after extra-time.

Walsall Football Club was and still is a lovely, friendly club. My Pal Dean Smith was the manager, with another pal Richard O'Kelly as his second in command. They did a brilliant job on a shoestring budget and to be honest didn't even have the shoestring. They now ply their trade at Brentford.

WOLVERHAMPTON WANDERERS

A few words from MATT MURRAY

Matt was a goalkeeper who spent his entire career at Wolverhampton Wanderers. His career was plagued by injuries, which eventually forced him to retire aged 29. He also played for England U21s and but for injury would surely have played for the full England team. Since retiring, Matt has worked as a match reporter and in-studio summariser for Sky Sports News while co-hosting the Friday night Banter Chat and Phone In on Free Radio 80s with Tom.

'With Tom Ross it is all about the banter.
'On Saturday afternoons when Tom is going round the Midlands grounds to get expert opinion from his pundits, Dave "Benno" Bennett and I would

always try to wind Tom up by calling him a silly name, usually a derivative of Thomas but he always got the final word because he would just cut us off.

'"Benno" was always giving us stick because he had won the FA Cup and the rest of us had won nothing!

'Tom is extremely well respected, he can be trusted and he is totally professional; if he was commentating on a Wolves v Birmingham City game and Wolves scored you would not be able to tell from his commentary how much that had hurt him – he is full of passion for football and particularly the Blues.

'He is a man with morals; if he was offered a better job and his current employers would not let him go then he would see that contract through to the best of his ability without holding a grudge.

'His understanding of the modern game of football gains him respect within the sport – he always gives an honest take on whatever you ask him – except when he is on air! I know sometimes that he agrees with me, but he will argue against me to ensure that the listener gets to hear the opposite point of view.

'Driving with Tom is an experience and you need to have had three Weetabix before you get in his car, having said that, the time flies by due to the constant banter. Tom has a mantra, which he calls YOLO – You Only Live Once!

'He will always help you if he can and I was always impressed by Tom's charity work. Even though he is so busy he always tries to help, especially for Help Harry Help Others. Anything you tell him you can 100% guarantee that it will go no further – people have absolutely trust in Tom which is unusual in the world of media.

'Things I recall:

'Tom's Crooked Quiz – when even though he knows he has read the question wrong he will not admit his mistake and will say "well I told you it was crooked".

'My suits – When he see's me on SKY TV he always says he can hear my suit buttons screaming "help" because my jacket is tight.

'He loves me being on SKY because then he knows he can pop round to see my missus, mind you he is definitely punching above his weight to marry Anne! We always tell him that.

'And if you ever get the chance ask him about what happened when he was playing for a radio station five-a-side team when a member of the opposition nutmegged him and laughed? (He chinned him.)

It was in the mid 80s when George sent me to lots of Wolves games home and away. I witnessed their fantastic post Chorley re-birth as they charged back up the divisions with Steve Bull and Andy Mutch in sensational form scoring loads of goals.

I loved it because I was friends with Graham Turner the manager and his assistant Garry Pendrey and they gave me great access.

Forum with Wolves striker Steve Bull a genuine guy who always gave me loads of banter about Blues

Being in the fourth-tier of the football league meant that I was visiting far flung places of the football world, like Halifax where the banter in the Press Room surrounded the club's financial situation: 'If you want a light at your seat in the press box you have to bring a light bulb with you'. It was great in my development as a radio reporter/presenter because grounds are so much better now

Sir Jack Haywood –Wolves owner

Covering the Wolves brought about my first appearance on television although it was only a photograph of me whilst I gave my post-match analysis on Channel 4.

I can still hear the Wolves barmy army singing their song, 'Everywhere we go people wanna know'. That travelling army did a lot to inspire the team to the great success they had.

I also had some funny and not so funny situations linked to Wolves games, which appear later.

I remember being in the middle of a volatile post match phone in when my producer Salty said next caller is Jack a Wolves fan. I went to him and was amazed to find that it was Sir Jack Haywood calling from his boat in the middle of the ocean off the Bahamas. He had been listening to our commentary on the Wolves game and had called to say how much he had enjoyed it and to talk about the game just like any other fan. What I found endearing about it was that he didn't come on to our phone answerer saying I am Sir Jack Haywood owner of Wolves get me on. He just waited in the phone queue just like any other fan. I said I was giving every Wolves caller a 'Wolves Bronx Hat', so I would send him one for being a great Wolves call and did, although I am sure he would have no need for it out in the Bahamas. A top man and I was privileged proud and honoured to be invited to his funeral In Wolverhampton

WEST BROMWICH ALBION

A few words from TONY 'BOMBER' BROWN

Tony 'Bomber' Brown played For West Bromwich Albion as an attacking midfielder who scored spectacular goals. He was part of an Albion team that built a reputation as a great side in the league and the cup. He won the 1966 League Cup Final and the 1968 FA Cup Final and finishing as runners-up in the League Cup in 1967 and 1970. He was the top scorer in Division One in 1970–71 and received his only England cap at the end of that season.

After relegation in 1973, he helped Albion to win promotion back to Division One in 1976. He scored 279 goals in 720 competitive games for Albion, both club records.

Tony also played in the USA for New England Tea Men. He holds just about every single record at West Brom and they recently erected a statue to him outside the main entrance to the Hawthorns. He was a pundit with Tom on BRMB for over 20 years.

> *'I would describe Tom Ross as "top notch".*
> *'I first met him after I had finished playing and was turning out for the West Bromwich Albion All-Stars. Tom played left-back for us along with Baggies' legends such as John Wile, Johnny Giles, Ally Robertson, Ally Brown etc and when he was on the pitch – as he was often a substitute – he*

would try to do one or two things with the ball. This used to infuriate Johnny Giles who would say "Tom, you just win the ball and then give it to me, someone who can pass it!"

'*Tom is well respected because he is so professional, he gets to know everybody and because he knows his football, l pros and ex-pros will talk to him.*

'*My first job working alongside Tom at football matches was as a summariser for an away game at Bolton, as Jeff Astle couldn't make it – I must have done a decent job as I was taken on permanently to a job that lasted for nearly twenty years. Tom was terrific to work with and he taught me that you need to work hard for the sake of the audience and hopefully I developed what Tom would call "good habits".*

'*We must have travelled thousands of miles doing the job, Tom always drove and I am a nervous passenger, but we got through the journeys listening to and singing along with music from the 60s which we had booming out of the car's speaker – we must have looked like a couple of loonies.*

'*Tom was a delight to work with, he's even-handed, impartial and he never switches off! That's his professionalism.*

'*It is not easy being a pundit but straight away Tom put me at ease saying he would give me a signal and then all I had to do was just say what had happened. As an ex-professional you have an insight to an incident, which the listener will not know and because I have probably experienced that incident during my career I can sympathise with what has happened and give a different perspective.*

'*We get on really well and have a habit of "corpsing" for no reason and I always get the blame for most things that go wrong!'*

The West Bromwich Albion All Stars charity team in the 80s.

I have always had a fantastic relationship with West Bromwich Albion due mainly I am sure to playing for the Albion All Stars charity team and of course being great pals with Bomber Brown, Bobby Hope, Garry Pendrey, Joe Mayo, Ally Robertson and many more.

One stand out game for me was during the club's promotion to the Premier League in 2003–04. The crucial game was away at Bradford. Bomber and I were feeling the tension ourselves with the score at 0–0. Don't forget Albion were neck and neck with the Wolves in the race for promotion. Bob Taylor had come on late in the game and won a penalty – Bob was injured in the incident and needed treatment meaning penalty taker Igor Balis had to wait some time before he could take it. This is stressful for any player but he scored and the place erupted. I don't know how many Baggies fans were in the stadium officially but when the ball hit the back of the net they emerged from every part of the ground. And I mean every single part of the ground. I remember looking down and there was one in the Bradford dug out – They were everywhere!!!

I got caught up in the excitement of the moment and live on air I said, 'They'll be running out of toilet rolls in Wolverhampton tonight!' which caused a few comments which Baggies fans loved and Wolves, I am sure, didn't.

A few words from BLIND DAVE HEELEY

About Dave...

The father-of-three from West Bromwich, who is known as Blind Dave became the first blind person to complete the seven marathons in seven days in seven countries challenge in 2008.

The first marathon was in the Falkland Islands via Rio de Janerio, Los Angeles, Sydney, Dubai, Tunis and culminating at the Flora London Marathon.

Dave, from West Bromwich, has run 10 marathons in 10 days travelling from John O'Groats to Land's End and cycled between each stage raising money for Macmillan Trust.

Prior to the 2012 Olympics in London, Heeley carried the Olympic Torch on a 300-metre stretch of the relay before taking part in the opening ceremony of the Paralympics on 29 August 2012.

He has also taken part in Seven in Seven, a 700-mile week-long bike ride between Zurich and Birmingham in aid of Help Harry Help Others.

'Tom Ross, well!

'Young man, I feel I have known you all my life, ever since I've listened to local radio, from Xtra am days to present day Free Radio 80s. I have listened to some great commentaries and at times some not so great! But that is the Baggies for you.

'Going back to the first time I ever came onto your show it still brings on *a smile, "I can't call you Blind Dave, it's just not right at all!" you said, but now it's like water off a ducks back and pleased to hear, It's Blind Dave all day! At a cricket match you made an appearance at, I would have said played, but can't remember whether you were LBW'd before you got to the wicket, but what I do remember you had my missus on her knees fixing your cricket whites! Talk about getting familiar!*

'You have made me smile with some of the pundit debates and comments from fans, a listening ear, with the "we'll agree to disagree" conversations, the wind ups, but all the fans love it and love you for what you represent.

'On the subject of pundits and the double acts, Matt the dingle 'keeper; fancy him putting his fingers to his lips to shhhh me up during one of my appearances on your phone in? And football chat from Tayls! What's he know about football? He played for Villa after all. But then I can forgive you, for at least introducing sense to your programmes with none other than the legend that is Bomber Brown!

'Tom please keep on doing what you keep doing, great commentaries, great banter, great shows, I hope the book is a great success and you know, one day you'll make a radio presenter yet."

Another memorable game, but for different reasons, was the Championship Play-off Final at Wembley against Derby County on 28 May 2007, which the Baggies lost 1–0. It was a disappointing performance and result for the Albion fans and they soon left the South Stand after the final whistle. All had left but one fan who was at the back of the stand waving an Albion flag in total defiance of the events of the day. 'Bomber' and I immediately christened him the 'Last Man Standing', This was particularly poignant as, as is the norm these days, some of the Albion players were telling journalists that they would have to consider their future now that they were not going to be playing in the top flight. The name stuck and I wrote about him in my *Birmingham Mail* column as he epitomised what supporting your club is all about. His wife made contact and I spoke to him on the Friday night phone in. Sadly he has now passed away through illness but recently his son came up to me and talked about his Dad's claim to fame as the 'Last Man Standing'.

Being a radio commentator is not all fun – I was covering a Baggies away game at Charlton Athletic which the Albion were comfortably winning 3–0. Now at Charlton the press box runs the length of the stand with the Charlton fans immediately behind us.

One over excited and probably drunk Addicks fan kept leaning over and shouting things down my microphone like 'f**k off you Brummie c***s'. Now I took this for so long, before I flipped. I just took off my headphones in mid commentary and stood up and turned around to remonstrate with this abusive Cockney loony tune.

Well I looked at him and needed a double take because he was around six feet six tall and six feet wide, skinhead with earrings and tattoos. I must admit to feeling a little nervous, however I thought in for a penny in for a pound, so I let him have both barrels. Telling him in no uncertain term that we had families listening and that he was out of order. I fully expected him to smack me one. However while I was giving him a piece of my mind I heard a voice to my right saying, 'you're on your own'. It was my hero Bomber. Thank God the thug's pals agreed with me and persuaded him to sit down and shut up. Another bout of constipation cured.

I had my worst and most embarrassing moment at Molineux at a massive derby game between Wolves and the Baggies on 11 March 2007. It was a tight old affair and poised at 0–0 which would have been a great point for the Baggies while Wolves needed all three because they were both battling to make the Play-offs.

Wolves boss Mick McCarthy decided to throw on Jay Bothroyd, as virtually his last throw of the dice in trying to win the game.

I remember saying something along the lines of, 'Wolves are bringing on the number 10 Jay Bothroyd and that's great news for Albion as he's useless'. Bomber Brown immediately said, 'Don't say that Tom he'll probably go and smack in the winner'. And that is exactly what he did with his first touch. I was mortified but not because I had made myself look a prat, as I have done that loads of times, but because I was disrespectful to Jay Bothroyd a professional footballer and it was not my place to say it. I wrote to Jay apologising and to be fair he said it didn't matter. I suppose because he had had the last laugh. I learned a very valuable lesson that day. Just stick to describing what had happened.

I was embarrassed when the commentary cock up was featured on Central TV's sports programme the following Monday night with Nick Hancock and Sara Jane Mee along with Tommy Mooney, who at that time was with Wycombe Wanderers, and former Villa Wolves and Coventry defender Stephen Froggatt.

To be fair they could have slaughtered me but thankfully didn't. Some of the Wolves fans made their feelings felt by accusing me of being a DIY expert.

It is still on You Tube and to be fair I have never lived it down and never will and to be honest I only have myself to blame.

After the dreadful Valley parade fire that cost so many lives Bradford played some of their home games at the Odsall Speedway Stadium. I can remember being there, I believe with West Bromwich Albion, and watching the grounds-men putting the large quadrant of turf in at each corner so the flags could be put in so the games could go ahead. They had removed them from the bend of the speedway track so the bikes could take the corner sharply.

A few words from GRAHAM WILLIAMS

Graham was West Bromwich Albion's Captain when they won the FA Cup in 1968. A one club man who also won 26 caps for Wales.

'What can you say about Tom? He's a legend in the West Midlands, we talk about footballers but after a game what do you do but listen to Tom on the radio. He's taught "Bomber" Brown all he knows about radio! Make no mistake Tom knows his football, but we can always tell when the Blues have won because he is nice to his callers, however if the Blues have lost he can be a "nasty little man" (only joking Tom). If you want a successful Q & A night – who you gonna call? – Tom Ross, if you want a good night out related to football – who you gonna call? – Tom Ross. We accept him as a Bluenose – he's a friendly foe!"

ASTON VILLA

The decline of Aston Villa 2011–16

Over my 35 years on BRMB/XTRAam/Capital Gold/Free radio covering West Midland's football I was certain I had seen it all, but the decline of Aston Villa over five years and in particular the events during the 2015–16 season amazed and staggered me.

You can trace the decline back to Martin O'Neill leaving the club after allegedly having a row with Randy Lerner about investment and use of players already at the club. Randy bought the club from Doug Ellis in 2006 for £62 million and for the first four years the team was chasing a top four place and although they didn't achieve it they were in the top six.

However since then, Gerard Houlier, Alex McLeish, Paul Lambert, Tim Sherwood, Remi Garde have all failed while caretaker boss Eric Black was put in charge to see out the season after they were relegated in 2016. Every one of those had to work within a financial policy that was designed to bring down the wage bill. They also replaced players with some abysmal signings that just were not good enough, although they paid good money for them. The recruitment policy that was so obviously a problem was never addressed. The club needs a complete and probably expensive overhaul from top to bottom to sort out the shambles it has become.

I am not just talking about relegation because that can happen to any team at any time and to be brutally honest dropping into the championship is a just consequence of everything else that is wrong at Villa Park. Everyone knows that relegation has been brewing for five years but this season has to go down as the worst with more business own goals than goals.

Three managers in one season were all charged with trying to mold players, that were so obviously unfit for purpose, into a side capable of staying in the top flight. Whatever cliché you want to use to describe the task would fit perfectly, from the job is a 'poisoned chalice' to it's the 'impossible job'.

Yet no one has really taken the recruitment department to task! In fact as managers, CEO's, directors all leave and hundreds of staff are facing the prospect of redundancy the head of recruitment Paddy Reilly appears to be fireproof.

I was at Villa Park to witness the most gutless display I have ever seen from one of the Midlands teams and I have seen quite a few contenders, but Villa's 6–0 defeat by Liverpool was without doubt the worst ever. After this game, even with 33 points to play for, most Villa fans knew their team was doomed to relegation.

Lerner appeared to fiddling while Villa burned, however we saw CEO Tom Fox disappear and Steve Hollis come in as chairman. He quickly brought in former FA Chairman David Bernstein and former governor of the Bank of England Lord Mervyn King and what a coup that was. All of a sudden there was a lift in positivity around the place and belief that the football board, which also included Brian Little and Adrian Bevington, could steer the club back to the Premier League at the first attempt.

However as quickly as they arrived Bernstein and King were gone having resigned over some email that had allegedly been sent to Randy Lerner. Villa were back to square one.

Bernstein and King used words used like 'untenable'. No one at the club will say anything about it, but it looks as if they have made football recommendations that have been turned down by Randy Lerner via Chairman Steve Hollis. Was it to do with the appointment of a new manager, the cost of getting rid of the current players who would not be wanted, or recruitment? What else could it be, if they were only ever responsible for the football side and charged with improving and implementing their review recommendations?

Remember King and Bernstein were also members of the main AVFC board along with Randy Lerner, Steve Hollis and General Charles Krulak. However, they can have as many names on the board, only one man makes the major decisions and that is the man that owns it.

Within hours of that news the fans were hearing newspaper allegations about their club captain Gabby Agbonlahor that resulted in him being suspended from all club premises pending an investigation. This just a week after fans were told he was not physically fit enough to play Premier League football? And the guy is earning more money in a week than most fans earn in a year.

You couldn't make this soap opera up – it's like a scene from *One Flew Over the Cuckoo's Nest*, it's no wonder Villa fans are up in arms and already wondering what will happen next.

As I write, head of recruitment Paddy Reilly is still at the club while others have gone? Now I do not know Paddy and he may be a nice guy and a top bloke, but all I can speak about is the poor quality of players brought into the club. That gave the managers problems, because they were good coaches not magicians. They found it impossible to give the players a heart. And therein was the biggest problem for all of them and that was getting players to show desire. True they ran about, but there is a major difference between running, working hard and desire. Desire is when you win a ball that is 60–40 in your opponents favour.

Does Paddy Reilly dictate the recruitment policy or does he just implement and work within a recruitment policy decided by the board or to be more specific Randy Lerner?

For the last five years they appeared to have made some seriously bad management/ business decisions and as a consequence they are now flitting from one disaster to another. If ever there was a time for Randy Lerner to come to Villa Park and explain what the future holds it was then. However the silence was deafening.

They will find life tough in the Championship, which promises to be the toughest for years. Whoever the manager is must be allowed to bring in the players he wants and needs to challenge for promotion.

A few words from PAUL FAULKNER
Former CEO of Aston Villa and now currently Chief Executive of the Birmingham Chamber of Commerce, a member of Birmingham Children's Hospital NHS Foundation Trust and owner of Paul Faulkner Consulting.

> *'Despite being such a well known Bluenose, the two characteristics that best define Tom for me are his fairness and his desire for all Midlands clubs to be as successful as possible. This is a man who is passionate about the region above everything else, and I am sure that is why he has been so popular for such a long period. Fans of other clubs might like some banter with him about his love for Blues, but at the end of the day they also respect him for his knowledge and balance when discussing the key issues relating to their teams. When Martin O'Neill was Villa manager I remember going to a number of local social clubs, packed with Villa fans, with him and Tom to record Q&As, and my abiding memory was how totally in control Tom was...comfortable asking searching questions of a leading football figure, but also encouraging and dealing with the crowd, ensuring a great atmosphere that never got out of control. A real professional and someone for whom I have the utmost respect.*

At Villa Park in the 80s I experienced the best entertainment I have ever seen – a Bruce Springsteen concert (only joking Villa Fans!)

Memorable games?

The League Cup Semi-Final Second Leg against Tranmere Rovers on 27 February 1994, Villa were 3–1 down after the first leg and can have Dalian Atkinson to thank for scoring a late goal at Prenton Park. The atmosphere for the second leg at Villa Park was absolutely brilliant as the game ebbed and flowed. First Dean Saunders popped up with a goal that was then followed up by Shaun Teale at 2–0 to level it at 3–3 on aggregate. John Aldridge put the Merseysiders back in front before Dalian

Atkinson took it into extra-time with a goal with just minutes to go and it was four all. The extra 30 minutes was in reality a non-event and so it went to a penalty shoot-out with the drama not over by a long way.

It was 'keeper Mark Bosnich who was the hero of the night. After four penalties Villa were 4–3 up and it was left to Ugo Ehiogu to send Villa through to Wembley but he hit the bar while John Aldridge scored to once again level it at 4–4. Kevin Richardson sent the fifth penalty into the stand. That gave Tranmere a great opportunity to reach Wembley but Bosnich brilliantly saved the spot kick, so after six penalties it was still 4–4. Tony Daley was next to take a penalty and he superbly put his past the 'keeper to put Villa 5–4 up and remember it was now sudden death. Tranmere's Ian Nolan had to score or Villa were through. The atmosphere was electric as he stepped up to shoot but Mark Bosnich again made a brilliant save – his third of the seven.

The place erupted with fans running onto the pitch as they realised they were going to Wembley to face Manchester United.

However Villa were not done with dramatic penalty shoot-outs. Later that year on 29 September I had the pleasure of covering the second leg of the UEFA Cup tie against Inter Milan. Villa won the game 1–0 but that meant it was level at 1–1, Villa won that penalty shoot-out 5–4 thanks to defender Phil King who scored the winning penalty. Again the atmosphere was amazing.

DOUG ELLIS

Sir Doug Ellis, OBE was a dream to deal with as long as you understood his eccentricities. Everyone has Doug Ellis stories so I will share a few of mine. He was known in the game as 'Deadly' and that had nothing to do with sacking managers, but to do with him bashing Salmon or trout over the head with a small wooden mallet when he caught them.

On the BRMB Saturday Sports show with George Gavin we had a feature called 'the Mystery Singing Sports Star'. George would send me out to get sports stars singing just one line of their favourite song. George would play it in the show and ask listeners to ring in and guess who it was.

I got Andy Gray singing, *I Belong to Glasgow*, Steve Lynex sang *This Old Heart of Mine*, Ian Botham warbled *Even the Bad Times are Good*, while Pat Cowdell murdered *You'll Never Walk Alone*, we had many more and to be fair it was great fun.

But as you might expect the highlight was Doug!

George told me to pop down to Villa Park and do an interview with Doug and then afterwards get him to sing one line of his favourite songs – job done.

So after the interview I asked Doug if he would sing one line of his favourite song for the competition.

Doug's reaction was priceless and went something like this: 'Ah you've heard!... BBC Cathedral Choir Chester 1936 what would you like me to perform?'

I said, 'No Doug just one line of your favourite song will do so that the listeners can guess who it is singing'.

Doug was having none of it. 'Leave your recording equipment and Peter (his son) will work that and Heidi (his wife) will play the piano,' well who was I to argue with him.

I went back a couple of days later and a cassette was waiting for me. Doug had done an album of his favourite songs by Josef Locke (Google him) including *Hear My Song* and *Ave Maria*.

Former Villa director Steve Stride still has the cassette to this day it was hilarious.

We played a clip out and no one could get it. One caller even said it was Barry McGuigan's dog? I saw Doug not long afterwards and told him we had received a record number of entries for the competition and he was chuffed and said, 'I Thought So'. What a man!

When MITA COPIERS renewed the shirt sponsorship deal for Aston Villa, they sent over a top man from Japan to hand over a cheque for around a million pounds to Doug Ellis at a press conference at Villa Park. It was a big deal in those days and everyone knows how much store the Japanese place in respect and manners.

Well Doug got up to say a few words of welcome and thanks, however, the first thing he said had the press absolutely biting the inside of their lips to stop laughing. Doug just smiled at the Japanese visitor and said, 'Do you know I spent most of my war years chasing you lot round the Pacific'.

Well we all sat there expecting World War three to break out and the Japanese dignitaries to up and take their cheque back to Japan. But all he did was smile at Doug because he didn't speak a word of English.

Thankfully the Japanese interpreter must have diplomatically said that, 'Mr Ellis welcomes you to Villa Park and hopes you have a great visit'.

During the war years Doug played for Southport and he used to carry with him the card asking him to attend for a trial.

Some years later Steve Stride and the late Tony Barton related a story to me about Doug that was hilarious. I am sure most fans remember when Doug had a brace on his neck and was in hospital.

Steve and Tony visited him and he said, 'They've found out what the problem is with my neck, it was because I kept heading the ball when I played for Southport'.

The next night they again visited him and he said to them, 'the doctors have changed their mind they believe it's because of all the punches I took when I boxed for the army'. Doug was priceless.

The former Villa boss Graham Taylor tells the story of when Doug turned up to the Bodymoor Heath Training Ground on a Christmas Day morning dressed in his Villa tracksuit with gifts for the players and staff. Doug would then stand behind the goal watching the training.

One of the players ballooned the ball over the crossbar and Doug raced after it. Well that was the only encouragement the players needed. They started belting the ball as high and far as they could and laughing as Doug was chasing every ball. In the end he went home knackered and breathing out of his backside but before he went he said to the manager, 'Graham aren't you worried about the strikers scoring goals as they haven't hit the target once'. Only Doug!

Not many people know it but Doug claims to have invented the overhead kick. Andy Gray tells the story better than anyone and it's hilarious. Apparently it was while Doug was playing for the Armed Forces when a cross came over and he instinctively threw himself backwards and smashed the ball into the net. As Andy tells it the crowd grows from a 100 to 50,000 before the story ends. Doug was definitely a frustrated footballer like most of us.

Doug's biography was entitled *DEADLY DOUG – Behind the scenes at Aston Villa FC* and was published in November 2005, in typical Doug style he gave a copy of it to Queen Elizabeth II on an official visit to Birmingham. I am sure it was a book she couldn't wait to pick up.

However no one should ever underestimate what Doug did for Aston Villa. The stadium and their time in the Premier league is a testament to his love, work and commitment to his beloved Aston Villa. When he sold the club to Randy Lerner for £80 million plus he insisted that £20 million of it was put into an account for new players.

He is a generous man and if he can he will always help and there is always an invitation into the boardroom waiting. I was at a Help Harry Help Others charity event when Doug donated £10,000 without any prompting or asking,

Recently he donated £100,000 to the Queen Elizabeth Hospital – in fact to the QEHB Charity's brain surgery fund after they performed an operation on Mathew Stride to remove a brain tumour. Mathew is the son of former Villa director and close friend of Doug, Steve Stride. Top man Doug!

Sadly there are very few characters like Doug in the game these days

FA CUP FINAL 2000

A few words from JOHN GREGORY

John was a manager of Aston Villa. As a player, he was a versatile midfielder who started his career at Northampton Town and later played for Brighton and Hove Albion, QPR, Derby and Aston Villa and ALSO won six caps for England.

> *'Whenever I meet up with Tom this is how our greeting goes. No hello's, how are you etc... Just the following...*
>
> *'Tom... (sung)... The Rangers had a homecoming in Harlem late last night*

Villa's legendary owner and chairman Doug Ellis.

'JG...*(sung)... And the magic rat drove his sleek machine over the Jersey state line*

'Tom... *Barefoot girl sitting on the hood of a Dodge drinking warm beer in the soft summer rain*

'JG... *The rat pulls into town rolls up his pants together they take a stab at romance*

'Tom… And disappear down Flamingo Lane…

'The opening verse to Springsteen's Jungleland.

'We're both Springsteen disciples and our greeting to each other has always been Jungleland. When I first met Tom I just presumed he was just like any other local sports journalist. But I soon found out that he was different. He mentioned to me one week that he liked Bruce. Then he reeled off the Bruce gigs he'd been to. I responded to him… "Yep I was there too!!!!"… We both soon realised that we had this huge connection with The Boss. We'd spend endless Friday's sat in my office at Bodymoor talking Springsteen. Suddenly about 2pm Tom would say… "Oh by the way better do an interview about the game tomorrow…"

'On any given Friday, I could tell Tom the Villa team for the following day, to give him a "heads up" with his preparation for the game the next day, always knowing that he would never ever tell a soul what my line up was. That is another reason why he's different.

'Totally trustworthy with any information that you give to him and that's why I always had a lot of time for Tom. As a Bluenose he has always had to stand and fight his corner for his team, and without doubt always got an enormous amount of flak in and around Bodymoor from the likes of Ian Taylor, Dion Dublin, Townsend, Bozzie, Stanley Victor and hundreds of others.

'But Tom is a Bluenose that we all love to see and to be with. Not many Noses are welcomed at Bodymoor. But Tom is. He is a special man. A very special man. He's a friend to everyone he meets and a huge supporter not just of the Noses but of Midlands football.

'Although I don't get to see him as much these days as I would like. I know the next time I see him he'll look at me and start to sing.. "The Rangers had a homecoming in Harlem late last night".'

Villa face Chelsea in the last ever FA Cup Final at the old Wembley and to be honest were lucky to be there after a poor but winning performance against Bolton in the semi-final, which was also at Wembley.

It was an eagerly awaited final as the expectation was for a match with both sides showing attacking flair, in the end it was probably the most boring final since World War II.

I was not the happiest because Blues had been beaten 4–0 in the first leg of their Play-off semi-final by Barnsley the day before.

Anyway before the game I was walking across the Wembley Car Park on my way to the Press Room when my mobile phone rang. It was Villa boss John Gregory. He was at the team hotel and I could hear all the lads laughing in the background it must have been at their team meeting ahead of the Final.

Interviewing my great pal John Gregory at a QPR v Villa game.

John said 'look would BRMB play a song for the lads as they get ready to head to Wembley'. 'Of course' I said, 'what would the lads like?' JG said, 'anything by UB 4 nil.' I could hear all the players laughing their heads off. Banter I suppose but the Blues defeat was still raw with me. I can't tell you exactly what I said but the second word was 'off'.

COCA-COLA LEAGUE CUP

A few words from RON ATKINSON

Ron is affectionately known as 'Big Ron' During the 1990s and early 2000s he was one of Britain's best-known football pundits. His idiosyncratic turn of phrase has led to his utterances becoming known as 'Big-Ronisms' or 'Ronglish'.

He spent his entire playing career at Oxford United, where he still holds the record as the club's highest appearance maker. He was twice manager of West Bromwich Albion and arguably had their most entertaining team in the 70s. He was manager of Aston Villa and led them to a Coca Cup Final win in 1994.

'The overriding factor for me with regard to Tom is that although he is a fanatical Blues supporter he likes all the Midland clubs to do well. Normally people who are fanatical about one club find it difficult to have time for any other club – not Tom he genuinely wants all the clubs to do well – don't get

me wrong if there is a game between Blues v Villa there is only one result he wants – a win for the Blues. I share that view with Tom whether I was managing West Bromwich Albion or Villa as well as wanting my team to do well I also wanted to see my local rivals and the likes of Nottingham Forest doing well.

'When I first came back to the Midlands to manage the Albion, the Villa had a good team as did The Wolves and even Birmingham had an entertaining side under the management of Jim Smith.

'St Andrew's is one of my favourite grounds, as I have never lost a match there as either a player or a manager.

'Like Tom I love the banter associated with football and an example of this was when we played together in Gary Newbon's All-Star XI along with the likes of Ron Wylie and Jim Smith.

'In a professional capacity I first came across Tom when he was a junior to Tony Butler on BRMB. Tony was a "funny" guy and I went to do an interview with him when I was managing at The Hawthorns. TB kept having a go at Jim Smith at the Blues, so much so that I started to stick up for Jim, which resulted in TB having a go at me for the whole season. I think eventually he got fired for punching someone and in came George Gavin with Tom as his number two and then Tom took over.

'Tom's the sort of bloke that would rather do you a turn rather than do you down, he's a genuine guy who is a "dyed in the wool" Midlands football fan.

'At the time there was a group of media people that the managers could trust and Tom was one of those, we had a good relationship and I would never turn down an interview with Tom because you could trust him.

'By the way he used to deliver the papers to my Mom and Dad when they lived in Lea Hall."

Villa were staying at The Compleat Angler in Ascot prior to the Final at Wembley. As I knew Ron Atkinson well he agreed for me host a 'Phone In' from the hotel. It all went well without any problems until the following morning when a former Villa skipper the legend that is Dennis Mortimer had a pop at Big Ron in the morning newspapers. Big Ron was raging especially at the timing of the article. I gave Ron the opportunity to respond via a live exclusive interview on the morning of a Wembley Final and he let Dennis have it big time. Now that's what journalists call a scoop.

After Villa had played the old Wimbledon FC team at Villa Park I was doing the post-match phone in and giving Wimbledon and their tactics plenty of stick when the producer said we have a call from the Wimbledon team bus. I remember it was not a player, but it may have been one of the coaches and he was not happy, but I told him I didn't care and to call someone who did. For days I thought I would get a visit from Vinnie Jones!

BIRMINGHAM CITY

A few words from ALEX McLEISH

About Alex…

Alex played for Aberdeen during their 1980s glory years, making nearly 500 League appearances for the club, and won 77 caps for Scotland. He started his managerial career with spells at Motherwell and Hibernian before guiding Rangers to two championships and five cup wins in five years. McLeish spent ten months as manager of the Scotland national team, which narrowly failed to qualify for the finals of the 2008 UEFA European Championship.

He took over as manager at Birmingham in 2007 and though they were relegated at the end of the season, McLeish guided them back to the Premier League in 2009. Birmingham then won their first major trophy in 2011 The Carling Cup.

'When I first came to Birmingham City I was aware that Tom Ross seemed to be a resident of the club, he was in and out when he wanted and had the "run of the club". I thought to myself, "What's going on here?" as based on my previous experiences with the media it had the potential to be a little bit dangerous, he needs to be controlled I thought.

'Anyway I spoke with Gordon Strachan and asked him if he knew this guy Tom Ross and he did, saying what a great guy he was and very different to the typical media men. Gordon said he was a big man who wasn't afraid to say it how it was and that he was the type of guy that would, "watch your back".

'Based on this assessment I did not press the "Access Denied" button, but the "Access Granted" button.

'I got to know him really well and we became friendly and I found him to be a superb individual who was totally, absolutely in love with the Blues. The only downside with Tom is his love of Celtic as I am a Rangers man!

'There a lot of good press men and sometimes too much access means that they know too much and they can use their position to influence other people, with Tom that was never an issue. He's totally loyal to the manager even if you are "shite" he will stay loyal but he'll tell you you're "shite".

'Tom has respect.'

Memorable games? All of them (only joking Villa fans!) but there are quite a few:

Of course the Carling Cup Final against Arsenal was the highlight of my 35-years. Arsene Wenger had disrespected Blues by saying before the kick-off that one of his injured players (Fabregas) would pick up the cup?

That moment when Obafemi Martins scored the winner will live in my memory forever. The 'keeper Wojciech Szcze͵sny and defender Laurent Koscielny to be fair cocked it up and Obafemi Martins was there to put it into the net. I just lost it in commentary, on what was an emotional day from the walk up Wembley Way before kick-off to going home.

I recall during the goal celebrations on the pitch Barry Ferguson running past Szcze,sny and Koscielny and patting the defender on the head as if to say, 'Thanks a lot pal'.

On the final whistle I said on air that, 'this is better than sex', to which my Jon McCarthy replied, 'it is the way you do it lad', genuine radio gold. Jon had also lost it but all he could do was giggle insanely.

Before the game my pitch side reporter Adam Bridge went to interview Blues fans in the stand. He spoke to one guy who was on his own but said to Adam I am here with my pal. Adam said has he gone for a drink or something to which the guy replied no he's here. He then picked up a paper bag that had an urn in it, which contained his friend's ashes. His bluenose pal had died and he wanted to bring him to the game. I was really touched by that.

Earlier Adam had spoken to a young Blues fan and said do you play football the kid said yes. Adam then said, 'I bet you would like to play on this pitch,' to which the lad replied, 'I did last week for the England schoolboys,' Brilliant

The semi-final against West Ham United was special as well for a number of reasons. 1 because the Hammers were now owned by the Birmingham City's previous owners David Gold and David Sullivan. 2) Because Blues were trailing 2–1 from the first leg.

The atmosphere at St Andrews that night was truly amazing as Blues won 3–1 (4–3 on aggregate) Craig Gardner's winning goal was brilliant and sent St Andrew's crazy as well as yours truly. In commentary I was in ecstasy and went mental screaming, 'you can hear the sound of bubbles bursting all over the East End of London'.

Sorry Villa fans but the quarter-final win was also special although any real joy was marred by the moronic and senseless behaviour of a few loony tunes who just have to make it a war. I hated that side of the game and to be fair the joy was muted because of what was going on inside and outside of the ground.

A few words from KEVAN BROADHURST

Kevan played 173 games for Birmingham City in all competitions and had a three-game loan spell at Walsall before his playing career was cut short due to injury. His managerial career began in 1999 when he was caretaker-manager of Northampton Town, becoming full-time manager of Northampton in 2001 for sixteen months.

In 2004 Broadhurst was appointed joint caretaker-manager of Bristol Rovers with Russell Osman, and when Ian Atkins joined the club as manager Broadhurst remained as his assistant. He also managed Walsall. He has been a pundit on BRMB for years covering the Blues games.

'Over forty years of friendship, twenty-four years as joint-managers of Birmingham City All-stars, hundreds of commentary games and many nights out, Tom Ross...I know him pretty well.

'I first met Tom in 1975 when I joined Birmingham City and we struck up an immediate friendship. I have seen him go from matchday PA announcer at Blues to being the voice of Midlands football.

'For twenty-four years we have co-managed the Birmingham City All-stars team, which has raised hundreds of thousands of pounds for Midland's charities. As a player Tom has the honour of being one of only two players to score from their own half, the other being Martin O'Connor. Tom's goal came at a game in the Black Country, the ball was laid back to him and his clearance sailed over the defence and over the goalkeeper and into the back of the net. I don't know who was more surprised, Tom, their goalkeeper or his teammates.

'About seven years ago, Tom, myself and Dean Holtham formed the Birmingham City Former Players Association of which Tom is chairman, and it has gone from strength to strength and we are now able to support former players and purchase equipment for local charities. We have travelled thousands of miles watching and commentating on Birmingham City fixtures, and we have shared the highs and lows of being Blues' fans. Tom's

Presenting an award to Darren Carter in 1996- little did I realise then that he would score the goal that sent Blues into the Premier League just six years later.

enthusiasm and passion for the game never ceases to amaze me, and despite being a Blues fan, Tom shows the same support for all Midland clubs.

'We have had many nights out over the years and as Tom is teetotal his recollections of a night often vary from my own. I have been fortunate to have shared 40 years of friendship with Tom and seen the incredible success Tom has had in his career. Long may this continue.'

Obviously Darren Carter's winning penalty in the Championship Play-off Final against Norwich City at the Millenium Stadium has a very special place in my memory. I can recall my pundit Kevan Broadhurst leaning over me shouting over and over again, 'Rossi we've done it!' a tremendous response from a Yorkshire man and proving that when you join the club it becomes ingrained in you. I was thrilled for Darren however I wonder how many Blues fans were waiting for the usual kick in the 'you know what's', as he walked up to take the penalty. But the teenager kept his calm and put it away nicely to put Blues into the Premier League for the first time. The atmosphere was amazing and watching all those bluenoses signing and crying with joy brought a lump to my throat. Ex-players, pop stars and ecstatic fans all joined in on the post-final phone in. Darren Carter missed the team picture because he was doing an interview live on BRMB from near the penalty spot.

A few years before I had presented Darren with his trophy when he was playing for Arden Colts as a ten-year-old, little did either of us know what was in store for us all?

The most important game in that successful journey to the Premier League was the semi-final second leg at Millwall on 2 May 2002, which is never any easy place to go as their fans are very intimidating and do like to have a face-off with opponents. It was especially so with Blues because there was history between the two club. And there had been trouble on a number of occasions.

Just four days before the first leg had ended 1–1 with Millwall striker Dion Dublin publicly saying he was confident they would win the second leg.

Blues were superb in that second leg at the New Den. They withstood everything Millwall or their fans threw at them. I remember Oliver Tebily losing his boot and still tackling like a tiger in midfield.

But Stern John earned his place in Blues history when he smashed home Steve Vickers cross after Martin Grainger had hooked the ball into the penalty area.

After the game it was like World War Three was going on outside the stadium with flares and police sirens. *The Birmingham Mail's* Colin Tattum and myself were told to stay on the pitch with the players until the police had dealt with the situation.

To ease the tension we recreated the winning goal with yours truly scoring – someone said it was a better finish than Stern John's but not as important – what an understatement that was. That though was typical of the banter going on the pitch while outside it was a war zone.

However to earn a place in the Play-off Final at the Millennium Stadium was fantastic especially after the fans had experienced so many disappointments at the semi-final stage.

The day at the Millennium will never ever be forgotten by any Bluenose, a day of emotion from start to finish. Lots of fans who had become Blues fans because of their parents dedicated the win to them. I know I thought of my dad and how proud he would have been of the team. It was a great game, one of those where you really never knew which way it would end. Going into extra-time and going behind to an Iwan Roberts goal and many Blues fans thinking here we go another disappointment on the way. But feed the Horse and he will score and he did just that to take it to a penalty shoot-out.

Blues had lost penalty shoot outs too many times for any fan to be uber-confident. But this time it was to be so different. After the Canaries missed their fourth penalty it left Blues 3–2 up thanks to excellent penalties by Stern John, Paul Devlin and Stan Lazaridis.

So it was simple score the fourth penalty and Blues were in the Premier League. Up stepped teenage midfielder Darren Carter and I have to say like many, my first thoughts were why is a kid taking such a high-pressure penalty kick? I felt the pressure myself as Darren was a friend of my son Jon and had spent a few nights sleeping on our sofa after nights out.

I remember urging him to score in the commentary and when he did the whole place erupted. My co -commentator Kevan Broadhurst shouting, 'we're back Rossi, we're back in the Premiership'. That penalty kick earned Darren a place in Blues folklore and he will forever be a legend at the club.

None of us could contain ourselves – it was just a magical moment that blew your mind and as I have said many times took you on an emotional roller coaster ride, which is why we all love the game. Which is why it is our religion.

The Leyland DAF Cup Final in 1991 was memorable because it was the Blues' first trip to Wembley since 1956.

It became very real after the win at Brentford in the area final second leg – Simon Sturridge the scorer to make it 3–1 on aggregate. I was thrown into the player's bath along with my tape recorder and had to borrow a pair of shorts to travel home with George Gavin. All I could say was 'Yes', 'Yes', as I was going to see my beloved Blues at Wembley even if it was in the Leyland DAF Cup.

I remember banging on about it to Big Ron Atkinson and him replying that his teams had never finished low enough to qualify for it. I think Ron was a little jealous (only joking)

The final itself was amazing but so was the build-up.

The team was based at Reading University and I was invited to stay with them by Manager Lou Macari, as was *The Birmingham Mail's* Blues reporter Colin Tattum.

It was not the most salubrious of places to stay but it fitted Lou Macari's philosophy and of course the clubs bank balance.

Training was totally amazing and to say it left me gobsmacked was an understatement.

On the first day we got on the coach and I was amazed to hear the manager say we are going to drive around and find somewhere to train. That is exactly what we did – we eventually came to a field stopped the bus and climbed over the fence.

Colin Tattum and I were allowed to join in the training, well certainly the running bits, which Lou Macari did a lot of.

At night I went to the pictures with Lou Macari as, like myself, he was teetotal. When we got back we would join his assistant Chic Bates and stand in the shadows by the gate to catch those players who had gone out after curfew. We only caught one and that was young goalkeeper Dean Williams.

I remember the team doing shooting practice in the grounds of the University up against a very high wall. Let me tell you that during that session John Gayle could not hit a cow's backside with a banjo. In fact he cleared the wall on a few occasions. I am sure he was saving it all up for the Final because we all know what he did there.

The day before Wembley we again jumped aboard the bus and headed out to find somewhere to train. We found what looked like a school running track. So again over the fence we went.

Lou suddenly said to the players I am not taking the training today – Tom Ross is taking it on my behalf which was a surprise to me.

Immediately two players John Gayle and Nigel Gleghorn said they would not train if I was taking it and looked to Lou for support, but he just confirmed that I was taking the training so I did.

In fact I made John and Nigel do twenty press-ups for refusing to train and then proceeded to run the arses off the players. What they did not realise I am sure was this was Lou's way of relaxing and getting them laughing, as all the main pattern play and shape had already been decided.

After the game I said, tongue in cheek, to the lads that they were fitter than Tranmere in the second period of extra-time so the success was in no small way due to my focusing on the fitness side, so they could cope with it – to be honest that went down like Bobby Crush on an oil rig. I could not repeat what they said.

Lou wasn't finished yet he allowed me to broadcast from the bench at Wembley, which was unheard of and I am sure against all the rules.

I was on the team list as the second physio and in my Blues tracksuit walked to the bench with my headphones in a bucket covered by sponges.

George Gavin was in the Press Box and regularly came to me for reports and insights as I sat next to Robert Hopkins who was one of the substitutes.

To watch from the bench as John Gayle scored one of the goals of the season at Wembley to help Blues lift the trophy was absolutely brilliant.

The team bus turning up Wembley way for the Leyland Daf Final

It was an amazing, thrilling, and exciting Roy of the Rovers experience for a massive Bluenose like myself and I also got to go into the dressing room. I can't begin to explain what this meant to me. All those years as a kid in the inner city slums dreaming of leading Blues out at Wembley and there I was sitting with the subs on the bench. I am sure I was the first to broadcast from the subs bench although Gary Newbon claims he was first.

I have to say one of my greatest memories in the 35 years I have been broadcasting on BRMB/Free Radio is being on the team bus as it turned up Wembley way in 1991. We had left the University and with a police escort made our way from Reading to Wembley going the wrong side of "keep Left" signs etc.

When it turned up Wembley Way (The last time it was done by the way) we were greeted by thousands of Blues fans all singing and cheering. That was quite an emotional moment for me as a Bluenose and radio man and because I was on the air by phone to BRMB painting the picture with words for those fans at home. I must admit I had a lump in my throat because, despite it only being the Leyland DAF Cup, Blues were at Wembley and fans had waited a long time to experience it. Talking to the players it was also emotional and inspirational for them. They were definitely stirred by what they saw and heard.

After the game I was on the pitch with the players getting interviews etc. but when I finished I got caught up in the celebrations and followed the players on their lap of honour. Big Ron was commentating on SKY TV and said, 'that's Rossco with the team' – I don't remember him playing for Blues? I didn't care I was living the dream.

On that night Blues held a celebration dinner at the Hilton Hotel at Wembley. I was the MC and had to introduce the directors etc. I introduced Samesh and Ramesh

Kumar to a tumultuous round of applause. I then had to introduce the wives and family of the directors and as they walked in a voice, sounding remarkably like Ian Clarkson's, shouted out 'strippers are here'. Samesh was not amused and went to have a word with the player concerned.

However it was a brilliant night and another fantastic memory in my 35 years.

I was invited to travel on the Blues team bus by a number of Blues managers to any away games where I was covering the game for BRMB. It was fantastic for me we had some brilliant times. It was a time where the players didn't have iPads, iPhones or any other electronic game, so it was banter and cards that made the time pass so quickly. I remember Frank Worthington used to get wound up by the lads to ply Jim Smith with a few red wines before they invited the Blues Boss to play three-card brag. Needless to say they took a few quid off Jim.

Travelling with the team under Terry Cooper the favourite game was 'Hearts' and Terry would play with me, Mark Sale, Trevor Mathewson and Richard Dryden who we all called Trigger for obvious reasons. TC used to go mad if you played a 'bad' or 'wrong card', so inevitably it was me or Mark who were on the end of Terry's wrath and witty banter type comments. We used to look at each other and hope that it was the others who would get hammered by TC for a change.

I remember playing three card brag with Nigel Gleghorn and was dealt a prial of tens – a great hand – I tell you I was prepared to bet my house on that hand. But Nigel was brilliant and folded his hand saying, 'I like you too much' and then showed me his hand a prial of threes an unbeatable hand. I kept my house – thanks Nigel.

Getting behind the scenes was great for me as a Blues fan and you saw the other side of the game. I remember once going to Rochdale and not having a press pass waiting for me. They said the press box was full but Terry Cooper came to my rescue and said, 'sit with me in the dug-out!' So there I was doing reports on the game from the bench on my phone? It was the game where Terry's son Mark got sent off. TC said to me as Mark was walking off, 'tell 'em what a stupid t**t he is,' I did but not in those exact words.

I remember one time being called into St Andrew's by manager John Bond. When I got there he was in his office with Blues owner/chairman Ken Wheldon and Everton boss Howard Kendall. Also in the room were striker Wayne Clarke and reserve team player Stuart Storer.

They said they had agreed to sell reserve Stuart Storer and Wayne Clarke to Everton for around £500k, valuing Wayne at around £100k and Stuart at around £400k, this didn't make sense to me, with all due respect to Stuart as Wayne had been banging in the goals and was obviously worth a bigger fee than Stuart.

However I found out later that Wolves were entitled to 50% of any transfer fee received for Wayne Clarke as part of the deal that brought him from Molineux to Blues?

Talking of the then Blues chairman Ken Wheldon, I remember his failed attempt to have Walsall ground sharing with Blues and in fact he even announced that the Walsall groundsman Roger Johnson would look after both pitches. Saddler's fans were rightly not happy and it never happened but many believed that ground sharing was Ken Wheldon's intention from the moment he thought about buying Birmingham City.

In 1986 Ken Wheldon sold Scottish defender Ken Armstrong to Walsall, whom the chairman had previously owned, for a fee I believed to be around £125k.

Kevan Broadhurst rang me and said he was surprised at the deal because Ken Armstrong had a serious ankle injury and predicted that he would never kick a ball for Walsall and he was spot on because he never played one single game for the Saddlers.

Ken eventually sold Walsall to millionaire racehorse owner Terry Ramsden.

Just after that John Westmancoat the secretary at Walsall left to join up with Ken Wheldon at Birmingham City.

A few words from GARRY PENDREY

About Garry…

Garry Pendrey, is a defender who made 345 appearances in the Football League, including more than 300 for Birmingham City, he also played for West Bromwich Albion. After playing he went into coaching, as manager of Birmingham City and as coach or assistant manager under Gordon Strachan at clubs including Coventry, Southampton, Glasgow Celtic and Middlesbrough

'Tom, a man for all men there when you need him, there when you don't need him.

Not enough hours in the day for Tom who supports every cause he can and travels the country in his profession. Godfather to my youngest son Adam and a great friend for over forty years. To sum up – good man, good values, good family and good grief!!!! An autobiography !!!!.'

Garry Pendrey was managing Blues during Ken's era, in fact it was Ken who gave Gary his chance to manage his boyhood club. Garry would say to me that Ken had told him to sell 'So and So', even though he never knew how good the player was and how important he was to the club. But Ken's philosophy was simple, 'we have tax bill to pay and we have an offer for the player on the table'.

I honestly believe this meant Blues did not get the best price for players like Julian Dicks and also it never really gave Garry a chance to be a successful manager although I know Garry disagrees with this.

Garry was there with Tony Brown as his assistant and when all the selling was going on etc Ken always said he would look after them but he didn't. He sold the club to the Kumars and Garry and Bomber knew nothing about it. Garry was still in the job when Dave MacKay was appointed manager.

Tony Butler always said to me that, 'the game is full of crooks, cheats and dishonest men with just a few honest ones in it and the difficulty was finding the few honest men.' How spot on was he?

In a *Birmingham Mail* interview Garry's sacking was covered.

Not much gets to Garry Pendrey. But the way he left his beloved Birmingham City as manager still rankles.

Ken Wheldon passed the baton to the Kumars who, according to Pendrey, were 'unprofessional' in the manner they replaced him with Dave Mackay in April 1989.

'The thing about Blues was that when it got really bad, in the second season, I could have moved on. I had a great chance to become an assistant,' said Pendrey.

'But I couldn't have walked out at that time. I had to see it through, even if it meant the knock on the door came and I got the sack, the right way. That's what happens in the game.

'You're in, you accept it, you get on with it. As long as people are open, straightforward, honest, look you in the eye and say "time's up", that's fine.'

At the D Club at St Andrews with Blues Players for a charity fund raising skittles night around 1978/9

One of the great Junior Blues nights with a very young Garry Pendrey, Kevan Broadhurst and Jimmy Calderwood with Vi on the extreme right.

When Dennis Shaw was commercial manager at Blues he asked me to help set up a club for the junior supporters and I was delighted to do so. Along with Vi and another lady whose name escapes me we organised junior Blues discos and fun nights. One of these entailed me and the girls dressing up as Boney M and miming to songs. Yes there are pictures NO they are not here. The players bought into the Junior Blues and turned up many times which captivated the kids.

ANGLO ITALIAN CUP

Blues were asked to participate in an Anglo-Italian tournament, which was part organised by Gianni Paladini. Blues boss Terry Cooper was keen to be involved to give the club, players and supporters a taste of foreign football. The Italian teams involved were AC Cesena, AS Bari, Ascoli Calcio, and Lucchese.

For most of us it was our first experience of overseas football and we were able to do all the sightseeing just like tourists: Terry Cooper and I went to The Leaning Tower of Pisa along with our colleagues from Central TV (ATV) who were there filming, what was an amazing time and whetted my appetite to see the world.

One game against AC Cesena was in danger of being postponed as the mist and fog descended, but one minute it was off and the next it was on as the mist rose and fell. This happened a number of times and a decision on whether the match was played or not was delayed as they spoke to the pilot about the problems of not playing etc. anyway it went ahead and Blues won with Mark Cooper scoring.

To be honest the games were of little importance and the fact that only a handful of Italians bothered to show up for the games confirmed how they felt about the Anglo Italian Tournament with only 139 turning up to see Lucchese v Blues.

However socially it was brilliant. I remember me and Terry Cooper being driven around San Marino by Gianni Paladini. It was terrifying to say the least. Gianni didn't drive so much as aim.

I recall going off with Jack Wiseman, his son Mike (now Life President of the club), Terry Cooper, Trevor Morgan (Assistant Manager), Colin Tattum *(Birmingham*

Evening Mail) and Gianni to a restaurant that Gianni said was superb and it certainly was food wise.

We had been there a short while when one of the waitresses was giving me the come on. Obviously I was flattered and played along with her flirting until I noticed everyone was laughing because they knew something that I didn't. She was a he. My first and only experience of a lady boy! Now I know where the term Arthur or Martha comes from.

My second experience of the Anglo-Italian was a few years later when Barry Fry was manager and was less humorous with one of the games being labelled the 'Battle of Ancona'.

The Italian coach had been a nightmare all night deliberately doing things to wind up the Blues players on and off the pitch eventually Liam Daish and the players and coaches decided enough was enough.

Liam led the charge after the game to sort it out in the dressing room area.

The bottom line was their coach ended up on a stretcher, and the team bus had to have a police escort to the airport – the passports of our black players were confiscated. I am not sure if Michael Johnson is allowed to visit Italy to this day.

But every cloud has a silver lining and Barry Fry and Liam Daish have dined out over the years recollecting and re-inventing their memories of that match!

I did a Q & A dinner with Barry Fry many years later and he regaled the audience by telling them exactly what had happened down to the last detail. I remember saying, 'if you knew all that why when I interviewed you post-match did you say you didn't see anything?'

I don't think Director Jack Wiseman, Manager Terry Cooper and Club Secretary Alan Jones ever got the credit they deserved for keeping the club going when the Kumar's clothing empire collapsed. Those were real dark days but those guys kept a smile on everyone's face despite the club being so close to going under.

Then one day I was sitting in Terry Cooper's office having a cup of tea when a very attractive young lady walked up the stairs and into the office to see Jack Wiseman and Alan Jones. Terry said she was representing possible new owners and was called Karren Brady.

Not long after it was announced that *Sunday Sport* joint owner David Sullivan had bought Blues. Shortly after that he was joined on the Blues board by David and Ralph Gold his co-owners at the *Sunday Sport* with Karren Brady appointed as Managing Director.

They had many critics, but in my opinion they were brilliant for Blues despite one or two own goals such as the away travel club debacle that ended up with Karren Brady in court to answer charges from Trading Standards. I discussed this on my Friday night phone in and was amazed to receive over 2,800 letters of support many containing petitions signed by hundreds of people all supporting Karren.

With former Blues MD Karren Brady who I got on with brilliantly

I had a fantastic relationship with them all and still do have with David Gold to this day. I was invited to Karren's wedding to Paul Peschisolido, who I am still great friends with.

Sadly since Karren left the club and became a television star and of course a member of the House of Lords I have not heard from her. I suppose she is very busy. However it is disappointing because we met up on Holiday in Marbella when she was there with Paul and the kids on many occasions and I also socialised with them here in the West Midlands.

I actually thought a lot of her, despite her having a lot of critics, I thought she was fabulous for Birmingham City and from a personal perspective I thought she was great. We spent many times chatting and she took me into her trust, but more than that we had loads of laughs during her time at the club both professionally and personally. She was part of the group that had some brilliant nights out at Umberto's restaurant in Shirley.

I only fell out with her on one occasion, let me rephrase that: Karren only fell out with me on one occasion and that was when Blues were due to play Derby. The pitch was in a disgraceful state just a mud-bath. I was told by the commercial director Perry Deakin that the game was doubtful and more than likely would be cancelled. I put that out on the radio to keep the fans up to date. I received a call from her and upon answering was subject to a stream of foul abuse as she demanded to know where I had got my information from.

I told her the truth but she was not happy. To be fair she rang me back a couple of days later and apologised for her outburst. I let it go as we all have bad days. My guess is that she was under pressure from David Sullivan and was concerned about people not turning up at the game and the club losing revenue.

I was trusted by the board and was privy to many boardroom conversations about a lot of things. One concerned Steve Bruce after he had lost 1–0 at home to Norwich in October 2006; it meant no wins in five games. The fans were not happy and voiced their feelings to the board during the game. To be honest this made the board nervous as well. I was in the boardroom after the game until very late – in fact there was only David Gold, David Sullivan, and Karen there. They were talking about Steve's future in so far as they did not know what to do, but really wanted him to stay because they all liked him immensely. They thought the world of Steve and Karen had also become close friends with him and his wife Janet. David Sullivan asked me how the fans would react if they were to make a change. I simply said if everything goes wrong they will end up blaming you and I said Steve had done more than enough to earn a chance as his team were not playing that badly, but were not winning.

To be fair to the board they always gave their managers a fair deal. I left them talking about it and of course history shows they were right to stick with Steve.

He went on to win five on the spin and in fact only lost one of the next 14 games drawing two and winning 11. And ultimately winning automatic promotion back to the Premier League. They proved that you must never make hasty decisions.

I really enjoy derby Games with a passion and started using the phrase 'ding dong derby' in the 90s. I love the atmosphere they generate and not just on match day but also in the weeks before when all the talk is about what might happen and for weeks afterwards when all the talk is about whose fault it was for whatever team lost.

I have been at many Celtic v Rangers games in Glasgow and without fear of argument can say the Brummie bust up is up there with the best. Sadly I am afraid that the foreign players do not understand it, highlighted by Aston Villa defender Olof Mellberg. His comments about the Premier League derby between Blues and Villa did more to wind Blues fans and players up than anything the manager could ever have said.

That game arguably ruined Villa goalkeeper Peter Enckelman's career. However you can't gloat too much as what goes around comes around. Having said that we all do enjoy the bragging rights and dishing out the banter to our mates who support the other team.

After Blues were beaten by Villa 5–1 I had to go to Villa's Bodymoor Heath Training Complex for a press conference and was greeted by John Carew leaning out of his car window indicated 5–1 with the fingers on his hands.

Shortly after that game I was hosting a BRMB Football Forum at the Kingstanding Warriors Club (definitely Villa Territory). The guests were Curtis Davies and Gordon Cowans, and the latter presented me with a Villa shirt on stage with my name on and the number depicted as 5–1 – you've just got to be big enough to take it on the chin which I did. And to be fair I was very grateful it kept the car clean for a very long time! Only joking!

I loved Martin Grainger, 'The G Man' his attitude to the game was fantastic. He played with a toughness and passion that every fan could relate to. So when I was asked to turn out in his testimonial match on Wednesday 9 November 2005 I couldn't say 'Yes' quick enough.

At the time I was skinny and reasonably fit as I trained every day of the week at Paddy Lynch's Boxing Gym. I have put on a lot of weight since then but it's a medical condition – I suffer from an over active knife and fork.

The match was between The Blues and a Martin Grainger XI, for whom I played. The teams lined up as follows:

Martin Grainger XI
Substitutes and time of substitution in brackets.
Kevin Poole – Jerry Gill (Jon Bass 46, Ian Danter 70) – Martin Grainger (Tom Ross 80) – Gary Ablett (Ian Clarkson 46) – Dave Busst (Michael Johnson 46) – Jon McCarthy (Steve Robinson 46, Mick Flaherty 70) – Nicky Eaden (Paul Devlin 46) –

Danny Sonner (Dougie Brown 46) – Tommy Mooney (Jeff Kenna 46) – Nicky Forster (Dean Gaffney 46, Trevor Francis 65) – Dele Adebola (Paul Furlong 46).

Blues

Substitutes and time of substitution in brackets.

Colin Doyle (Andy Bagnall 70) – Mario Melchiot (Chris Cottrill 58) – Martin Taylor (Sam Oji 46) – Matthew Upson (Alex Bruce 46) – Marcos Painter (Carl Motteram 58) – Nick Wright (Njazi Kuqi 58) – Neil Kilkenny (David Howland 46) – Nicky Butt (Asa Hall 58) – Jamie Clapham (Mat Sadler 46) – Jermaine Pennant (Sone Aluko 46) – Walter Pandiani (Oliver Allen 46).

Attendance: 4,428

Referee: A. Wiley

It ended Blues 6 Martin Grainger XI 2.

I came on with 10 minutes left to go replacing the 'G Man' and what an honour that was. Earlier Mario Melchiot had given way to one of Blues' youngsters, Chris Cottrill who was an Aston Villa fan and just 21 years of age.

Anyway I got a rather too short ball from Trevor Francis and while desperately trying to get to it suddenly found myself flying through the air. I ended up on the ground and looked down to see blood pouring from my leg. The young Blues defender had nailed me good and proper.

Now I had a problem, don't forget I was brought up playing football on park's pitches and I was programmed not to show pain or that you were hurt, so even though my leg was bleeding I got up and said something like 'Is that the best you can do?' but let me tell you inside, I was crying with pain!

If he did that tackle in the Premier League he would have got a 20 game suspension at least. However yours truly, this 50 plus nugget of a radio presenter stupidly stayed on and kept trying to jinx past him. In fact I immediately ran at him and tried to goad him into another moment of rashness. What planet was I on, but remember I was playing on the St Andrew's pitch and that does things to your mentality.

To be fair Collin Tattum told me the people in dugouts were open mouthed – with some saying they thought I had broken my leg. TF was certain I had. Even the crowd gasped in disbelief although at the time I thought it was for my skill. What a dreamer.

Seriously though it was a bad injury, which needed a number of stiches.

After being stitched up in the medical room I went into the Blues dressing room and said to Chris in front of the Blues first team, 'If that is the best you can do then you better look at another career son,' the lads were howling and giving him some stick. Great banter.

Later I received a letter of apology from Chris on a BCFC letterhead, which I suspect Steve Bruce had persuaded him to do.

A few words from GARY ROWETT.

Gary was appointed manager of Birmingham City in October 2014. He played in the Premier League for Everton, Derby County, Leicester City and Charlton Athletic and in the Football League for Cambridge United, Blackpool, Birmingham City and Burton Albion. He is also a former BRMB pundit travelling around the country covering Blues games with Tom.

'I was obviously aware of Tom from my days as a Blues Player but I didn't get to know him until I joined BRMB around ten years ago.

'Tom was looking for someone to act as his pundit for the Blues' matches and when he spoke to me about the opportunity, not surprisingly I jumped at the chance.

'You really get to know someone when you are travelling from game to game in their company and I realised very quickly how passionate and professional Tom is in his approach to his job. He will not allow anything to stop him doing his job to the best of his ability like the time when we were late turning up at Anfield to cover a Liverpool game. Tom needed to get parked up and prepare for work, but this steward said we couldn't park in our designated car park. I have never seen anyone get so angry so quickly and he gave the steward five barrels and berated him in no uncertain terms – needless to say we were allowed to park up as planned.

'That's the first thing that springs to my mind when I think of Tom Ross!

'Having said that he is really professional and totally trustworthy – I let him know my Blues team at lunchtime on match days certain in the knowledge that he would not give it away to anyone.

'He can be quite feisty and when he tells you about his footballing days he describes himself as "the toughest full-back of all time".

'It was a pleasure to work alongside his unique style of commentating and hopefully in my role as a pundit I was able to explain the "bones" of what had happened from a professional footballer's perspective.

'He is passionate about Midlands' football and although everyone knows he is a Blues fan he is admired for the diplomatic way he deals with the other local teams.

'Tom Ross – a good guy.'

While Ron Saunders was boss of Birmingham City I received a call from his secretary saying I was to report to his office at 2pm on a certain date. Now those that know Ron would realise that this usually meant a bollocking for something either said or written. However he was all sweetness and light (unbelievable I know), but he definitely was and it was because he wanted me to be the secretary of his new charity Soccercare. He had persuaded all the local players to donate a sum from their wages for local charitable children's causes. I have to say I thought it was a brilliant idea and jumped at the chance to be involved. We were able to provide adapted computers, learning machines etc. for disabled children.

I really enjoyed it but to be honest when he left Birmingham it just sort of fizzled out. How good would that be of the modern players did the same? Just think how much good work could be done!

TOM ROSS – BLUES BOSS?

Radio Stations are always looking for something different to fool their audiences on 1 April every year.

I was at BRMB while Barry Fry was managing Blues who were then owned by David Gold, Ralph Gold and David Sullivan. The BRMB programming and marketing people came up with an April fool hoax that I was to be a part of.

We announced that 'TOM ROSS HAS BEEN APPOINTED BLUES' MANAGER' with immediate effect.

Obviously we needed to give the announcement some credibility, so we had David Sullivan saying in the news bulletin that, 'he was sorry to see Barry go, but Tom is the best man for the job'. Then Barry was in the bulletin saying, 'I am gutted but pleased for Tom as he is the best replacement.'

The telephone lines were on meltdown, the faxes were red hot while the club were also inundated with calls as were *The Birmingham Mail.* Everyone wanted to know, 'What the hell was going on?'

I could not believe that I had messages of support for my new job – how bizarre and crazy was that? But lots thought the club had lost the plot and threatened all sorts of things. I was even on the end of personal threats.

I never really was and still am not a fan of April Fool gags, but it was funny at the time. However the biggest threat to my safety came from our receptionists who had to deal with the calls and faxes.

KEITH COOMBES – END OF SEASON DO

Keith Coombes decided to host the Blues' player's end of season party at his swish Solihull home. I was asked to be the DJ for the event and loved doing it; it was no job but a labour of love.

These were great dos with a never-ending supply of drink and food. I remember Frank Worthington turning up with Mandy Rice Davies. She was part of the Profumo political scandal along with Christine Keeler that rocked British politics.

Jim Smith who had already had a few was, shall we say impressed with Many Rice Davies and told her that he dreamt about her or words to that effect.

I remember one player who shall remain nameless but he played left-back throwing up all over the snooker table.

Some of the lads were in awe of Frank and to be fair I think they were more than a little envious.

I was also the DJ for the players do at Lorenzo's. They always used to be in fancy dress and were brilliant parties. I can still see Tony Want playing the guitar to entertain the lads. Strange seeing my hero's dressed as Andy Pandy or Bill and Ben.

THE GOLDS – AT THE HYATT

I used to get celebrities to come into the studio to contribute to an idea I had developed called 'A Funny Old Game.' The guests would talk about their careers in football and we played ten of their favourite songs. I invited Ralph and David Gold in and we talked about Ralph boxing for England and David playing for West Ham boys and lots of other things, as well as what they hoped for Birmingham City. It went really well.

They were staying at the Hyatt Hotel just off Broad Street and so we all headed there for a few drinks and a chat and to meet up with Barry Fry.

In the reception area of the hotel there was a grand piano and Ralph fancied himself as a player, but in reality he made Les Dawson seem like Liberace. There was no stopping him so he got on the piano and began playing *Here is My Heart* badly or as Eric Morecambe would say, 'he was playing all the right notes but not necessarily in the right order!'

David, Barry and I were howling with laughter particularly when Ralph finished and came over and asked if we had any requests. David quickly said stop playing, but I said Ralph we would love to hear *Here is My Heart*. Ralph didn't think it was at all funny. So he headed back to the piano. However while he was talking to us, the hotel manager had raced to the piano and locked it. We consoled Ralph telling him we were gutted that it was locked but I am sure the smiles gave away just how gutted we were.

After home games our regular venue was Umberto's on the Stratford Road where Karren Brady, Terry Cooper, Mike Wiseman, Jack Wiseman and quite often David and Ralph Gold would have a meal and chat the night away sometimes until four am. Fantastic nights although not for the waiters.

LEE HUGHES

One night David and I were at a Sports Dinner at the Aston Social club when we were approached by a young man who told me he and his family were big listeners to the football on Xtra AM so we had an amiable chat with him. I asked him why he didn't listen and why his mom had to record the Baggies games for him. He told us he played on Saturdays for Kidderminster Harriers and I suddenly realised this was Lee Hughes the non-league goal scoring sensation. He told us that he was certain he could play in the Football League and did he think Blues would be interested, as Kidderminster would only want around £200,000 for him.

David told me to mention him to the manager Trevor Francis, which I did after the next press conference. TF said that he knew about Lee and that Mick Mills had looked at him and they thought he was no better than what they had at the club. So that was that. Lee eventually signed for West Bromwich Albion and scored loads of goals.

It's funny how things turn out because some time later Trevor tabled a bid of around £5 million for Lee and I say that with no disrespect to Trevor, because he has proved many times to be not only a great manager but an excellent judge of a player.

You get a lot of this from some professionals when you have never played the game at the pro level, they don't respect your opinion and that is understandable and to be honest it's perfectly OK with me. However as I always say when faced with this, 'Remember the professionals built the Titanic but the amateurs built the Ark'.

IAN BENNETT

Benno is one of the funniest footballers I have ever met. Nothing bothers him and he just plods on and on. I recall one incident when Blues were in the final of The Worthington Cup at the Millennium Stadium in Cardiff. I had been invited to stay with the players at the very posh St Piere Golf Hotel in Chepstow. I was hosting a live phone in/forum for BRMBs sister station 1152 am Capital Gold on the Friday Night. Every one of the players came into the room where I had set up the equipment and they were brilliant with some great banter and I guess in a way it helped to take their minds off the game the next day and it was fantastic radio.

I was talking to Stan Lazaridis and a Blues fan on the line when unbeknown to me goalkeeper Ian Bennett walked into the room stark naked and stood in front of me and Stan. The whole squad fell about laughing especially Stan who was trying to talk on the radio without laughing. One thing was for sure; Benno wasn't doing it to show off!

A few words from LEE CLARK
Lee is a former Manager of Birmingham City and Huddersfield and also played for Newcastle United, Sunderland, and Fulham and is currently managing Kilmarnock.

'Tom I first met when I became Birmingham City manager – I quickly formed a friendship that went beyond manager and radio presenter. He had terrific knowledge of the game and understanding of West Midlands fans feelings. Also Tom would give constructive criticism, which we all need to help us. He became a personal and family friend with his honesty integrity and loyalty.'

TAMWORTH FC.

In November 1998 I was invited by Tamworth manager Paul Hendrie to travel with the team to Exeter for their first round FA Cup replay. I was doing live kick by kick commentary on the game so jumped at the chance.

The Lambs were a more than decent team with quite a few players that could have played at a higher level including Willie Batchelor, Gary Smith and Darren Shaw. Batchelor had an outstanding game against Exeter despite losing 4–1.

We arrived at the hotel for a pre-match rest and meal and I remember saying to Paul after the meal that they looked a little bit nervous. At that time one of the injured squad Denis Mulholland got up and started to play the piano in the restaurant and he was truly amazing. When he finished all the players and the rest of the diners in the restaurant gave him a standing ovation. He took a bow and promptly lifted the lid of the piano and took out a cassette recorder that had been playing the music. The whole place fell about laughing and I am convinced it helped to relax the players. Mulholland was absolutely brilliant and is well known on the non-league circuit as a joker/prankster.

WORLD CUP

I was fortunate enough to be part of the Capital Radio team covering the 1998 World Cup in France. This came at a time when I was not flying, so I elected to drive myself and Jim Proudfoot from stadium to stadium across France. Our pundit David Speedie was also with us for many of the trips across the country. David was a player's agent at that time and spent most of the time setting up deals to transfer players. Imagine all the exclusive story's we had sitting in that car. We covered games in Lyon, Paris, Marseille, Toulouse, Bordeaux and Lens. We were based for quite some time at a five-start hotel in Avignon (where the Pont de Avignon only goes halfway across the river – Oh just google it).

During that time I struck up a great friendship with Tony Gale (ex-Fulham, West Ham and Blackburn Rovers central defender) I also hosted World Cup Phone Ins for the Capital Radio Group from the 'Chicago Pizza House Restaurant' on the the Avenue des Champs-Élysées. And also did a lot of interviews with people such as Arsene Wenger and Billy McNeil.

I remember being on a Bridge right by the Eiffel Tower recording some of the fantastic atmosphere for a feature and saw a man in a kilt playing Scottish tunes on the bagpipes. So I went to interview him about Scotland's hopes etc. only to find out he was French and didn't speak any English.

I also went to the 1982 World Cup Finals in Spain with my brother Frank to follow Scotland and again drove all the way to Malaga. We were based in Nerja just a short drive away from Malaga where the first Scotland game was being played. That was against New Zealand, which Scotland won comfortably. The second saw Scotland play Brazil in Seville. Without doubt one of the best atmospheres I have ever known anywhere. Outside the ground the Brazilians Samba'd with Scotland fans and then tried to do the Highland Fling. It was truly amazing. Sadly Scotland upset Brazil by taking the lead through David Narey.

Brazil were brilliant and tore Scotland to bits winning 4–1.The final game was back in Malaga against Russia where defeat would send the Scots home early and it did. To make matters worse we had booked our car on the train from Narbonne to Boulogne. However there was a festival in Barcelona and we got delayed and missed the train and instead had to drive through the night to catch the ferry back. – Happy days.

A few words from BRENDAN BATSON

Brendan played for Arsenal before moving to Cambridge United in 1974. He spent four years at Cambridge, captaining the side to the Fourth Division Championship under manager Ron Atkinson in 1976–77. When Atkinson moved to West Bromwich Albion in 1978, he brought Brendan to the Hawthorns. He was capped three times for the England 'B' team.

After retiring in 1982 he developed into an extremely able and active administrator at the Professional Footballers' Association. He was made a Member of the Order of the British Empire (MBE) in 2000 and Officer of the Order of the British Empire (OBE) in the 2015 both for services to football.

'I joined West Bromwich Albion in January 1978 which was when I first met Tom, however it was not until I had retired prematurely due to injury that I really got to know him. That would have been in 1984 and I was turning out for the West Bromwich Albion All-Stars and Tom became part of the squad. How he got there I don't know! But he became a friend.

'The best I can say about his footballing skill is that he was enthusiastic, but we all realised how much he loved the game which made the ex-professional footballers happy to have him on the same pitch as them.

'The great thing about Tom is that whatever you tell him it will be held in 100% confidence, in that regard he is "old school" and it is a pity there are not more like him in today's media people.

'As someone said, "What is there to dislike about Tom Ross other than he is a Bluenose!'

To make a list of my all-time favourite footballers is very difficult because one thing is for certain players like Jimmy Johnstone, Pele, George Best, Maradona, would have been sensational in todays game because they would be playing on perfect pitches with laws and referees to protect them from assault.

My favourite footballers of all time include and in no particular order:

- Jimmy Johnstone
- Bertie Auld

- Jim Baxter
- Jimmy Greaves
- John White
- George Best
- Pele
- John Giles
- Terry Cooper
- Tony 'Bomber' Brown
- Kenny Dalglish
- Trevor Francis
- Gordon Cowans
- Johan Cryuff
- Christiano Ronaldo
- Bobby Lennox
- Lionel Messi
- Denis Law
- Bobby Moore
- Gento
- Jarzinho
- Paul Gascoigne
- Maradona
- Paulo Maldini
- Roberto Carlos
- Liam Brady
- Lou Macari

In April 2016 I got a phone call that I had always hoped I would get. It was asking me if I wanted to interview Pele. Did I want to interview the greatest player who ever walked the planet? Are you sure! Pele was coming to Brum as part of a UK tour of venues to a talk about his career. I got five minutes chatting to Pele, he was a dream and to be honest I was like a kid in a sweet shop. I was disappointed that he couldn't remember playing for Santos at Villa Park in the 70s. What a legend and I enjoyed my five minutes although it was nowhere near long enough to cover the life and career of someone like Pele. A man who scored in a World Cup Final at 17. Played in the top league at 16 and won three world cups. He scored around 1,236 goals in around 1,300 appearances.

I was on a number of footballers' and cricketers' testimonial committees and had a great time raising money etc. for players who did not have the wages levels today's players have.

My lovely Gran and Grandad Sullivan whom I lived with for a few years.

Mom and Dad with my son Jon. Still miss Mom and Dad every single day

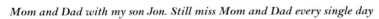

Taking a beating from former World Champion John H Stracey and also raising 17k for Acorns

The Bluenose Brothers - me and Ian Danter live on SKY TVs Premier League Show - singing Can't Keep Us Down

One of my boxing heroes the legend that is Sugar Ray Leonard.

The lad from the inner city slums with the Prime Minister David Cameron.

With a young man who changed my life - the inspirational Harry Moseley

Playing the Part of the Plumber in Mrs Browns Boys with the fantastic Brendan O'Carroll.

With The Raging Bull – The boxing legend that is Jake La Motta

My second family in Spain The Teagues

My Brothers and sisters the last time we were all together with Mom and Dad

At Jeff Lynne's party to celebrate his Star on Broad Street

My great pal Jasper Carrott Telling me my gags are rubbish

My Wedding day June 25th 2015 Marrying the love of my Life Anne

An amazing day inside the beautiful 850 year old St Nicholas church in Curdworth with some of my family and friends

With some of my pals at the wedding - Adam Bridge, Mark & Jo Hunt, me & Anne, Paddy Lynch, Emma Lynch and David Salt.

He flew mover 6000 miles to be at my wedding-a great friend Roger "Bomber" Fewtrell

With some of my great friends at my wedding

My "adopted" son Salty (LOL)
and his beautiful fiance Emma

My large and wonderful family with only my
sister Cathy missing

At a fund raising night for Garry Pendrey's testimonial.

The Garry Pendrey committee included Jasper Carrott. Gary, Jasper and I were invited to be members of a private members club called the Stechford Private Members Club, where we could play snooker and have a quiet drink etc. We were all given a key to let ourselves in at any time and to be honest it was brilliant. However we made a mistake of selling fund raising scratch cards for Garry's testimonial fund. The committee found out and, apparently because this is the most heinous of crimes, we were told that the committee had blackballed us and our keys were removed? It is the only time I have ever been a member of any private club and never will again, as it is far too pompous for me. Other players I have had the privilege of serving on testimonial committees for are; Kevan Broadhurst, Joe Gallagher and John Frain. While I was delighted to help out on the benefit committee for Warwickshire cricketers Geoff Humpage and Andy Lloyd.

CHAPTER FOUR
WAKING UP BRUM

In 1998 I was asked to take over the prestigious Birmingham Capital Gold breakfast show slot of 6–10am for two weeks replacing Paul Burrell who was on holiday. I somehow ended up staying for ten years until the summer of 2008. Paul Jackson, my boss at BRMB and Gold, and the Capital Gold Group Director Andy Turner both gave me total responsibility for the content outside of the playlist, which was pre-determined and sacrosanct. Or so they thought.

Paul told the Birmingham Mail in Oct 1999 in response to why he had appointed me that "We want our presenters to be less slick-we want real people having fun with local knowledge". I suppose there was a compliment in there somewhere.

I thought long and hard about the show and what I wanted to achieve on the breakfast show. I wanted it to be friendly and interactive with lots of laughs. In my view it had to be a happy escape route for all the people off to work to do mundane jobs – music, chat, engagement and interaction-make them smile on their way to work and I was absolutely certain that I had to enjoy it as well. If I did then I was at my best.

Four hours of great music, a bit of fun, engaging with the listeners – all designed for everyone to have a good time. What more could you want from breakfast radio.

I also realised that very often it would be families listening so it had to involve everyone. So that was the plan, for an audience that wanted cheering up a show that was entertaining with a mix of great music from the 60s/70s/80s, interaction, and sprinkled with humour.

I started throwing in one liner gags mostly aimed at myself and sometimes bounced them off the travel reporter in the Capital Gold Flying Eye (BRMB's aeroplane that flew over the region reporting on travel problems). I had four travel reporters in my time. Jimmy Franks, Chrissie Reidy, Kate Nicholls and Ian Danter and they all played the foil for my gags brilliantly.

Dants absolutely got it and loved the humour. As an example he would say something about drivers and I would then say something like, 'Dants I am feeling great because someone left a note on my car yesterday complimenting me about my driving'. He would then be surprised saying, 'what did it say?' To which I would reply, 'It said parking fine,' well I thought it was funny! Oh please yourself.

If there was an article in the news or papers about safe sex I would say, 'Safe sex at my age is a padded headboard,' or 'you know you are getting on when you are told to slow down by your doctor instead of the police'.

I never told jokes per se, but mainly dropped in one-liners that in most cases took the micky out of myself but never the listener.

I knew that the listener wanted the presenter to be happy and uplift them as well and that was something I was comfortable at doing, if I was not as slick as some of the radio jocks in the town.

I was determined it would not be an extension to the football phone in so would not talk football unless something very newsworthy had happened.

We also had Steve Dyson from the *Birmingham Mail* on the show every morning talking about what was in the paper and happening in our area.

I was up against Les Ross and others and let me tell you that was a challenge.

The playlist meant that the same songs would come round quite regularly, so to freshen it up and put my stamp on the show I created some musical features.

Beatles B sides

Dynamic Duos

Reggae Rewind.

Chill Out Tune

Best of Brum

Hall of Fame.

The interaction with the listeners came from phone in and text competitions. However I would still get 15/18 songs away an hour so to the listener the music appeared seamless.

We needed prizes so we did a deal with Greggs to give away four doughnuts, which was perfect as I regularly called listeners a 'doughnut' in a friendly, cheeky, banter way that your mate would do. It was the same with my other word used regularly and that was nugget used similarly to doughnut so we commissioned some Capital Gold Nuggets, which were sweets that the listeners loved to win.

We would always have a daily gold prize pack containing CDs books and DVDs

Listeners loved the competitions. For example I would have my top ten holiday destinations and the listener would have to try and correctly guess one. If they did they would get the doughnuts and also go into the draw for the Gold Breakfast Show prize pack. Simple but effective.

Others competitions included:

Tom's Top Ten Totty

Toms Top Ten favourite chocolate bars
Toms top ten retro biscuits
Toms Top Ten Movies
Guess the intro
Guest the TV theme
Top ten dogs names
Top ten boys/girls names
And many more.

But as in any radio show the listeners were the real stars. I remember one hilarious caller who rang up to take part in our competition called 'Guess the song'. The idea was I would play a line from a chorus of a big popular hit song from the 60s 70s and 80s and stop the song and that was the cue for the caller to sing the next few words.

So I had the caller on and the song was Manfred Mann's massive hit *Do Wah Diddy Diddy*.

I played the first line of the chorus, 'There she was just a walking down the street singing...' To be honest I thought it could not have been easier but how wrong I was.

I am sure that everyone reading this will immediately know the next words. This guy was silent so I repeated it. Still no answer let alone the correct one. Then he asked for a clue.

So now I am enjoying it and to be fair you really had to be there to appreciate how funny this moment was.

So what I did next was play the whole thing for him so blasting down the speakers was, "There she was just a walking Down the Street singing Do Wah Diddy Diddy Dum Diddy Do.

So then I said, 'OK lets go again' and I played the bit, 'There she was just a walking down the Street singing...' To which he said, 'hang on I think I know it now, it's on the tip of my tongue'. I just corpsed with laughter. The West Bromwich Albion manager Gary Megson called me after the show and said he was listening while driving to training and had to pull over because he was laughing that much. There's nothing funnier than real people in real life. Too many presenters forget the listeners are the real stars.

Another strange call I got was from a woman who had a go at the competition but spoke in a whisper, which sounded rather strange. Before letting her go I asked her why she was whispering and she said, 'I am at work'. So I got into my stride and asked her what she did for a living and to my utter amazement she replied, 'I am the receptionist at the BBC at Pebble Mill and I am not supposed to be listening.' I loved it.

HOLD YOUR PLUMS

'Hold Your Plums' as the name suggests was a competition that was innocent but tested the minds of people. Basically it was a quiz competition based on a fruit slot machine.

The listener got up to three goes, 'pulls on the handle'. If they correctly answered the first question they won four doughnuts, which they kept regardless! If they correctly answered the second question they would win a current CD or DVD, which they could keep or have a third pull on the handle and risk the second prize for a chance to win a Television or SKY subscription. Great fun!

Unfortunately over time a number of rules and regulations have been applied to radio competitions by the broadcasting authorities, with terms and conditions needed for every competition no matter how small it is. It has become a 'minefield' for radio presenters.

Competitions have to also be entertaining and fun, but you could argue they are too much trouble these days.

In hindsight we did let some usual moans from listeners along the lines of 'It's a fix!' or 'We couldn't get through on the number given' etc, but no real genuine complaints because they were just too popular.

However believe it or not there are people who are professional competition entrants and would use different names and numbers to have more than one go for big prizes. They would also be on every single radio station in the area.

A part of the show I loved was chatting with star guests – I don't do interviews but have a chat with no prepared questions. The memorable ones include:

LIONEL RICHIE

He was brilliant. I thanked him for all the fun me and other men had while listening to his songs. He said, 'It drives me crazy women get all romantic when they listen to my songs! So I seduce 'em and you guys get the fun!'

Now remember this man was a mega star and still is. He had me chuckling when he said that his kids just didn't get their dad was a major recording star. He said, 'I thought it was changing and they were beginning to get what I did when my youngest asked me how famous I was, so I asked him why he wanted to know?' he just replied, 'because I want to know if you were famous enough to know New Kids on the Block'.

HANK MARVIN

Hank Marvin was another down to earth proper bloke. He said that he was touched to be so well known among the younger generation. I was taken aback by this until he started to laugh and added, 'they don't know that I played the guitar, or was in the Shadows with Cliff Richard, but they all say to their moms, 'Mom I am Hank Marvin what times tea?'

MIKE PINDER OF THE SEARCHERS

I was a massive fan of the Liverpool group 'The Searchers' and played them regularly on the breakfast show so it was a real pleasure to speak to Mike Pinder live one morning. He explained how they had come by their name. They had gone to see John Wayne's classic movie *The Searchers* and just loved the name and so that was that.

Interestingly that film also inspired Buddy Holly to write his classic song *That'll Be The Day*, as that was one of the lines John Wayne used many times in the film.

SPENCER DAVIS – SPENCER DAVIS GROUP

I had Spencer Davis in the studio and we were talking about the band and how it all started in Brum and how tough the search for a vocalist was. Spencer told me that Stevie Winwood almost didn't get the gig and was on a short list of two for the job. I was gobsmacked when he told me that Reg Dwight was the other in the frame, who of course ultimately became Elton John.

ANDY WILLIAMS

Andy Williams was a massive star and yet was as friendly and down to earth as anyone. I really enjoyed my chat/interview with him down the line from the USA and probably overran a little. He was not angry about me overrunning, but came up with the best get out line ever. He said, 'Tom I am so sorry, but I have to go as I am playing golf with the President (of the USA)". The President or me? – no contest really!

MIKE D'ABO – MANFRED MANN

Being a fanatic about the music of my teens – the 60s – it was a real pleasure to chat with the lead singer of the pop group Manfred Mann – Mike D'Abo. He had a great voice but was also a very talented writer and lyricist having written *Handbags and Gladrags* for Chris Farlowe, a song that was also a massive hit for Rod Stewart and the Stereophonics. He also co-wrote B*uild Me up Buttercup* which was a multi-million seller for The Foundations. I remember saying, 'those great songs and the royalties from them must be your pension?' 'Oh no,' he said, 'you will never guess what is?' And he was right I couldn't. I was amazed when he told me that he made most money from a piece of music he wrote for a Cadbury's TV ad promoting their Fudge chocolate bar. 'A finger of fudge is just enough,' amazing!

As I said I had always loved my music and twice got the opportunity to sing along with two legends on the radio during the breakfast show. Gene Pitney and Bobby Vee.

One of the things that often happens when chatting to a singer, especially if you say you are a fan. They will nearly always test you by asking what is your favourite one of their songs, and if you ain't got one it could be embarrassing and make you look stupid and false.

When I met **Gene Pitney** it was shortly before his death and he asked me that question – to which I replied that I loved *I'm Gonna Be Strong* and that I was going to play it in a few minutes. He said, 'OK lets go' and asked me to sing the opening with him as the record started. So there I was singing with the legend that is Gene Pitney, 'I can see you're slipping away from me' – what a thrill and what a nice guy, he was in making me feel so comfortable. Lots of listeners were not so enamoured with my singing and started the banter by suggesting I left it to Gene. He could have thought, 'what a muppet', but he definitely made me feel great. I was devastated when just weeks later I heard he had sadly collapsed and died.

With **Bobby Vee**, who's still going strong, my reply to the question was, *Staying In* which was the B-side of his biggest hit single *More Than I Can Say*. He was surprised because it was a B-side but he invited me to sing with him and I did so off I went with, 'I punched my buddy in the nose after lunch Now I'm in trouble 'cause the Dean saw the punch'. If only there was an X Factor show in those days? Well maybe not!

Another fantastic genuine guy, and I have to be honest I cannot believe that I have had the chance to chat with genuine legends that I grew up listening to as a teenager. How lucky am I?

One guy I loved interviewing was the fantastic **Neil Sedaka**, one of the great pop stars of all time who was a brilliant songwriter and lyricist and also a brilliant musician and performer. His stories about Carole King left no doubt with the listeners that he genuinely loved her to bits. An awesome guy.

I had a great time when **Kid Creole** came into the studio. The interview revealed that he was a huge fan of black and white gangster movies on TCM, as was I. Because of this we became great friends. Like myself he loved James Cagney and would always greet me with, 'What do you hear? What do you say?' which is a Cagney line from the brilliant film *Angels with Dirty Faces* although Cagney's drawl came out as 'Whadda ya hear whadda ya say'. That love of 'gangster movies was the reason Kid Creole always wore a Zoot suit on stage'.

One of my favourite interviews was with **Antonio Fargas** better known as 'Huggy Bear' from *Starsky and Hutch* fame. He was appearing at the Alexandra Theatre and from the moment he walked in he was amazing. Friendly with no side to him at all and was happy to talk about Starsky and Hutch and the film *Carwash* as well as his theatre roles. The office staff were also captivated by him and he took the time out for photographs and chats.

Great times, great memories and I know I have said it a few times, I cannot believe how lucky I have been in having the career I have had.

A few words from BRENDAN O'CARROLL

Brendan is the writer, creator and star of *Mrs Browns Boys* the hit BBC TV Programme. He is also an author and has been in films such as *Angela's Ashes*.

143

'Long before there was a BBC TV series of Mrs Brown's Boys the city of Birmingham had taken Mrs Brown to their hearts. In a very large part thanks to Tom Ross. My very first radio interview about the show happened in Birmingham one rainy Tuesday morning over ten years ago, with me on one side of the microphone and what looked like slightly balding Santa's elf bouncing with energy on the other. He introduced himself as 'Tom' and I wondered if his surname was Thumb?

'It turned out to be one of the most delightful interviews I have ever done. Tom is insightful without making you feel uncomfortable, friendly without being patronising and always, ALWAYS, fun!

'Over the years we have become friends. His support has never weakened, his friendship is valued not just by me, but by my entire family, and indeed the Brown family too. Have a great read here and, if you get the chance, try and meet this man. You will come away from him feeling a lot better about the world... and he might even put a good word in for you with Santa Claus!

'Know that you are loved.

'Brendan xxx'

I remember being asked if I would like to give away tickets for a show at the Alexandra Theatre called *Mrs Browns Boys*. It was about a dysfunctional Irish family, with the mother Agnes Brown played by a man called Brendan O'Carroll. Well that was too close to what my own family was like as a boy growing up in Brum, so I was delighted to do it.

Now remember Brendan was very famous in Ireland and in some parts of England but was relatively unknown in Birmingham in his words, 'When I came to Birmingham I couldn't even get arrested'. Oh how that was to change.

I gave away loads of tickets. I could not believe it the following morning when everyone who went to the show was calling in to say how brilliant it was and how hilarious it was. So I went to see it that night and was mesmerised by this guy dressed as a woman and it was amazingly brilliant and funny as hell. So I asked the Alex Press Office to set up an interview. I fell in love with Agnes Brown because she was so like my Granny Sullivan.

A couple of days later I met Brendan for the first time when he came in for a chat with me on the breakfast show. We immediately hit it off, as I said I saw a lot of my Granny Sullivan in Agnes Brown. And Brendan said that every family has an Agnes Brown in it. And I did as my Mom was Mary Agnes Ross.

I absolutely loved the show and laughed from the first minute when he did the safety procedure instructions, to the last minute when he read out some thank you's. I had given away tickets and Brendan always graciously credits me with helping with his success in Brum. Well let me correct that and put that record straight right now, I got people to the Alex in the first instance but it was the quality of show and Brendan's immense talent that made people spread the word. Brendan is a comedy genius and a naturally funny man and to top it all he is a genuinely nice kind man.

Anyway I had scheduled five to 10 minutes with Brendan live on the breakfast show however he virtually took over the whole hour between 9am and 10am and was brilliantly entertaining and hilariously funny. He was just like Agnes and said what he thought. The listeners loved it as he hilariously did the travel and weather as well.

I can't begin to explain how much I loved his live show and went a few times on that first week he was at the Alex. And like all great comedy genius's, no two nights where the same.

I became great friends with him and his gorgeous wife Jenny and would often go out after the shows to have a bite to eat in a local casino. The whole family made me welcome.

Every time he was appearing in Brum he would come in and entertain the listeners for an hour or so. All the Irish football players at our clubs wanted tickets to see him. Sometimes I would do my evening show from the Alexandra Theatre when he was appearing, so I could talk to him and some of the other cast members.

One day during one of our on air chats he suddenly said, 'would you like to appear on stage in the show as I have a walk on part for you'. Well I said yes straight away because I can walk on anywhere and thought, even I can't cock that up. After the show I was handed a mini script with a list of lines for me to speak in an Irish accent. I was to play the part of the plumber in *Mrs Brown Rides again*.

The Birmingham Mail had gotten wind of the story and featured it with a picture of me with a toilet on my shoulder outside the Alexandra Theatre – Oh the showbiz life I lead.

I started to panic because I had never acted in anything since school, which made my nerves worse. Peter Kay had played the part in Manchester and Ronan Keating in Dublin – No pressure then?

I rehearsed every day with my breakfast show producer Lisa and to be honest was word perfect when the big day arrived – word perfect and terrified.

Basically I was a plumber wearing overalls and a flat cap who was hired to install a new loo underneath the stairs inside the cupboard in Mrs Brown's house. Now unbeknown to the plumber (me), Agnes earlier in the play had asked her son Dermot what a blowjob was and he replied £20. So in her mind if I did a good job she would give me a blowjob? Are you getting it?

So I am standing backstage with the toilet on my shoulders going through my lines in my head waiting to go on and getting more nervous and panicky by the moment, remember there were 2,000 people in the audience. When suddenly Jenny, Brendan's wife who plays his daughter in the show, says to me, 'have you rehearsed your lines?'

and I said quite confidently, "yes I think I am word perfect.' To which she replied, 'it's a waste of time because no one knows what Brendan will say or do next'. Well let me tell you that did nothing to relax me and I was wondering what they would do if I suddenly legged it?

The moment came and I was on. There were lots of BRMB/Capital Gold listeners in the audience and they gave me a warm welcome while I am sure the rest were thinking, 'who is this nugget?'

Brendan was brilliant and tried to 'corpse me' – It was truly a memorable experience and was yet another time I have stepped outside my comfort zone and challenged myself to do something different.

He offered me another chance to be in another of the Mrs Brown Trilogy but this time I said no after I found out I would have to wear leather chaps and flash my backside – no audience deserves that so I said no way, which let me say, was a blessing to everyone.

It was without doubt one of the most exciting things I have done and yet although I thanked Brendan for the opportunity I have never really told him what an honour and privilege it was to be on the same stage as him and Jenny and the rest of 'Mrs Brown's' family. A truly remarkable never to be forgotten experience for which I will always be grateful to him for.

Brendan makes it look so easy and yet it's far from that. It looks easy because he is an extremely talented individual with perfect comic timing.

It is no surprise to me that he is now a massive TV star thanks to the BBC screening the *Mrs Browns Boys* series.

One day I was driving to Southampton for a game when he called me and asked me to put him in touch with Jasper Carrott. He said he had been offered the chance to do a series of *Mrs Browns Boys* on the BBC and wanted to talk to JC about the ins and outs and pitfalls of TV.

Jasper told him to insist the BBC let him be himself and not dumb him down – in other words to do it his way just like the brilliant stage shows.

He did just that and the rest as they say is history – now a worldwide success and deservedly so. It's great when the nice guys win.

And, unlike some, he doesn't forget those he met on the way up – he recently got angry with me because I bought tickets to his show at the NEC. He insisted I had tickets left by him with backstage passes for me and Anne to see him afterwards. When we saw him he and Jenny and the family were brilliant with us – nothing big time about them whatsoever and made us feel so welcome.

By the way you should read some of his books *Me Mammy* is my favourite and tells the story of Agnes Brown. He was also in two big films *The Van* and *Angela's Ashes* while he also appeared in *Max and Paddy* a spin off from Peter Kay's *Phoenix Nights*.

Other memorable guests include **Steve Harley** of Cockney Rebel fame who did some great 'drops' for my show. A drop is a line that I play over the start of a song. He did a great one to play over the start of his biggest hit *Come Up and See Me (Make Me Smile)*. He said, 'Hi Steve Harley here on the breakfast show with Tom Ross come up and see him make him smile'.

Steve was doing an unplugged set at Ronnie Scott's in Broad Street and funnily enough it was Steve Stride, then a director of Aston Villa and a huge fan who got him back performing again,

Jeff Wayne (*War of the Worlds* composer and a senior tennis player on the ATP Seniors circuit) was a lovely person and very down to earth and a joy to interview.

I was apprehensive about interviewing pop star **Will Young,** whom I had been led to believe was a very difficult interviewee. He was in reality a real pleasure and delight to talk to. I think he enjoyed the informal chat style and I got a few brownie points early on when I said I loved his first album. Now I was out of his demographic and he must have thought I was coming the old soldier, as my Mom would say. He asked me my favourite song and when I replied, *Love is a matter of distance* he preened as he told me it was the only song he had written and was his favourite too. The rest was easy

Motown soul legend **Martha Reeves** of Martha Reeves and the Vandellas fame came in to the Breakfast Show with **Mary Wilson** one of the original Supremes. Now as a Motown fan and music lover I was in my element to be sitting having a cup of tea with Tamla mega stars who had recorded *Jimmy Mack, Dancing in the Street, Baby Love* etc.

They were lovely down to earth women who spoke about everything and anything. Mary speaking frankly about the fallouts with Diana Ross, while Mary regaled us with stories of Gordy Berry, Marvin Gaye etc. She had been a secretary/receptionist at Motown Records before she got the chance to be a backing vocalist. The rest is music history. Interestingly she found it strange that over here it was always Tamla Motown but not in the USA where it was just Motown.

Both Mary and Martha raved about Dusty Springfield who they say was probably the only English female who quite easily could have been a Motown star.

Motown artist **Edwin Starr** who recorded *War, SOS, Contact* and *Happy Radio* was a regular visitor as he lived locally. He was one of the most engaging humble men I have ever met. Sadly he died at a far too early age.

Graham Gouldman of 10cc was a welcome visitor although to be fair I was never a big 10cc fan, although I loved some of their songs such as *Dreadlock Holiday*. But Graham was extremely interesting and we enjoyed a chat about some of the songs he had written for other artists especially *No Milk Today*, which was a massive hit for Herman's Hermits. It contains one of the great song lines 'No milk today my love has gone away-the bottle stands forlorn a symbol of the dawn' fantastic!

I interviewed **Duran Duran** ahead of their gig at St Andrew's in the 2000's and to be fair I don't really think they wanted to be interviewed at all and at times they seemed disinterested, so I didn't really enjoy it.

I mentioned to them that it was a great co-incidence that they were playing at St Andrew's where the very first playing of their first hit *Planet Earth* took place in 1980. They seemed genuinely surprised at this because Radio One had always claimed the first public playing of the song. I explained to them that footballer Frank Worthington was a great friend of the Berrow Brothers who ran the Rum Runner nightclub in Broad Street where the band were effectively based. The Berrow Brothers were also the band's managers. They gave a cassette copy of *Planet Earth* to Frank Worthington on one of his many visits to the Rum Runner. On the following match day Frank appeared in the commentary box and gave me the cassette to play, which I did.

I remember also going to school in Acocks Green to review this young band called Duran Duran for the *ABC Advertiser* in which I wrote a pop column. This was long before they had a record deal but even then they showed talent.

Gerry Marsden (of Gerry and The Pacemakers) was brilliant and very funny. He came in for a chat on the breakfast show and we had a great time. We talked about his career and I remember saying that one of my all-time favourite songs of his was *Don't Let the Sun Catch You Crying*.

He explained, all deadpan, that he wrote it after splitting up with his girlfriend when he was 14 years of age. He sent her the tape of the song and it touched her so much they got back together.

He then said, 'that girl has been my wife for over 40 years (pause). Sometimes I wished I'd never written the thing'.

UB40 were always a pleasure to interview and always gave you the impression they were doing it because they wanted to and not because they had to. They were always entertaining, honest and informative and not just plugging their latest album or single.

I have been great friends with the band for lots of years, especially Astro and had the greatest of pleasure to introduce them onstage at the Café Du Paris in London at a Capital Radio gig. I remember we took a coachload of Brummie UB40 fans down to London and had the best of times. It was like 'the Jolly Boys Outing' in *Only Fools and Horses*.

The UB 40 band are Brummie guys who were employers in the city and still lived in the area. It's a mystery how they have never had a star on the Broad St. Walk of Fame.

When they acrimoniously split over money it was one of the saddest things. All the band were friends as youngsters and started the band while broke.

Astro and Micky are now touring with Ali Campbell who is without doubt the voice of UB40. Robin, Brian and the rest of the guys enlisted another brother Duncan Campbell to be their lead vocalist. Lovely man though he is and as talented as the band still is, Duncan is not Ali. I just wish they could reconcile and once again entertain us as the complete UB40.

Paul Carrack was another brilliant artist who regularly came in to have a chat. He was lead singer of ACE who had a massive hit with *How Long* and was also lead singer with Mike and the Mechanics who had fantastic hits with *The Living Years* and *Over My Shoulder*. He was a big Sheffield Wednesday fan and a big friend of Trevor Francis who introduced him to me. One of the best voices you will ever hear.

I once interviewed top chef **Ainsley Harriott** on the Breakfast show. He starred in *Can't Cook Won't Cook* and brought a fun element to the art of cooking. I was amazed when he asked me on air if I would go on his TV show as a celebrity guest (his words not mine) I could think of nothing worse than making myself look like a right nugget in front of the TV cameras. I do a good enough job in front of a radio mic (there I said it while you were thinking it.) It was a perfect title because it was spot on for me *Can't Cook Wont Cook*. Most of my radio presenter colleagues thought I was crazy not to want to go on National TV. Now, while I like a challenge, I just did not fancy it because I just have no interest in cooking, end of story.

I was asked to interview the **Stereophonics** ahead of a new album release and was told Kelly Jones could be difficult. What a load of rubbish! He was a dream and we had a great chat.

He arrived with guitarist and vocalist Adam Zindani and after talking about their new album we got onto football because I knew Kelly was a fanatical Leeds United supporter. It turned out that Adam was from Kings Heath in Birmingham and was a massive Bluenose as were his brothers.

Adam has since invited me to all the Stereophonics gigs when they are local and I have become a big fan of the band.

I have never been as excited as when I was asked if I would interview actress **Gwyneth Strong** and I literally jumped for joy. Gwyneth plays the part of Cassandra Trotter in my favourite TV programme of all time *Only fools and Horses*. She was appearing in a play at the Rep in Birmingham but that was secondary to me. I was meeting Cassandra – wow.

She was lovely and very posh, well posher than me anyway. She was comfortable and enjoyed the chat about *Only Fools and Horses* and I was delighted to hear her say it was as much fun to act in as it was to watch it. She said she was a soccer mom who had to take her kids to practice and that they were Arsenal fans. I was that excited I forgot to get a photo with her, I was gutted.

Anna Karen was a dream to interview and nothing like 'Olive' the part she played in *On the Buses* She was very warm and eloquent and an actress of note and it was the same when I interviewed the late comedian **Victoria Wood** who was a very warm and lovely and made me feel so at ease. They were so different out of character and just being themselves.

I have interviewed some of the modern pop stars as well and I have to say **One Direction** were brilliant. A couple of them were massive football fans and just wanted to talk football. Really nice kids but I am not sure how they would be now they have lived in the USA for a while and are now massive stars worldwide, but they were brilliant.

I am not the biggest fan of the way the pop music business has become pre-occupied with all the reality shows such as *X Factor*, *The Voice*, *Pop Idol* and *Britain's Got Talent*. I must admit I view the pop business world as pretty vacuous.

However **Olly Murs** was a real breath of fresh air. He was a lovely guy and always made a beeline to talk football with me as he is a huge Man United fan but he is also a proper grounded bloke. To be fair he also has a great voice and is a proper pop star with no pretensions to be anything else. When my daughter Amy was not too well he picked up the phone and gave her a call and had a long chat with her that gave her a lift when she needed it. Top Man.

I don't often get overly excited about interviews but I must admit I was thrilled to be given the chance to chat with actor and 60s pop star **John Leyton** (*Johnny Remember Me*). He was in one of my favourite films. *The Great Escape* you may remember he was the young blonde man who help Charles Bronson through the tunnels. It was fascinating to hear him talk about the making of *The Great Escape* He said that Steve McQueen kept himself to himself and wasn't really sociable but the rest of the cast were brilliant and he became great friends with Charles Bronson.

I once interviewed **Freddie Starr** and he was both brilliant and hilarious. After we finished the interview he would walk around the office Introducing himself and telling the staff gags and doing impressions. He appeared in reception a couple of times after that without anything pre-arranged. I had the feeling he was a lonely man in terms of friends. But still showed how funny he was and had the office in stiches.

Another one who would just pop in was **Tony Christie** (*Is This the Way to Amarillo*) I didn't realise at the time but he lives locally and if he was appearing at a local theatre he would drop in for a chat.

One of the strangest interviews was just two years ago when I was asked by my bosses to interview the **Prime Minister David Cameron**. Only it wasn't so much an interview as me putting listener's questions to him. Sadly I was warned that I had to ask those questions and not to add in any questions of my own or even to question his answers. I really could have had some fun with that. After Mr Cameron had left the building with his armed security guard I was thinking about it and how it had gone etc. When I suddenly thought who would have thought when I was sitting in the tin bath in front of the fire in the inner city Birmingham back-to-back slums of the 50s that one day I would be chatting to the PM. What a life I have had. He did chat about genuinely being an Aston Villa supporter and how he got to see them when he had the chance.

Jeff Lynne was amazing to interview. I had not seen him for over 20 years but as soon as we caught up at the Birmingham Library ahead of him getting his star on Broad Street he was brilliant and he made me feel so comfortable. And while the interview was smashing it was better when we were just chatting about the old days etc. A top man and one of the most talented people I have ever interviewed.

After the presenting of the star on Broad Street to Jeff at a private ceremony at the new Birmingham Library Jasper Carrott hosted a Q & A with Jeff and it was truly awesome. Jeff talked about his early live with various bands and about growing up in Shard End.

In his down to earth way he also explained how he came to form the Travelling Wilburys. He and George Harrison had decided to start a band and wanted other members so Jeff rang Roy Orbison and said, 'Roy do you wanna be in our group'. Then he rang Bob Dylan and said the same in his Brummie accent, 'Bob do you wanna be in our group'. No pretentious projects etc. – just brilliant.

After it was over the Lord Mayor invited a few of us to his parlour for a little private get together. I was chatting to this guy who asked me why I was not drinking I said, 'I don't drink what about you?' He replied, 'I am not drinking because I am working tomorrow'. We chatted for a few minutes before I suddenly realised I was talking to rock star **Bryan Adams**? I didn't know whether to say, *Summer of 69* was one of my all-time favourite songs or that the Robin Hood song was shite.

I said nothing and continued a nice chat with him and what a humble bright friendly man he is.

In May 2016 I got a call from Steve Hewlett asking me if I would like to host a special event in Brum City centre which would involve interviewing Black Sabbath frontman **Ozzie Osbourne**- the Prince of Darkness himself. I could not say yes quick enough as he is a rock legend. People told me he would be difficult but he was a dream to talk to and had the thousands who had gathered in Corporation Street in his hand. He has led some life that's for sure and crammed more in his time than most.

Some of the other stars that I have loved interviewing
Johnny Cash Band
Barry White
Sheila Ferguson (The Three Degrees)
Dionne Warwick
Shaking Stevens. Who gave me one of my best lines? I would say to the producer before playing a Shaky song "do you like Shaking Stevens" he would say "yes" and I would reply "well you're not shaking mine" Please yourself!
Meatloaf
Manic Street Preachers
Scouting for Girls

JLS

Lemar (It's Not That Easy)

Cyndi Lauper

Eddy Grant

Apache Indian

Lenny Henry – although I had to give him a Baggies Bronx hat for his friend

Sir Cliff Richards

Gilbert O'Sullivan

Anthony Cotton (Sean Tully in *Coronation St*)

Claire Sweeney (*Brookside*)

Tom Watt. (Lofty in *Eastenders*) Tom was an unassuming lovely man and we clicked right away. Even though I am not and never was an *Eastenders* fan. We still catch up on the football circuit and through social media as he is a massive Arsenal fan.

One of the worst was **Boy George** – who appeared to me to be a very angry man. I asked him if he liked football and his reply was, 'are you taking the piss'. I couldn't wait to end it and that's what I do if I feel they are not really interested and are only doing the interview because they have to.

TOWER BALLROOM

The Tower was situated by Edgbaston Reservoir. It was a popular dance venue and nightclub. It was also the venue for the Xtra-AM 'Soul and Motown' nights. They were great fun and always packed out by listeners who just wanted a great night dancing to great music.

I and another Xtra AM presenter Mike Hollis hosted them as the Blues Brothers. We would always have a live band and usually it was 'the Official Receivers' who were a brilliant local soul band. Mike and I would join then on stage for a song or two usually The Temptations classic *Ain't To Proud To Beg*. Perhaps now you can see how I was loving life in radio.

CHAPTER FIVE

SPORTS BARMY

Don Cherry, one time coach of the Boston Bruins Ice Hockey team, led them to glory when they won the Stanley Cup against all the odds. In his autobiography he wrote, 'Never underestimate the power of desire over ability' and that has stuck in my memory from that day to this. He also said he wanted both in a player, but if he had to choose one he would pick desire because, 'ability without desire is a waste of time.'

I believe that applies to any sport and also to any aspect of life. And I have always been extremely competitive with an overwhelming and at times obsessive desire to be number one.

I never needed telling that I wasn't the best broadcaster, but I am sure there were not many who worked harder at their trade than I did. I knew that I had to work harder to be more successful than those with more natural broadcasting talent.

My involvement with the Solihull Barons Ice Hockey Team is mentioned elsewhere in the book, but I must have been mad when I agreed to play in a charity ice hockey game against the Solihull Vixens women's team. I had to learn to skate and to be fair ended up being able to skate quite well. However stopping was the problem thankfully the rink boards helped. I ended up with more bruises than I did in my charity boxing match with former world champion John H. Stracey!

I was once asked to play in a charity pro-am golf tournament at the Belfry on their Ryder Cup Course. Now let me make it clear I am not the best golfer in the word, in fact I am useless. I was playing with two top ex-professionals. They both smashed the ball about 200 yards off the tee and then it's my turn. There are around 150–200 people around the first tee and one or two Villa fans who were trying their best to put me off. I had a few practice swings as it went very quiet. I then took my shot and missed! A voice erupted from the quiet shouting 'One'. Well that did it for me I was swinging wildly and divots were flying everywhere until I eventually hit the ball. It shanked to the right and hit the tree by the starters hut and flew over my head? I was 25 yards further away for my second shot than when I started. The crowd were howling with laughter. It was like the Martians in the Smash Advert (Ask your Dad). Lying around and laughing until tears fell. I made a decision then that I would never play the stupid game again.

The only other time I was embarrassed was in a charity pro-am cricket match at Edgbaston. I am not sure what professional cricketer I was batting with, but my memory says it was Imran Khan. One thing for certain is that Jimmy Cumbes the former Villa and Baggies goalkeeper, who of course had also played County Cricket, was bowling at me. Now he sent a ball down to me and to be truthful I didn't see it but it hit my bat and went down to third man. I looked up and Imran shouted 'yes' so off I went racing down the wicket when all of a sudden he said, 'I am not coming'. I was run out amid great hilarity from the footballers who were also playing.

However worse was to come in terms of embarrassment for yours truly? This time I am bowling at Jimmy Cumbes, he described my bowling style as right arm crowd pleasers, anyway I had the longest run up ever known to man and Jim just leant back and smashed it so high and far it went out of Edgbaston and into Canon Hill Park and that takes some doing. He leaned on his bat and said, 'Rossi I wonder if there is a stewardess serving drinks on that'.

We had a BRMB charity cricket team, which was captained by George Gavin. In the team was Tony Trethewey, News reporter Brian King, Jimmy Franks, John Buust, Football reporter Tony Leighton, racing results man George Reeves and a

The BRMB Charity Cricket team in the 80S

few others. We played Sunday afternoons and had a great time all over the Midlands although we were not the best, we were competitive. As an example of the standard our wicketkeeper George Reeves once famously said, 'he was a good wicketkeeper, but didn't like catching'. That summed up our ability.

The cricket team folded after a game we were playing against 'The Sportsman' in Harborne, Birmingham ended in a brawl, which upset the vicar who was there at the charity event. There was a bit of needle in the match although for the life of me I can't remember why. One of our civilian bowlers (in other words he didn't work for BRMB) bowled a Sportsman batsman out and said, 'now f**k off'. Well that was it all hell broke loose.

The BRMB Football team was started by Tony Butler and helped to raise loads of money for local charities. I loved playing for them and we played in front of some big crowds. George Gavin was the skipper and to be fair George was a more than decent player, Jimmy Franks also played and had a sprinkling of top non-league players. We had some real tough games and Tony Butler would not be too pleased if the tackling got too tasty. He had to speak to me on more than one occasion for getting involved as he called it. I remember when we played the Winson Green prison officers and I was left wing and more than got the better of their right-back who was not the quickest or slimmest in fact he was built like a brick outhouse.

I tormented him and said a few not so nice things to him and he was ready to explode when I swapped wings with Jimmy Franks. Within seconds this loony tune right-back did no more than nail Jimmy with both feet. Jimmy's leg was in tatters and needed plenty of treatment and one or two stiches. Jimmy tried to blame me and to this day mentions it every time we meet. All I did was know exactly the right time to get out of the war zone.

One of the things I really enjoyed was covering the AAA's Athletics meetings at the Alexander Stadium, reporting into George Gavin's Saturday afternoon Sports Show. These were usually qualifying events for the Commonwealth games or the Olympics. The Athletics people were a dream to deal with and nothing was too much trouble interviewing any of the Athletes, well apart from one.

I was at one of these meetings when I asked if I could speak with Daley Thompson the Decathlete and was told he had almost finished training and I could wait trackside for him so I did just that. When he came up I said quite politely, 'excuse me Mr Thompson could I have a word for BRMB radio. He just looked at me and told me to "f**k off". So I did but I was very upset at the time, as I was a big fan of his brilliant and cavalier way of competing. I have to say it's the only time any sportsman or woman has spoken to me like that. I have never forgotten it and when a few years ago I was asked if I wanted to interview Daley about his new book, I can't tell you what my answer was but I bet you can guess. Perhaps he was just having a bad day, but it upset this naïve inexperienced reporter at the time.

GLASGOW CELTIC

After Birmingham City my second football club is Glasgow Celtic and once again I have to thank my Dad for getting me involved.

He was an ardent 'Bhoys' supporter and for a time was Chairman of the Celtic Supporters club in Birmingham, organising the coach trips up to the big games. He took me to many games in Glasgow including plenty of Auld Firm games when I was thrilled to stand with him in the 'Jungle.'

In the late 60s I went to see Bertie Auld in Glasgow and he took me around Celtic introducing me to Jock Stein and the whole of the 67 Lisbon Lions team. However it was no posh hotel we went to but to a pub on the London Road called 'The Sidelines' owned by a couple of the players. I used to sit with the team just talking football and being mesmerised by the banter from these European Cup winners, but I was the only one drinking Vimto.

When Garry Pendrey was assistant manager to Gordon Strachan at Celtic I was invited to the Champions League game against Manchester United in November 2006 with Eric Black (who was Assistant to Steve Bruce at the time). I had forgotten how special the atmosphere was at Parkhead as the *Fields of Athenry* rang around the terraces followed by *You'll Never Walk Alone* it was fantastic especially as Celtic beat Manchester United 1–0. On this occasion I was privileged to be a guest in the manager's office after the game where Sir Alex Ferguson and lots of other footballing legends were. I was like a kid in a sweet shop.

Before the game I was in the VIP lounge with Eric Black talking to Bertie and also to Walter Smith and Archie Knox two Scottish legends.

I was back in November 2008 when they again clashed in the Champions League and it was made all the more special because my son Jon was with me experiencing a European night at Parkhead. All Dads will understand when I say how special it was. Garry Pendrey gave Jon his official Champions League tracksuit. He also took us out into the centre of the pitch and what an experience that was for the both of us! I thought of my Dad while out there and just wished he could have been with me. He did so much for me as a boy and yet I never really got the chance to repay him by taking him to these games when he was fit and able to enjoy them.

Because of my Dad I am a Scotland fan, however I am not anti-England. When England are playing of course I want them to win unless they are playing Scotland. I saw all the Home International games at Wembley and at Hampden. We had a little group that went to these internationals including Paddy Lynch, Pat Van den Hawe and Jimmy Calderwood. One time we had to stop Pat getting battered by Scotland fans because he was talking very loudly in his 'cockney accent'. Thankfully he was OK when I gave him my Scotland scarf.

There was one Scotland game when I arrived buzzing with excitement and left feeling a little ashamed. It was in 1977 when I went to the Scotland v Wales World

Cup qualifier at Anfield. I have to say the atmosphere was absolutely electric. One of the best I can remember.

A coach was organised by Andy Gray and others to take us and bring us back. With us, from memory, were Jimmy Calderwood, Ricky Sbragia and other Scots from all the local clubs. Also with us was the *Birmingham Mail* reporter David Leggatt, a great journalist who loved a few sherbets.

The trip was awesome until the French referee awarded Scotland a penalty for handball. However everyone in the ground knew that Joe Jordan had handled it and not a Welsh defender. That knocked the stuffing out of the Wales team and Scotland went on to win 2–0. It left a bitter taste in my mouth and the trip back was not quite so awesome although it was for the others. I must have been the only teetotal man on the bus.

BOXING

I love boxing and one of my long time great pals is Paddy Lynch who along with his brother Tommy did so much to make Birmingham famous for boxing. They promoted great fights in the city as Prescott-Sweeney-Lynch promotions and after that with Dave Roden as Roden-Lynch promotions. Dave went on to work for the British Boxing Board of Control.

Paddy is one of the most knowledgeable men I have ever met about the noble art of Boxing. He and his brother Tommy coached nine boxers to win British Titles. They were: Gordon Ferris (heavyweight), Wayne Elcock (middleweight), Costas Petrou (welterweight), Pat Cowdell (featherweight and superfeatherweight), Roy Rutherford (featherweight), Lloyd Christie (middleweight), Robert McCracken (middleweight), Tony Willis (lightweight) and Hughie Ford (featherweight).

He also took Pat Cowdell and Wayne Elcock to world title fights. Probably one his best nights was masterminding Wayne's British Title win over the incredible Howard Eastman.

Paddy and his brother Tommy have given and continue to give so much to the sport of Boxing in fact I think they have won more titles than any other management team. They have invested hundreds of thousands of their own money into the sport without ever worrying about getting it back or making any money from it.

Paddy always talks about fighters needing to have the "Holy Trinity" of boxing: a good chin, a big heart and power. If you have those three you will always have a chance but to rely on boxing ability on its own is just not enough.

How their contribution to the noble art has not been recognised with an MBE or OBE for services to boxing is totally beyond me.

Paddy also had to win his own personal battle against cancer, but if there was one man you would bet on when the odds are stacked against him it is Paddy Lynch. He undertook a new treatment that really was a kill or cure treatment. Thankfully he won that battle. He has supposedly retired from training boxers however he has been looking after Stuart Hall and has been helping out Frankie Gavin who, with his trainer Max McCracken, uses Paddy's gym.

At BRMB I have been fortunate to interview some great fighters and none bigger than Muhammad Ali. Dave Hadley, who was the Commercial Director at Blues, got me the opportunity to talk to Muhammad Ali (Cassius Clay) when he made a trip to Birmingham City.

He was not at all like the upfront lippy character I had seen on the TV. He was charm personified with a great sense of humour.

I remember getting up in the early hours to listen to the world title fights on the radio with my Dad and so to meet this great man was something else. I reckon you could drop Ali anywhere on the planet and everyone would know him – that is a genuine legend.

One of the highlights for me was when boxing promoter Ken Purchase invited me to his home for an exclusive interview with non-other than **Jake La Motta** – The Raging Bull. I could not believe it! For God's sake they had made a film about this guy's life and here I was sitting having a chat and a cup of tea with him.

He was brilliant, warm and funny. He told me how he coached actor Robert De Niro who was to play him in the Oscar winning iconic movie. He said that De Niro boxed hundreds of rounds to get ready for the movie and look authentic. Jake said by the time they had finished he was convinced De Niro could have been a contender. A genuine highlight of my radio life.

I was invited by promoter John Pegg to a sporting dinner at the Holiday Inn in Birmingham where **Mike Tyson** was a guest. John managed to get me an exclusive interview in Mike's room. Now I have to confess I was a little nervous because I had heard from some boxing journalists that Mike could be quite intimidating and threatening.

So on my way to his room with my son Jon I decided that if Mike said it was Christmas I was singing carols. However I was more than pleasantly surprised to find Mike Tyson quite engaging and friendly which was more than could be said for his minders.

The legendary **Sugar Ray Leonard** was making a rare visit to Birmingham when I was invited down to interview him at Villa Park. I could not believe how good he looked. There was not a mark on him, which probably sums up how good he was. He talked at length about the Golden era of brilliant middleweights that featured him and Thomas 'Hitman' Hearns and 'Marvellous' Marvin Hagler. The like of which we will probably never see again. He made me feel so welcome and enjoyed the banter about boxing during the interview.

Evander Holyfield came into the studio to promote his autobiography and again I was told he is difficult and will not pose for photographs or sign things etc. However he was superb and the interview was hilarious, in parts as he talked about Mike Tyson biting part of his ear off during their world title fight. Holyfield was a true warrior a humble man. I did get to have a picture with him but have searched high and low and can't find it. It was pre-cameras on phones days. But I am just happy he signed my book.

On behalf of BRMB I was invited by Gary Newbon to interview Azumah Nelson at ITV ahead of his world title fight with **Pat Cowdell** at the NEC.

I had seen Pat in action many times and felt that with his unorthodox awkward style he could beat Nelson and that the African would not like Pats doggedness. So during the interview, which was going quite well I said to Azumah 'lots of people think you have come a long way to get knocked out,' well the look he gave me sent me pale. What I meant to say was, 'what would you say to those people who think you have come a long way to get knocked out?' It came out disrespectfully and that is not what I meant because every man who gets into the ring, good bad or indifferent, is a true warrior.

Richie Woodhall has become a great friend and was a fantastic interviewee even after tough world title fights. He tells it like it is and doesn't hide anything or make any excuses. Just after I joined BRMB I was given the task of making a programme about local athletes who were competing in the 1988 Olympics. I chose Richie and one of his boxing colleagues and called the programme *Going for Gold*. Original eh?

Richie and his late Dad, the brilliant Lenny, were super with me and so it was fantastic for me to cover his world title fight against Sugar Boy Malinga in Telford when he won the World Super Middleweight Crown. Richie wouldn't mind me saying that he was never the classiest of boxers but he definitely had the boxers Holy Trinity, Chin, Heart and Ability. He was one of the most dedicated trainers I have known. He trained hard every single day. I was lucky to cover most of his fights and it was a pleasure. I went with Paddy and Tommy Lynch to Len Woodhalls funeral last year (2015). He will be sadly missed by the close boxing fraternity.

It was the same with **Robert McCracken** I travelled all over the country covering his fights and always believed he would one day be world champion. He had everything in his armoury to be a long time world champion. However unlike Richie he might not have been as dedicated. I loved watching him in action though he had the heart of a lion and a great punch. I believe he would have been a multi-millionaire had he done the hard running.

His knockout punch brought him back from the brink when he fought Smith on the Frank Bruno bill at the NEC in Birmingham. He had virtually lost every round but came up with a brilliant punch in the last round that poleaxed Smith.

When he fought the Manchester Viking Steve Foster at the NEC both sets of fans had a running battle in the arena and that damaged the City's reputation. Frank Warren and Don King said to me afterwards they would think twice before putting on high profile boxing bills in Brum. Thankfully they did.

However it was no surprise to see him coaching the Great Britain team while also being trainer to World Champion Carl Froch. Robert knew every trick and excuse in the book, in fact he probably wrote most of them, to get out of training so no one could ever pull the wool over his eyes. Brilliant to see him awarded the MBE for services to boxing.

At the time of Robert's fight with Steve Foster the legendary American boxing promoter Don King came into the studios in Aston and joined me for an hour on a boxing phone in and he just took over. He was brilliant and absolutely hilarious. He entertained the listeners and me with some brilliant boxing stories and anecdotes and this will surprise you...I couldn't get a word in!

I recall BRMB doing live boxing commentary at the NIA In 1992 when Nigel Benn fought Sugar Boy Malinga. George Gavin was hosting it while I was out and about doing what I was best at, getting interviews.

On the same bill was a relatively unknown Naseem Hamed (Later to become Prince Naseem Hamed) He was fighting Steve Bloomer in only his third professional fight. Naseem had won the first two by knockout in the second round and did the same to Bloomer. I went into the dressing room and spoke to Naseem who suddenly launched into a Cassius Clay style rant about how I was talking to a future world champion and he was the best ever etc. I remember saying to George Gavin who is this nugget-little did I know that he would do exactly what he had said he would in the interview.

Pat Cowdell was an exceptional fighter with a difficult style that gave opponents loads of problems. Pat had the Boxing Holy Trinity in bucketful's. Lots of heart. Great chin. And super ability as his record shows.

I loved covering his fights ever since his dodgy controversial defeat by Dave Needham at Wolverhampton Civic where Pat won all 15 rounds by a distance. No one in the building could believe it when the referee help up Needham's hand. It went off big time with chairs thrown. Thankfully justice was done when they met two months later. This time Pat got the decision in what was a closer contest.

They met a third time for the British Featherweight title and Pat punished Needham forcing him to retire after 12 rounds. It was extra sweet for Pat because that was his third successful defence of the title and meant he kept the Lonsdale Belt forever.

Pat took the legendary Salvador Sanchez to a split decision for the world title in the USA in 1981. No one should ever underestimate just how great a performance that was from Pat.

One of the best fights I have been at was at the Aston Villa Leisure Centre when Pat won the European Super Featherweight title by beating Jean Mark Renaud. Pat was brilliant that night.

It was always the case he would get another world title fight and it came when they matched him against African Azumah Nelson at the NEC. Pat was caught cold in the opening 90 seconds and knocked out. His chance had gone, I and many other boxing journalists believe but for that he would have given Nelson plenty of problems. But of course we will never know.

After the fight we media men were allowed into Pat's dressing room to interview him. I was second behind Gary Newbon. Gary said, 'Pat didn't you see the punch?' to which Pat replied, 'If I had f*****g seen it Gary I'd have got out the way.' Brilliant.

One of the biggest disappointments was that Pat never got it on with Barry McGuigan. In my opinion McGuigan or his manager Barnet Eastwood never wanted to fight Pat and always ducked it.

I know Paddy and Tommy Lynch tried so hard to make the fight happen and despite the Lynch's offering big dough it never did. In fact Paddy and Tommy had posters circulated around Belfast saying 'WANTED BARRY MCGUIGAN'. He sadly never took up the challenge.

Liverpudlian **Tony Willis** another member of the Lynch Brothers stable of boxers was a great guy. A typical scouser who had a one liner for every occasion. He won a bronze medal at the Moscow Olympics at Light welterweight and was British Lightweight champion for two years in the 80s. Overall he only lost four of 29 fights and he could bang with either hand knocking out 14 of his opponents.

He was invited to a garden party with the Queen at Buckingham Palace after competing at the Olympics. After a while he called one of the Queen's aides over and asked where and how he got his expenses for travelling down from Liverpool for the event. She was definitely not happy and explained to him that they did not pay expenses as it was an honour to be invited to Buckingham Palace.

Anyway Tony kept banging on about his expense so much that the Queen's aide demanded to know his name and threatened to report him. Without a moment's hesitation Tony said, 'Pat Cowdell'.

Wayne 'Mad Dog' Elcock was another boxer Paddy and Tommy took on quite late in his career. He had already been British Champion, but was thought by many to be past his best when he joined the Lynch Brothers. Paddy and Tommy still managed to guide him to a brilliant British Light Middleweight title win over the legendary Howard Eastman in Coventry at the age of 33. He was the first British fighter to beat Eastman and that win secured him a Lonsdale belt outright. They also got Wayne a shot at the World title against Arthur Abrahams in Germany in 2007 but that proved to be a step to far for the likeable Brummie.

Hughie Ford was another fantastic guy who won the British and Commonwealth super-featherweight titles. Had he been with better management in my opinion he might just have done even better.

I was given the opportunity by promoter Ken Purchase to interview heavyweight champion Anthony Joshua. He is one a proper unit, a beast of a man and physiologically perfect. I am convinced he will unify the world titles eventually. I found him to be a very humble guy and more importantly dedicated to his sport. He will never take short cuts in training or preparation and that will be the key to his certain success.

CRICKET

A few words from JIM TROUGHTON

Jim was mainly an attack minded left-handed batsman but also an occasional slow left-arm orthodox bowler. He played for and captained Warwickshire and has played for the England one-day international team. He is now on the coaching staff at Edgbaston.

His grandfather Patrick Troughton, starred as the Doctor in the science fiction series *Doctor Who* in the 1960s.

After retiring because of injury Jim is back at Edgbaston as one of their coaches.

'I remember meeting Tom for the first time at backward point. He was batting (or attempting to bat) in a Bunbury cricket match played at Walmley Cricket Club. Charging in to bowl was Gordon Cowans, who was no slouch with the ball and Gordon, along with a number of other ex-Villa players, who were fielding at the time, had the express intent of "knocking that bluenose's head off". Tom took it all in his stride with a huge smile on his face. There was no way anyone from the Villa was gonna knock his head off and to be fair he was right. His first delivery arrived and he backed away so far he couldn't even reach it, let alone worry about it hitting him on the head. With his stumps in tatters, he strode off defiantly with the nattering Villa contingent giving him a proper send off.

'Tom is a legend of a bloke. When I think of Midland's football, I think of Tom. If you want to listen to proper footy commentary – listen to Tom. If you want someone to have a good night out with, who will make you laugh and enjoys a good piss take – look no further than Tom.

'Has he got a star on Broad Street yet? If not, it's a travesty.'

In the 1980s George would send me to Edgbaston one week and New Road the following week. I loved covering the cricket. It was much more laid back and civilised than the crazy world of football.

WORCESTERSHIRE

They always made me very welcome at New Road and I like other reporters were often allowed into the dressing room at close of play to interview players such as Ian Botham, Graeme Hick, Graham Dilley, Neal Radford, and Stuart Lampitt and everyone of them was brilliant. They would never refuse interviews, win, lose or draw.

Unlike Edgbaston BRMB had no radio line at New Road so I had to do my twice an hour updates from a red telephone box, which was situated inside the ground at the opposite end to the river stand.

So that was my task to ring the studio at a set time to speak to George Gavin and update the score for the listeners. Sounds simple? If someone was already using the telephone box I had to get them out and then I had to speak to the telephone operator to get her to ensure that the 'pips' didn't go off whilst I was giving my report.

When it came to interviews with the players I was required to send them down the line. Our engineers showed me what to do which was, I am sure, illegal. Today we conduct on-site interviews with the players via iPhone and just email them back from the phone without moving.

In those days it was a lot more complicated and required me to appear to be a vandal to those looking on or waiting to use the phone box. I had to take off the mouthpiece of the Black Bakelite telephone and connect my recorder by way of a wire with 'bulldog' clips on one end. I would connect these to the insides of the phone mouthpiece and press play. As I said it was totally illegal but although I knew I was taking a risk I knew, 'it was easier to ask for forgiveness rather than permission'.

By the way the ladies tea room at New Road was magnificent and sold homemade cakes and cups of tea – I just might have been one of their best customers – halcyon happy days.

WARWICKSHIRE

These were great days for The Bears. I was at Edgbaston more often than I am now in fact I was there virtually every time they played at home. I just loved going there to catch up with and interview Dennis Amiss, Asif Din, Alvin Kallicharan, Dermot Reeve, Paul Smith, Brian Lara, Andy Moles, Geoff Humpage, Gladstone Small, Jason Ratcliffe, Andy Lloyd and others. I would be invited into their dressing room without any fuss or drama and the banter flying around was superb even though I was often on the end of a lot of it.

I had the pleasure and honour of covering a lot of their matches in their history-defining seasons. They were a good lot of blokes and thought nothing of inviting me, at times, join them for lunch after I had done an interview. They would invariably answer any question put to them honestly and sometimes I had to remind one or two of them that they should not say certain things.

The club were also fantastic to me in terms of it never being a problem to get interviews etc and they were extremely helpful and had a brilliant relationship with BRMB. For example: In the 90s the West Indies were playing England at Edgbaston so I got a call from my boss, Richard Park saying he wanted to go to the match with a very important contact from the record label Polydor International. So I asked the club and they immediately invited them to the private committee area and included lunch. My boss Richard ended up sitting alongside John Major and Mick Jagger. I got a few brownie points that day let me tell you!

In recent years I have found Ashley Giles, Dougie Brown, Ian Bell, Jim Troughton, Chris Woakes, Ian Westwood, Richard Jones, Will Porterfield, and Jonathan Trott to be absolutely brilliant to us at BRMB/Free Radio despite us not doing cricket apart from updates in sports bulletins.

They would come into the studio for an hour's chat and phone in without any drama or press officer with them. Most were football fans as well so we had plenty of good-natured debate and banter. Football could learn so much from the cricketers.

Every year I arrange tickets for them for the World Darts Championship at Wolverhampton Civic and we would have a great night. Jokingly I said to the fitness guy Chris Armstrong that if you were caught out playing up with someone other than your wife or girlfriend then I genuinely believed it was an illness like any other addiction. So Chris held up a card at the darts saying, "Tom Ross said I am ill". It was seen on TV and his Mom was soon on the phone to him asking what was wrong?

When Brian Lara, one of the greatest cricketers ever, joined Warwickshire I received a phone call to see if I would do a live link up with the radio station in Trinidad and Tobago. My job was to describe his arrival to his countrymen at home and also to the Prime Minister and other dignitaries who would be listening. I described him arriving and then the questions started! Where would he be living? What was it like?

Warwickshire's Chris Woakes and Richard Jones with me Bomber Brown and Pat Heard at a Baggies v Villa game.

Was it a nice place? Etc. I had no idea that I would be live for around half an hour. He was their greatest sportsman and they wanted to know every little detail.

I had the privilege of doing two one-hour cricket specials on the life of two of the games genuine legends, Sir Garry Sobers and Imran Khan. Sir Garry was one of the most humble gentlemen I have ever interviewed. Modest and with a great sense of humour. My only regret was not having a photograph with him. It was pre-mobile phones with cameras.

Imran had a fantastic story to tell and I was gripped from the minute he started talking, not only about the Pakistan cricket team, but also about the culture and way of life in Pakistan. Sadly he was not as warm and friendly as Sir Garry. However the women in the office were drooling over him as he was a very handsome man – or so they told me.

DARTS

Every year on my Free Radio 80s Goalzone (formerly Capital Gold and Xtra AM) Banter Chat and Phone-in show we do the draw for the Grand Slam of Darts, which takes place at Wolverhampton's Civic Centre. Dave Allen from the PDC and the SKY commentator Rod Harrington come to the Free Radio studios to talk about the tournament and also to make sure the draw is fair.

One year my Monday night co-host, former Aston Villa midfielder Ian Taylor, was doing the draw in FA Cup style pulling the balls out of a bag.

We are on air and I set the scene explaining to the listeners what would be happening etc. I then say 'right now is time to get the draw underway' and asked Dave to run through the seeded players Dave read them out and just said right 'Ian have you got your black balls ready' to which Ian responded immediately 'of course I have, I take them everywhere.'

Well I just fell about and was apoplectic with laughter. Dave, Rod and Ian were all laughing their socks off. Live radio eh?

SOLIHULL BARONS ICE HOCKEY TEAM

In the 80's I bumped into Gary Newbon in New Street and he said I have a great job for you! I want you to be the game announcer for the Solihull Barons at Solihull Ice Rink.

I had not got a clue but started finding out what it was all about and came to love the sport and eventually started travelling all over the country with them and have remained friends with many of them to this day including Chuck Taylor, Jay Forsland, Rod Turner, Marc Piovesana, Paul Frankum, Paul Hand, Ian Pound, Warwick Hammerton, Chris Pugsley, Luc Chabot, Steve Small, and David Simms to name but a few. We had some terrific times under the ownership of Gary Newbon playing in the top flight. The weekend road trips were awesome.

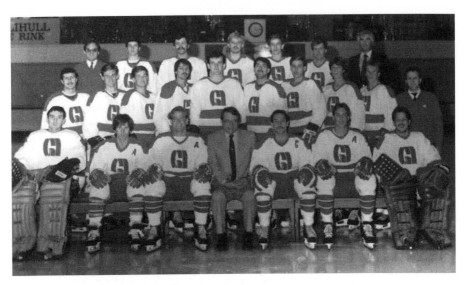

With the Solihull Barons Ice Hockey Team in the 80s

FACING UP

A few words from ROBBIE SAVAGE

Robbie played for Manchester United, Crewe, Leicester, Birmingham City, Blackburn, and Derby County and also played 39 times for Wales.

'Tom Ross what can I say...One of the nicest, honest, passionate, professional people I've come across as a player and a fellow pundit/presenter! His honesty and passion in his interviews and commentaries comes across on the radio and that's why he is one of most recognisable voices in the Midlands! Every time I see him now in pressrooms I get a big smile on my face as the banter (which I always win) never stops! I now regard Tom as a close friend, even if he thought when I signed for Birmingham I was an expletive I can't repeat...Tom Ross #legend!'

I have been accused many times of being too close to managers and players and sometimes directors, however, my whole career has been based on building relationships and relaying facts to the fans which are not always what they want to hear.

Sometimes they have been told down the pub, by someone who knows someone who used to work at whatever club and therefore it must be the truth.

The advent of social media means that these Chinese whispers can spread far more quickly these days and very often 'send reinforcements I am going to advance' ends up as 'send three and fourpence I am going to a dance'.

However despite always wanting a good relationship and creating a banter-like atmosphere I am and always have been prepared to face up to anyone who does not like what I say. I decided early on that if I was brave enough to say something on the radio then I should be brave enough to say it to their faces.

Over 35 years I have not had many fallouts and enjoy getting on with people and having the banter. However like most of us in life there are those whose company I much prefer to others.

One incident that really upset me involved **David Sullivan** in 2001. It all revolved around the sacking of Trevor Francis in December 2001, just five months after they reached the Worthington Cup Final.

You may remember the team were going to play at Crewe on 29 September and it was hinted on the website that TF was to go. I thought this was dreadful and I know some of the players also though it was a disgrace.

It was the subject of my post-match phone in at Crewe and on my Monday night football phone in with Blues fans ringing in their droves to voice their opinion.

Apparently David heard the phone in and was unhappy and blamed me. He savaged me in his *Sunday Sport* newspaper, which absolutely devastated me. Especially as I got on so well with him. I had even been to his home and stayed the weekend for a dinner party. I also had an open invitation to visit the Boardroom any time I wished. So to see this totally unwarranted and in my opinion unfair criticism in the newspapers was hurtful at first but that hurt quickly turned to anger.

I immediately listened back to the tape and sent him, Karren Brady and David Gold a copy of it too because I knew there was no problem with it.

At first I thought someone was being devious and winding him up because a few fans did speak direct to David Sullivan at his home. One in particular I knew to be a nasty devious piece of work whom I had had many arguments with and who on a few occasions had spoken untruthfully and detrimentally about me and it didn't stop until I fronted him up and warned him what would happen if it continued.

I could not believe it when I got a fax from David Sullivan thanking me for the tape and then ranting on about how fed up he was with Blues fans criticisms on my phone in's and also in letters to the *Birmingham Mail*. He also said he listened to the tape on the way home from the Barnsley game, he said he had also listened to the phone in after the Crewe Game and also to the Karren Brady phone-in.

I knew then someone had been stirring it because he also said he had to listen to it. Yet I was slaughtered in his *Sport* Newspaper before he had heard the tape? Imagine me amongst all those naked women – hardly bears thinking about.

He also copied in Colin Tattum and Karren Brady and David Gold.

He was very critical of TF and the media and in particular me for what he called three month of non-stop attack on him by the media.

I wrote back explaining that the reason I sent him the tape was because I had nothing to worry about and that it was not angry or hate filled and also that in my opinion it was very fair.

What he didn't know was that Karren Brady and David Gold had listened to the tape of the phone in and both said there was nothing wrong in it.

It all centred around an agreement the club had supposedly made with TF when he was sacked whereby neither side would publicly 'slag' the other off. Yet David had done an interview in the *Sunday Mercury* doing just that. In that interview with Roger Skidmore David Sullivan was said to have called Trevor Francis a spoilt 16-year-old.

During the phone in I made it clear that this was unacceptable in light of the agreement TF had made with Karren and David Gold and that agreements should be honoured. However David said in his fax to me that he knew nothing about any agreement signed or otherwise with Trevor.

I also pointed out that my criticism of the website message was based on the timing of it. For anything negative to be made public just before a big game was just wrong. I also made it clear on the air that if it came out after the game had ended it would have been OK.

He went on, in his fax, to heavily criticise Trevor, however because it was sent Private and Confidential I cannot re-produce them here.

I offered to go down to London and talk with David face to face but that never happened and to be fair when we saw each other afterwards he was absolutely fine with me. However from my perspective the relationship was sadly never really the same again.

I suppose what hurt most was the fact that I had had such a fantastic relationship with David who had invited me to his home for dinner along with Terry Cooper, Jack Wiseman, Karren Brady and Gary Newbon.

We always spoke regularly and got on well. I remember him saying at a Birmingham City club AGM, when questioned about Xtra Ams exclusive commentary deals, that he would let BRMB have the commentary deal for nothing because of our relationship. He and David Gold gave me a standing invite to the boardroom and his inner sanctum so you can understand when all this blew up it came as a shock to me.

Dinner at his palatial home was an experience let me tell you. A marvellous place with beautiful views overlooking the Essex countryside. And David was very hospitable with nothing too much trouble for him to ensure you had an enjoyable stay.

Downstairs was a full size bowling alley, which was amazing. The rooms were beyond dazzling. I stayed in the Indian Room and it was plush as befits a millionaire home.

He only had 12 couples for dinner in a massive dining room and you would look up and at the far end would be the Four Tops getting ready to perform for the guests – amazing.

What I will say is that in my opinion no Blues fan, and I am one, should ever forget what David Sullivan, David Gold and Karren Brady did for Birmingham City. They restored a sense of pride for the supporters, which was in short supply following the Kumar's and previously to that the reign of Ken Wheldon. I would have them back at the club in a heartbeat.

One incident I really got angry about concerned **Nicky Butt**, who had joined Blues from Manchester United and had won everything in the game and had also played for England. However when the time came I looked him in the eye and told him straight.

Let me explain. Blues were playing away at West Ham United one night under the managership of Steve Bruce. Nicky Butt was not selected and chose to go home under his own steam rather than stay and support the players who had been selected.

I was incensed because in my opinion he had disrespected the club, its fans and more importantly his teammates. I criticised his behaviour and attitude in my *Birmingham Mail* column.

A week later I was at the Blues Wast Hills training ground talking to Steve Bruce and the general manager John Benson when they told me I should keep out of the way of Nicky because he was extremely angry about my comments and criticism and that he felt it was too easy to sound off in a newspaper. They made it clear to me that they worried that he would lose it with me and were concerned for my safety.

My response was to say to John go and get him and tell him I am waiting in Steve's office. Despite some protestations John agreed to do so. He came back and said Nicky would be up to see me after training.

I sat there until around 1pm before he came into the office. I looked him straight in the face and told him why I had written what I had and repeated it to his face.

He said I did not know the full facts and when pressed he refused to say what they were. I ended by saying that he would never have done that to Sir Alex Ferguson and Manchester United so why did he think it was OK to do it at Blues? We never reached agreement on it but he did thank me for fronting him up.

Another time was when Steve Bruce told me he was thinking of signing **Robbie Savage.** I said to him "you must be mad, he's a w****r and he will get you the sack".

A couple of weeks later Steve called me and said he had signed Robbie. I said to Steve that I could not interview Robbie at his unveiling at the club until I had looked him in the face and told him what I had said.

To be fair Steve was great and said, 'you will love him once you get to know him' and arranged for me to meet with Robbie at the training ground before he did his press interviews.

I was introduced to Robbie and said to him, 'look I didn't want Steve to sign you' and then repeated exactly what I had said to Steve about him.

Robbie smiled at me and said, 'I've been called worse' and added that, 'I will change your mind about me' and then shook my hand. From that day to this we have been

With Robbie Savage and Rusell Grant at the Grass Roots Football Show at Birmingham's NEC

great friends. I was disappointed when he wrote in his own book that he deliberately played badly against Newcastle to force a move away from Blues. I also told him he was wrong to do that.

I quite liked **Paul Lambert** especially as he had played for Celtic however I remember having words with him. It was at the Friday pre-match media conference. I was with BBC reporter Mark Regan when Paul Lambert made it clear the FA Cup was unimportant and that all that really mattered was the Premier League games. When the interview finished I just looked at him and said, 'In over 30 years of broadcasting that is the saddest interview I have ever done and summed up exactly what was wrong with the game,' He waffled a bit before saying to us that, 'if I win the cup but get relegated I will get the sack'.

I had not known **Tim Sherwood** long when I had an issue with him at Aston Villa. I was at Bodymoor Heath for his pre Crystal Palace media conference. He was asked a question about Adama Traore and replied that he was just a development player. Now Villa had paid a lot of money for him and so when it came to my turn to ask questions I pushed him on it asking what he meant. Was Traore not physically fit or match fit or what? He replied that he was a development player who had been playing in the Spanish second division and that we, 'would not see much of him this season'.

So that is what Free Radio and other media outlets went with. However the next day Traore was sub against Crystal Palace and came on as sub so you can imagine how I and other radio journalists were feeling.

Now I understand managers wanting to 'play down' new players to reduce the hype but all they have to do is work with us and say, 'don't ask me about him' etc. and we will help.

I spoke to the Aston Villa Head of Communications Tommy Jordan and said that I could not work with or trust a manager who would not tell me the truth and that I wanted to speak to him face to face to tell him just that.

Tommy said that before the next media conference took place would be the best time to do it although I would rather it be one to one.

So just ahead of the next media conference I was there with Mark Regan, the local BBC guy, and I just said, 'Tim you might want to tell me to sod off but I am not happy about the Traore situation'. He allowed me to get it off my chest as I also explained how we could be useful and helpful to him and then he just said, 'it's not my job to worry about you guys'. And that was that – or so I thought.

However on the Saturday I was covering Villa v Sunderland with Micky Gray for Talksport when I was asked to pop down to the tunnel to see Tim Sherwood. To be fair Tim handed out an olive branch in the form of an exclusive story. From then on everything was OK.

I will continue to be the same until I pack up. I don't lie to people and I don't want anyone to lie to me. And if I say or write anything about anyone then I must be prepared to say it to their face and I am. Since then Tim has been super with me and before he was sacked we got to the stage of having banter before and after the pre match interviews.

As my Dad taught me-never let anyone take the piss.

One of the Outside Broadcast Sports forums in the 80s was at the Dog and Partridge pub in Hall Green. The guest was **Jack Charlton** who had played for Leeds and England.

George was the host and I was the producer with Jimmy Franks doing all the technical work. The live programme had just started, when the door burst open and a group of animal rights campaigners/protesters ran in screaming killer and worse at Jack Charlton. Remember he was well known for his love of fishing and shooting. To be fair Jack tried to answer questions from the protesters but they keep chanting and spoiling the event for the football followers.

George was live on air and shouting, 'get them out' etc. So Jimmy and I tried to get them to leave peaceably but they started throwing punches, well Jimmy and I were not going to take that so we threw some back and all hell broke out. Eventually we got them to the door and they ran off.

One of the first things I had to do when George left was to host a Sports Forum with Blues boss Barry Fry. This immediately brought Villa fans out accusing me of being biased towards Blues and they were worried that as I had taken over the station it would become Blues biased. They didn't realise that before I took over the reins George had organised this forum before he left.

I loved hosting the forums at social clubs around the West Midlands and we had some belters. Baggies bosses Roberto Di Matteo, Alan Buckley, Bryan Robson and Gary Megson were brilliant. Wolves with Steve Bull and Jez Moxey, Blues with Karren Brady, David Sullivan, and David Gold were awesome. Alex McLeish, Craig Gardner and Liam Ridgewell before Blues Carling Cup Final against Arsenal. Steve Bruce before the Play-off Final and TF before the Worthington Cup Final. Villa with John Gregory, Big Ron, Brian Little, Gareth Southgate and Andy Townsend are just a few of the very popular series we did across the Midlands. I also did them with Premier League referees including Dermot Gallagher, Mark Halsey, and World Cup referee Howard Webb and they were fantastic giving the fans an insight to how referees applied the laws and they dispelled the myths surrounding refereeing.

I got on brilliantly with Howard and one time when he was in charge of a Villa game he looked up at the press box and gave me a red card – brilliant banter.

One forum caused me a lot of mixed emotions. It was with Villa boss Martin O'Neil at the Kingshurst Labour club. The forum went brilliantly but afterwards we went out to our cars only to find Martin's car had been daubed with paint and my rear window had been smashed. It left a sour taste in my mouth.

However the positive is that it was this forum that won me a Sony award (radio Oscar) and you can read more about that later.

CHAPTER SIX
NAME DROPPING

I am a massive Bruce Springsteen fan and have been to almost every gig he has ever done in Britain. One of my favourite Boss gigs ever was Villa Park in the 80s. It was the Tunnel of Love tour and the Boss was just brilliant. Thanks to Steve Strike at Aston Villa I got the tickets 00001 and 2. I have kept them and would never part with them. I was invited to sit in the director's box area, which was close to the stage. Doug kept turning round and saying, 'He can't sing Tom', That did it for me so I took my daughter Tracy down to the pitch and worked my way to near the front so I could stand with the Solihull Barons fanatics including Paul Heavey who, like myself, were all crazy about Bruce.

Just a few days later I went to Brammall Lane in Sheffield to see the gig again and it was just as brilliant. I was invited as a VIP guest of Sony Records. After the gig I was enjoying some food and drink in the hospitality room when in walked Nils Lofgren and other members of the band, however I was gutted the Boss didn't join us.

Bruce's official photographer signed a book to me, "To the Boss's number one UK fan," I don't know if that is true but I am definitely in the top one! LOL. John Gregory will no doubt be seething reading this because he thinks he is. John even called his house 'Rosalita' after a Springsteen song title. At our Wedding in June 2015 I named the tables at the reception after Springsteen songs.

I remember Trevor Francis ringing me and saying, 'Guess who I am having dinner with in London?' I said no idea and he said, 'The Boss'. I was gutted and told him to 'F**k off' and almost put the phone down. I was genuinely upset because he is the one man in the world I would love to meet. I have been privileged to meet many famous people from screen, stage and music and none of them have phased me. But I would probably go ga-ga at meeting the Boss.

My daughter Amy is also a Springsteen fanatic as are others in my family and that is because I have brainwashed them with his music. When Amy was four years of age at Walmley Junior and Infant school she had to do a party piece at Christmas. Most

Something I will cherish forever a Bruce Springsteen gold disc from Columbia records to celebrate my 35 years at BRMB/Free Radio

of the kids did Ba Ba Black sheep or other nursery rhymes however Amy sang her version of Glory Days. That's my girl!

Tom also holds the record for being the oldest centre-page spread in **Smash Hits!** *When Robbie Williams went missing from pop group Take That, the world's media were searching for him. Tom found him watching Birmingham City and got the exclusive interview with him and, within hours, it was all over the world on every TV station and newspaper in Britain.*

Do you remember when Robbie Williams went missing from the massive pop group Take That in the 80s? While the world's media were searching for him I found him and got myself an exclusive interview that was sent all over the world through TV, newspapers, and radio.

It was amazing and quite lucky really. I was commentating on Blues v Liverpool when I noticed Robbie Williams sitting just below the commentary point at St Andrew's. He was there watching his pal Neal Ruddock play. At the end of my programme I went into the 'D' club where he was and asked him if he would mind having a chat with me. He was fantastic and said no problem. He talked about his love of football and following Port Vale. But he also talked about why he went missing from what was pop music's biggest boy band at the time. He said he was frightened of one day maybe getting stabbed or whatever because of the intenseness of the bands fans.

174

Centre page in Smash Hits-Oh my days the game really has gone

I was so excited I rang our news editor Nicole Pullman at around 11pm to inform her we had a massive story and what did she want me to do with it. I have to say she was not overly impressed perhaps it was because I had woken her up.

I also sent the interview to Capital Radio, who were BRMB and Xtra Am's parent company in London and they put it out in full the next morning. The London media soon picked up on it and it was soon all over the world in newspapers and on TV stations. I suddenly became Tom Ross of Capital Radio when it was BRMB that should have had the credit.

The next thing I knew the whole interview was printed in the centre pages of the teenager's music magazine *Smash Hits*. There I was in the magazine that every one of our young FM jocks wanted to be in and yet this old Xtra AM breakfast presenter beat them to it. I did laugh.

One downside was the way some of newspapers sensationalised the story and made it something it wasn't. I was so angry I vented my feelings in the UK Press Gazette mainly because I did not want Robbie to think I had stitched him up.

A few words from GARY NEWBON

About Gary...

Gary began his television career at Westward TV in the 1960s, and then as an ATV sports reporter for their ATV Today programme in the early 1970s.

He became Controller of Sports (West Midlands) for ATV and, later, Central Television, he reported on football and hosted boxing and darts programmes for the

ITV network, whilst hosting sports coverage on ATV and Central, He retired from ITV after 36 years, and is now currently a Sky Sports presenter.

'Tom Ross is the best known sports broadcaster in the West Midlands these days. He is a work alcoholic who does not drink! His enthusiasm and appetite for sport and radio knows no bounds and he has been rewarded by being voted by his peers as Midlands Sports Journalist of the Year.

'His story is one of determination and effort to change his career path from businessman with a background in accountancy to life behind the microphone both at football matches and in the studio.

'I first met Tom through Trevor Francis. I was looking for some new lounge lights and Tommy came round to sort it out. This was in the 1970s and I was the sports presenter for ATV.

'I was also organising and managing the ATV All Stars. It was a football team that I formed for Charity with big names such as Jasper Carrott, Robert Plant, Bev Bevan the drummer from ELO; Dave Hill of Slade, Trevor Oakes of Showaddywaddy; Ron Atkinson, John Osborne, Ron Wylie, Nick Owen, Don Maclean, Jackie Turpin (Boxer), Dave Ismay and so on. Tommy asked if he could play. I was looking for someone to wash the kit after matches...deal done!

'So it was Tom's first taste of the big time as thousands used to turn up for the games. We also played on Football League grounds as well such as Wolves, Derby and Birmingham as warm-ups before the testimonial matches. With full houses present it helped us fulfil our Sporting dreams if somewhat deluded!

'Then one day he asked to see me in my home. I remember we sat in my dining room and he asked my advice. George Gavin at BRMB had offered him an assistant's job. The salary was small; half of what Tom was earning in the outside world.

'"Are you sure?" I asked him. "It's what I really want to do," was the reply. "Then go for it."

'I have always believed that if you get the opportunity in life to do what you really want to do especially in work then you should take it. Tom had the desire, attitude and chance to make it....and he has done just that.

'When I owned the Solihull Barons Ice Hockey team in the early 1980s I had no hesitation in asking Tom to be the matchday announcer on the PA system. It was an important job to keep the home crowd maintaining the noise level in the rink. He did it brilliantly.

'Tom is respected, trusted and is a popular and successful broadcaster. No one in radio would ask for more than that. He has lasted a long time and deserves to survive. He also happens to be a top person.'

Gary Newbon always says I only got in his celebrity ATV All Stars team because I agreed to wash the kit. Once again Gary is re-writing history. I played for the team for a few years after being taken to a game by Jasper Carrott and I believe they were short and didn't have a sub and I was asked to be on the bench, which I was delighted to do.

One day Gary said that we had a problem because the person washing the kit couldn't do it. So I asked my then wife Maureen to do it for a short time and she did, although she did moan about it when it was all muddy.

I absolutely loved playing for Newbon's ATV All Stars because as well as giving a football nutcase a chance to play in front of huge crowds it was also helping to raise money for charitable causes.

Non-league Saturday and Sunday footballers will understand how thrilled I was to get the chance to play at St Andrew's, Villa Park, The Hawthorns, Molineux, Fellows Park, Derby County's Baseball Ground, and Oxford United's Manor Ground in testimonials and charity matches. For a football nutcase like me it was just amazing.

Playing with the likes of Robert Plant − Bev Bevan − Jasper Carrott − Ron Atkinson − Jim Smith − Keith Bradley − Hugh Jamieson − Ron Wylie − Don Maclean − Jackie Turpin − Trevor Oakes − Trevor East − Jimmy Greaves and Nick Owen In fact I was the only one I didn't know!

It was an amazing experience and to be honest at first I was in awe of them, but everyone made me feel a part of it. Being a part of this wonderful bunch of guys allowed me to play at Wolves. Oxford United, Coventry City, Derby County (in Kevin Hectors testimonial), and also at Telford United when none other than Sir Geoff

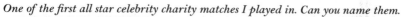

One of the first all star celebrity charity matches I played in. Can you name them.

Hurst called me the dirtiest full-back he had ever played against. Well when a world cup winner tells you – you listen. He also said the same thing to Trevor Francis a few weeks later when he bumped into us in the player's lounge at Wembley after an England game. I would prefer to say hard and enthusiastic rather than dirty. But from Sir Geoff it was a compliment.

Trevor East of TISWAS fame was a very good player and I persuaded him to play for my Sunday team Rosander and he was brilliant for us and he also enjoyed it. Through Trevor I was also fortunate enough to also play for the TISWAS charity team as Tele Cine three, which included Peter Tomlinson and Chris Tarrant.

Gary Newbon's ATV All Stars played one game where we all had to line up and be introduced to the Lord Mayor who was in all his mayoral chains etc. When he got to Big Ron, all Ron said was have you got a pal in the Jewellery quarter? We all fell about laughing.

Ron was the life and soul of the dressing room and I soon found out why players would run through a brick wall for him.

We were playing one day at Oxford when I kept drifting in from my left-back position when Ron, who was then the West Bromwich Albion manager, shouted, 'get out and mark the winger'. I replied, 'Ron he hasn't done anything he just stands there,' quick as a flash Ron came back with, 'I've just paid a million pounds for one of those, (Peter Barnes).

Another Gary Newbon ATV All Stars line up.

Another time after he had lost a game on the Saturday he walked into the ATV All Stars dressing room wearing a motor cycle crash helmet (he had obviously borrowed) and said to Jim Smith, 'Jim one defeat and the Jag's the first thing to go,' we were all in bits although you had to be there.

Every game he would announce to the team, 'Today I am going to be Bonhof,' (Rainer Bonhof –German World cup star) or Cryuff or whoever. He was brilliant and had the knack of making you feel brilliant. No wonder he was such a great manager.

Through the ATV All Stars football team I became friends with Robert Plant who, despite being one of the world's biggest rock stars, was one of the nicest blokes you could wish to meet. One day I arrived back in the BRMB office from a press conference to be greeted by the receptionist who said there was an old bloke called Robert asking for you an hour ago and he seemed to know you. She said, 'he said his full name, but I can't remember it but he left you a note'. One look at the note confirmed that it was the world's greatest and most famous rock star Robert Plant of Led Zeppelin fame who had walked into the radio station. *Whole Lotta Love* and *Stairway to Heaven* are just two of their songs recognizable anywhere on the planet.

Sadly the receptionist did not know him although I am sure she would have instantly recognised some no-mark who finished third on X Factor three years ago. That is the state of this instant gratification reality TV world we live in.

All Robert wanted to do was an interview about a gig he was playing locally. Radio stations worldwide would jump at the chance to interview a rock legend of his stature.

Gary Newbon's ATV All Stars charity team in the 80s

Without doubt he would be instantly recognised anywhere in the Western World. Can you imagine Bruce Springsteen turning up at a radio station in New Jersey and not being recognised? Of course not. This isn't a knock at young people but perhaps more of a dig at the modern world of radio, TV and the pop world that appears to get shallower by the year.

While talking about Robert my first radio interview with him was done in a toilet at Newport County's old Somerton Park ground in April 1988. Wolves were top of the division four under Graham Turner and I was covering the game for BRMB. Wolves won 3–1 with two goals from Steve Bull and one from Andy Mutch (no surprise there). I saw Robert afterwards and he was thrilled to bits with the win and readily agreed to an interview but there was no pressroom or anywhere else to do it. So I asked the world's greatest rock star f he would kindly follow me into the toilet for the interview, which he did. We both remarked that it was a first for both of us. Sadly Newport County went out of business shortly afterwards.

MY FAVOURITE SONGS INCLUDE:
I find it hard to do a list of my favourite songs because I love music and have so many songs I love, however with a gun to my head I would pick the following although having said that it would probably change overnight. There are so many I have left out I would prefer to choose my top twenty by genre.

- HUNGRY HEART – Bruce Springsteen
- THIS OLD HEART OF MINE – Isley Brothers
- TIRED OF BEING ALONE –Al Green
- I'LL HAVE TO SAY I LOVE YOU IN A SONG – Jim Croce
- IN MY LIFE – The Beatles
- I WAS ONLY JOKING – Rod Stewart
- BROWN EYED GIRL – Van Morrison
- BORN TO RUN – Bruce Springsteen
- OPERATOR – Jim Croce
- HEART OF GOLD – Neil Young
- HAVE I TOLD YOU LATELY THAT I LOVE YOU – Van Morrison
- DON'T LET THE SUN CATCH YOU CRYING – Gerry and The Pacemakers
- L.O.V.E. – Nat King Cole
- PRETEND – Gerry and The Pacemakers
- GENTLE ON MY MIND – Dean Martin
- JOHNNY TOO BAD –UB40
- MACK THE KNIFE – Bobby Darin
- ELUSIVE BUTTERFLY – Bob Lind

- TRY A LITTLE TENDERNESS – Otis Redding
- YOU NEVER CAN TELL – Chuck Berry
- MR BLUE SKY – ELO
- SUMMER OF 69 – Bryan Adams
- TELEPHONE LINE – ELO
- WALK LIKE A MAN – Bruce Springsteen.
- YOU'RE THE DEVIL IN DISGUISE – Elvis – the first song I ever bought
- JOHNNY TOO BAD – Jim Capaldi
- DAKOTA – Stereophonics
- THEN HE KISSED ME – The Crystals
- RAVE ON – Buddy Holly
- YOUNG HEARTS RUN FREE – Candi Staton
- ITS ONLY ROCK AND ROLL – Rolling Stones
- HARD TO HANDLE – Otis Redding
- I'M GONNA BE STRONG – Gene Pitney
- BETCHA BY GOLLY WOW – Stylistics
- FIELDS OF ATHENRY – The Dubliners
- THE GREATEST LOVE OF ALL – George Benson
- ONE LOVE – Bob Marley
- WHEN THE GOING GETS TOUGH – Billy Ocean
- JUST WHEN I NEEDED YOU MOST – Randy Vanwarmer

- However add to that any song by Bruce Springsteen.

IN PRINT

I find it uncomfortable to see myself mentioned in other people's articles or books. I don't mind writing columns etc and shooting from the hip or lip has never been a problem, however when I am the focus of attention I don't like it.

Still it comes with the territory and you have to be prepared to deal with what comes, be it in newspapers, radio, TV or social media. That can be difficult at times especially on social media because in a lot of cases you are not dealing with rational people, so it is impossible to have a conversation. They just want to be insulting because they are looking for a reaction or they get a buzz out of it. There are more cowards on social media than anywhere else on the planet.

I have covered my first meeting with Robbie Savage in the 'Facing Up' chapter but Robbie wrote about it in his autobiography called *Savage* he wrote;

'There were doubts when I arrived. Not for me. I have always moved for the right reasons and not for money, which a lot of people find hard to believe. But Birmingham fans weren't exactly jumping up and down at my arrival. I had a reputation as a

181

nuisance, a big mouth, maybe a liability. The doubts and fears were summed up by a local radio commentator in the city called Tom Ross. I respect him greatly now and regard him as a friend. He's also a great radio presenter. The only problem is no one can find his station – it's next to Radio Luxembourg! Tom was Mr Bluenose, the man who interviewed all the Birmingham players. 'What are you signing that wanker for? He'll cause nothing but problems,' Tom warned Steve Bruce, my hero, the man who had just bought me.

'I don't like you, and I think you'll be a waste of space,' Tom said to me when he eventually met me. 'Fine,' I replied. 'I'm going to change your opinion of me.

'We laugh about it now, but I did change his opinion of me,'

And he did!

I was also mentioned by **Ted McMinn** in his autobiography, *The Tin Man* let me explain why. I have always wanted to play for Blues since I first saw that St Andrew's pitch sadly I was nowhere near good enough and to get the chance to play on the St Andrew's pitch was pretty damn awesome.

However what many fans don't know is that I was given the chance to play in the first team by Terry Cooper in a testimonial in Yeovil.

I couldn't believe it, my boyhood dream had come true I would wear the Royal Blue shirt even if it was as a sub and in a testimonial.

However, as you might expect there was a catch – Trevor Morgan Terry's assistant said I would also have to be the physio, as they didn't have one on the trip? So even though I didn't have a clue what to do I thought what can go wrong – it was a testimonial for Gods sake.

Mid-way through the second half Ted McMinn went down injured so I rushed on with my medical 'physio's' bag. Ted had a massive gash in his leg and so be honest I didn't have a clue what to do. I looked through the bag and found some 'Vicks', which I rubbed on his cut. Now no one told me it would sting and to this day I can hear Ted's screams. However on a positive note the lads reckoned it was the fastest Ted had run since he signed for the club. We laugh about it now – well I do anyway.

When **David Gold** wrote his autobiography *Pure Gold* he mentioned myself on a few occasions and to be honest I was quite proud of the things he said.

He wrote; 'I think humility is very important, and it is good to have Lesley, my fiancée, watching over me, making sure I don't become Billy Big-time, as my friend Tom Ross often calls me.'

He also wrote, 'I began to learn very quickly who could be trusted at both local and national level. There are journalists like Colin Tattum, Graham Hill, John Curtis of the Press Association, Russell Kempson and Alison Kervan of *The Times*, Janine Self of the *Sun*, Vince Ellis, Bob Hall, and Jim White of the Daily Telegraph and of course my friend Tom Ross, broadcaster and Head of Sport at Capital Gold, who are professional people and trustworthy.'

'When you are comfortable with the media, there are parts of it you can enjoy…I can sit with Birmingham journalists like Colin Tattum, Graham Hill and Tom Ross, our local broadcaster, and enjoy just having a chat about football, regardless of the interview. I am genuinely interested in their opinions, and interviews often turn out to be two-way discussions. We talk about players, fans and the rest, and it is all immensely enjoyable, even though it means I am still working at nine o'clock at night.

'Later in the same season we were doing well, sitting comfortably in the top two and almost certainly guaranteed promotion back to Division One. We were driving back south listening to Tom Ross, the local broadcaster, who answered a telephone caller who said he wanted to thank David Sullivan and "those other two geezers" for what they had done for the club. We had been there almost two years by that time and we were still just "those other two geezers". We were in the background. Financing, supporting and helping to transform the club. We were quietly getting on with our jobs, because this is the way we have always been.'

Talking about the sacking of his friend Barry Fry he wrote, 'The decision was taken on a Wednesday, and on the Saturday Birmingham were to play Aston Villa in the Final of the Senior Cup at St Andrew's at 7.30 pm. That night Ralph and I were at the Burlington Hotel for the Midland Football Writers' Dinner, sitting on the top table with Villa chairman, Doug Ellis, ITV's Gary Newbon and local broadcaster Tom Ross.'

David paid a lot of money to buy the original FA Cup to keep it in the country and wrote about it in the book.

'I also went to a workingmens' club in Birmingham where I do a question and answer session every couple of years with Tom Ross, the local radio presenter, as the host. As he finished with the players, two exes and one current, he called me on to the stage as the next guest. Out came the cup, rather like another guest, and everyone rushed forward to have a closer look. Such was the interest that afterwards Tom announced the first ten out of the raffle could have their picture taken for £10. Then he had twenty people at £20 per head, and eventually we raised over £500, and this at a workingmens' club. And it didn't finish there. When Tom called a halt to the event, one man rushed forward and was so desperate to have his picture taken with the cup that he offered £250! This, for me, showed the absolute passion roused by this inanimate object.

'I have, of course, been ribbed unmercifully by everyone in football, telling me Birmingham couldn't win it so we had to buy it. But I do believe we have the ability to win a trophy, and it would be unbelievable if it was the FA Cup.'

This event I remember so well was organised by the Bluenose Executive Lunch Club and was entitled Tom Ross and Friends and raised funds for the Promised Dreams charity.

I remember Capital Radio MD Paul Davies calling me and saying, 'I loved the

Ross finds ways to turn airwaves blue

Sat April 19th 2003

Malcolm Boyden
Brum's the Word

A TINY ELECTRIC guitar sits on the shelf next to a replica of the World Cup. Near by, a tattered season ticket book containing passes for Aston Villa's official car park lies beside a box of Birmingham City after-dinner chocolates.

The office walls are randomly scattered with signed gold and silver discs. This is the world of Tom Ross, "Rossy" is a 100 per cent radio man — and fiercely proud of it.

Soon, he will take a brisk walk from desk to microphone to host Britain's longest-running football phone-in, a show invented by Tony Butler, a broadcasting legend far beyond the boundaries of Birmingham, more than 30 years ago. Ross is a disciple of his predecessor, but he does things very differently. He will sit with his feet up, virtually sprawled out across an area no bigger than the famous sound-proof booth, once used by contestants on the 1970s quiz show, Mr and Mrs. It's his way of talking to the fans. "I try and create a pub atmosphere," he said, eager to demonstrate his broadcasting stance.

"This is not just a job, it's my life. I'm the luckiest man in the world." He's quick to add a note of caution, though. "But I'll be a working-class Brummie until the day I die."

Ross is known as one of the hardest grafters in the radio industry. He day starts at 6am when he hosts the breakfast show from the headquarters of

BRMB/Capital Gold in Birmingham's fashionable Brindleyplace. After that, as the station's Head of Sport, he begins a routine tour of the training grounds on his patch. Often, he will then travel to commentate on a match (he calls every commentary game "an event"). If it's a long trip, he will arrive back in the city at around 2am to start all over again, after less than four hours' sleep. On top of that, he will somehow squeeze in two hours at the gym.

The boy from "two back of 437 New John Street West — Aston" has done good. So good that he's been nominated for a Sony Award — the Oscars of the radio business. The ceremony takes place in London next month.

"Sometimes I have to pinch myself," Ross said. "There were six kids in our house and we had nothing. Mum was a cleaner and barmaid at the Britannia pub." Dad was amazing. He could get four hundred slices from a Swiss roll."

As an eight-year-old, Ross fell hopelessly in love with Birmingham City after his Scottish father, also Tom, began walking to St Andrew's

to watch his fellow countryman, Alex Govan, in action. Govan was the man who first sang the Blues anthem Keep Right on to the End of the Road on the way to Birmingham's 1956 FA Cup quarter-final against Arsenal. The song spread quickly among the players — and then to the fans.

"We reached the FA Cup Final that year," Ross said, with a twinkle in his eye. "I remember thinking — this is the team for me, even in division one and a visit to Wembley. How they led me on that football slowly seeped into my blood. I used to stand on the Kop with my school pal,

Connie Walsh — and I always took my boots, just in case."

Ross dreamt of a career in professional football. He played left back for Hinckley Athletic in the Southern League. "We got ten bob a week and our own shirts leaving the kit was worth more than the money. And I never worried how quick the wingers were, as long as they could hurdle. I'd go in hard on anybody, always giving everything to win a game of football for my lads. But I would never cheat."

That sums up Tom Ross. "I'm a perfectionist. A 100 per cent man. I worry about every radio show. I do. My Dad once told me. 'Never be ashamed to pick up your wages.' Since then I've always worked my socks off. If they put the words, hard-working, loyal and honest on my tombstone I'll be happy."

Ross knew his dreams of

becoming a professional footballer were doomed when the Hinckley manager left. He stranded in Castle Bromwich one weekend. "I'd used to give me a lift to every game — so one afternoon he didn't turn up. He rang me the following week to say that because I was his most enthusiastic player he hadn't got the heart to tell me I wasn't good enough. Good job he phoned — I'd still be waiting now."

Instead, Ross set out on his media path, although he's still player-manager of Birmingham City Old Stars. His first match as a radio reporter was a Blues friendly against Ajax. He has hosted the Friday night phone-in for almost 2 years.

"One of his most memorable moments came during Birmingham's Leyland DAF Cup final against Tranmere Rovers in 1991. "I became the first reporter to commentate from the bench at Wembley," he said. "Lou Macan, the Birmingham manager, put me down on the touchbench (a seat) and physio. We smuggled in a microphone and headphones past officials to a bucket."

Now, despite his unashamed Blues bent, he is largely accepted by fans of both Midlands clubs, but he always a target for friendly rivalry. People remember their first record and the first game they went to. I'm passionate about both. "I'm a Bruce Springsteen fanatic."

malcolm.boyden@bbc.co.uk

> There were six kids at home. We had nothing. My Dad could cut a Swiss roll into four hundred slices'
>
> — Tom Ross, Capital Gold radio host

The kid from the inner city slums being written about in the "Times" in 2003. Must have been a bad news day.

article about you in *The Times*'. Well most of my pals read The Sun or the *Daily Sport* so I had to confess I had not seen it.

I had been interviewed by Malcolm Boyden some months before and had forgotten all about it. Still the boy from 2/437 New John Street West in *The Times*? What would my Mom and Dad have said?

Clive Tyldsley wrote a brilliant and very complimentary article in the *Daily Telegraph* where he called my Friday night phone an 'essential listening'. I was extremely flattered as I did not think Clive even knew who I was.

I love writing my column in the *Birmingham Mail*. For a Brummie to get the chance to write in the main newspaper was a privilege and an honour.

Previously I had written a column for the *Sports Argus* and also enjoyed that especially

It is always special when respected peers say something nice about you as Clive Tyldsley did in the Telegraph

INSIDE VIEW
The derby where black humour is always called for

CLIVE TYLDSLEY

THERE is something about the Brummie accent that is perfectly suited to gallows humour. The hangdog tone of Frank Skinner, Jasper Carrott and Ozzy Osbourne makes for the blackest of comedy. Why, even Tony Hancock was born in Birmingham. The second city's football supporters certainly need a sense of humour. Too many second class performances again this season. But salvation may be at hand for half of them at least. Birmingham City and Aston Villa share their woes at St Andrew's tomorrow lunchtime.

Both clubs have made their worst starts to a Premiership season. They inhabit the bottom six, along with West Bromwich Albion. It is a great time to be a Wolves fan. The current generation of suffering supporters have seen a grand total of three major trophies paraded round the West Midlands since the mid-eighties — Coventry City's FA Cup in 1987 and a couple of Villa League Cup since. There has been one European game played in the region since 1994, the year that Villa made their last title challenge. You could still buy tickets for the derby at the St Andrew's box office yesterday.

And yet, when Tom Ross opens the phone lines to Ron Atkinson and his other guests at the ground tomorrow morning, the local radio switchboard will be as jammed as Spaghetti Junction. Ross has been listening to the fans' frustrations on BRMB Radio throughout these 20 largely barren years, and insists local passions are running as high as ever. Yesterday's St Andrew's annual meeting was just what their supporters needed to raise the temperatures and clear the throats. They have not beaten Birmingham since Big Ron was their manager. There is previous. This is not a derby where the fans of both clubs cheerfully travel to the match together.

But who else really cares? The high noon kick-off time is not at the insistence of Sky Sports. The rest of the nation's interest in this very

Enckelman at St Andrew's three years ago. It is a fixture where security and safety are particularly sensitive issues.

The security of the losing manager may just be an issue by tomorrow evening, too. Birmingham have not won a home game this season. No manager ever has enough money to spend but Steve Bruce has had more than most. After two years of wheeling and dealing at Villa Park, David O'Leary is also fielding what is regarded as 'his' team now. Expectations inevitably exceed reality at the kind of football institutions that mean so much to so many. The question of which of the city's two clubs has the greater potential is just one of the arguments that rages around the fixture. But average attendances at both are down on last season. Villa's last home gate dipped below 36,000 for the first time in 21 months.

Ticket prices have been hiked for tomorrow's game, too. Up £15 to £45. Birmingham fans do not need reminding that four years ago, this weekend, Bradford City were the visitors to St Andrew's. Maybe the club need reminding that the same 27,000 fans were turning up then as now. Loyalty counts for a lot in MG Rover households. So does disposable income. Value for money is a Birmingham derby that gives the clubs a chance to move into the top six, not a chance to move out of the bottom six. Charlton Athletic are sitting in second place on a comparable budget.

The country is full of supporters that deserve better and clubs that belong at a higher level. Newcastle and Sunderland meet next weekend amid similar sentiments. How they would love a Premiership derby in Bristol or Sheffield, East Anglia or East Midlands. But the highlight of the season for clubs of Birmingham's and Villa's standing should certainly be something more substantial than a win over their local rivals. No matter how much excitement and noise is generated at St Andrew's, it will only dawn out the clamour for improvement for so long.

It looks as if Villa will give Stuart Taylor his debut in goal. Last season their regular keeper, Thomas Sorensen, made basic errors in both derbies and Birmingham completed the double. In 2002,

What a transformation

LEE HENDRIE

Inside Villa Park

Playing for England has changed my life. I dreamed what running on to Wembley in an England shirt would feel like – no-one ever told me what a profound effect it would have on my life.

Those first few days after the game were a constant high. I had fulfilled a childhood dream and there was a permanent smile on my face.

As the days and weeks have gone by that feeling has subsided (although the memories are still sweet). But one factor hasn't changed – the phone, it's never stopped ringing since Glenn Hoddle told me to get my tracksuit off and give the Czech Republic hell!

At home, in my car, when I'm out, the phone never stops. But I have found the solution to the problem – I just don't answer it.

Most of the calls come from the media or agents and while it's flattering that they are interested in me, after a while it begins to wear you out.

And it's not just the number of people calling me which has changed. I seem to get noticed whereever I go now.

Before, when I was just a Villa player I could go out and remain annonymous. Not anymore. If I just pop down to the shops people stop and ask me how I am.

It's incredible. I never knew playing for England could change my life so much in that respect.

In a lot of ways it has changed the things I can do, but one thing I will never alter is my approach to the people who say hello and want a chat.

If they are England fans or Villa fans then I will always have time for them because the club's supporters, in particular, are the people who helped get me in the Villa side.

When I was struggling to make it into the team, I used to hear fans ringing up Tom Ross's show saying I should be playing and, to be honest, it gave me a lift.

There were times back then when I was really down in the dumps. I used to worry I would never get back into the side again.

But those calls helped me through and I will never forget how much the supporters got behind my career.

Tom was another big help. He championed my cause on the radio. He's always been behind me.

I am reaping the rewards of playing for Villa and England now. Only a couple of days ago I signed a deal with Nike to wear their boots and clothes.

But I won't forget the people who helped put me in this position.

Lovely words from Aston Villa's Lee Hendrie in his Argus Column.

when you think I used to have to run and get it for my Dad every Saturday night. I also delivered them on my paper round in Lea Village.

Because of the nature of the job over the years I have been mentioned lots of times in the local and national newspapers, some good and some not so good. However when you do a job like mine you have to accept that everything you say or write will be scrutinised and that even more so in this modern world of social media. At one time you needed drink to turn cowards into brave men now you just need a keyboard.

My first chance to pen my opinions came when I was asked to write a pop column in the *ABC Advertiser*. I loved that and it gave me a chance to review pop gigs as well as promoting new local bands like Duran Duran.

Over the years I have also written columns in match day programmes for West Bromwich Albion, Blues, and Coventry. I was never asked to write in the Villa programme – I wonder why?

And also for various sporting magazines.

I was never a natural or gifted writer – never a wordsmith. So I made it clear to anyone who asked me to write that it would be my opinions without censorship and in my words. I wanted people to read what I wrote and believe they could hear me saying the words. It's been the same for this book.

CHAPTER SEVEN

CHINESE WHISPERS

My first contact with the Carson Yeung Empire came just before he made a failed attempt to buy the club from David Sullivan and David Gold in 2007. It came in the shape of Sammy Yu who wanted to get a feel for the area and the Blues fans. He spoke to me and the *Birmingham Mails* Colin Tattum.

However that initial attempt to buy the club failed because he could not raise the money to complete the deal by a November deadline. Even so it left him with 29.9% of the shares.

The deal eventually happened in October 2009 after Yeung's company Grandtop had paid Sullivan and Gold a staggering £81.5 million. Staggering because the club was only worth around 30 million at best.

However there was mass excitement and expectation among Blues fans who sadly were happy they not only got rid of Sullivan and Gold but now had a multi-millionaire owner who they believed would take them to heights they had only previously dreamed about.

At his press conference Carson was off the wall and to say the least he was visibly caught up in all that was going on in front of the world's media. He made promises to spend £40 million on new players, which rose to £80 million when he answered his next question.

I asked him why he had bought Blues and he said he had been trying to get the club for some time and he believed it could be a successful club, this through his translator Peter Pannu.

Two months previously I had written my column in the *Birmingham Mail* that I was unsure of Carson Yeung's motives in buying Blues.

My first meeting with Peter Pannu was with Sammy Yu and *the Birmingham Mail's* Colin Tattum at the Radison hotel.

Colin and I also met him at the Radison on a second occasion when he got up and walked away every two minutes to speak to Carson Yeung in Hong Kong. Colin and

My Birmingham Mail column before Carson Yeung completed his purchase of Birmingham City

I wanted to find out what he would do at BCFC and how he planned to take the club forward. However he was more interested in girls and said, 'where do you go for chicks?' Colin and I in true *News Of The World* style made our excuses and left.

The arrival of the Chinese signalled the start of a new and promising era at St Andrew's (or so we thought) and I spoke with my pal James Wong who owns the 'Chung Ying' Chinese restaurant in the city centre. He was excited about the Chinese owners at BCFC and so with BRMB we decided to put on a special welcome event at his restaurant for around 100 fans/listeners plus members of the media. Carson Yeung did not turn up but Peter Pannu, Sammy Yu, Vico Huii, and many others did.

We had a brilliant night as I welcomed then to Birmingham in Mandarin (how big time is that). We had dragon dancers and gave them a welcome they would never forget.

However I should have known what was to come when the Chairman Vico entered into a drinking competition with Pete Colley of SKY Sports and easily beat him before taking on all-comers. I have never seen anyone drink so much in my life and remain standing. I should have realised that these men were far from professional but they did love to party.

At another event he also took on Colin Doyle to see who could down a pint fastest? Colin beat him and so had to pay for the players Christmas party.

Peter Pannu was always likely to say the wrong things when he has had a drink. I compered the Birmingham City end of season players awards do in front of 1,100 people at the prestigious ICC in Birmingham. I invited Peter Pannu on to the stage to make a pre-arranged speech. What a disaster that was. He started by telling the audience that he was an Arsenal fan, but went on to tell smutty jokes and innuendoes. I saw the clubs management signalling that they wanted me to shut him up. But he was effectively the main man so I let him hang himself with his loose lips.

To be fair Carson Yeung was in charge of the club when they finished in their highest Premier League position in 2009–10 season, when they ended the season in ninth place.

Yeung was also in charge when Birmingham City won their first ever major trophy in 2011 beating much fancied Arsenal 2–1 at Wembley in the Final of the Carling Cup. They were also relegated that season, but in my opinion that had nothing to do with winning the Cup but was more to do with not being good enough over 38 Premier League games.

But rumours about his financial position were starting to filter in from China while Alex McLeish was under orders to reduce the wage bill and to start looking at a much cheaper player.

Interestingly that season I hosted the BCFC Academy awards night and sat next to Peter Pannu. He confided in me that he didn't get on with, or like Alex McLeish and that he was 'going' and that he had already 'put out the feelers for Sam Alladyce'. However Alex McLeish beat him to it and resigned to take over at Aston Villa that summer.

How much truth there was in the Alladyce story I am unsure, it may just have been bravado from Pannu, however, what was true was that Pannu wanted McLeish out of Blues. I suspect because Big Eck was making it known that he was having to get rid of the clubs better players and replace them with those not quite so good.

After the news that Carson Yeung had been arrested on money laundering charges Blues were sinking further into the financial mire and it was made public that the club was up for sale.

However I was contacted by an old pal of mine Gianni Paladini who told me that he was in negotiations with Peter Pannu about buying Blues. I spoke to Peter Pannu who denied any contact with Gianni whatsoever. Gianni sent me copies of documents that had been sent to Peter Pannu so I knew Peter Pannu was being more than economical with the truth.

One time the *Birmingham Mail's* Colin Tattum and I were invited to see Peter Pannu in one of the executive boxes. On that day Pannu was dismissive and in my opinion disrespectful about Carson Yeung and his influence on the football club. This was probably because it was obvious that Yeung was going to prison. I suspect PP thought he would end up being the main man with Yeung out of the way.

He was disgusting when talking about Italian businessman Gianni Paladini, when I asked if he would ever sell to the Italian's consortium. He used an analogy where he likened Paladini to an old lady toilet cleaner saying that, 'if you went out to a club to pick up a good looking chick and an 81-year-old toilet cleaner was interested, you would keep on looking for the gorgeous one but if that, failed you would go back to the toilet cleaner,'

That made me angry because Gianni was a pal of mine, although Pannu never ever knew that. My Mom worked as a cleaner at the MEB for a long time so I was also angry at his snotty and snobby disrespect for hard working people who clean for a living.

Over time he appeared to become even more paranoid and aggressive about things. I suspect because he felt his power slipping away.

NB the following emails and text messages from Peter Pannu are replicated exactly including any spelling, punctuation or grammatical mistakes.

In November 2012 I asked Peter Pannu if Gianni Paladini was in talks to buy the club. I received this text;

> *15th Nov 2012*
>
> *Guys, there are no talks with Paladini people. I hate to deal with people who has a big mouth but no money. Only if their pockets were as big as their mouth. Their improved deal was rejected long time back.*
>
> *If the plan is to unsettle BCFC , it fails. Given the unprofessional way they are handling things, I doubt if they are a suitable party to lead the club to the next level, let alone lack of funds and the terms which no sound minded person will accept. I respect what is an NDA and thus will not go in to details. Suffice to say, this is history they are talking about as their last email was rejected.*

In December 2012 I asked for an update on what was happening re selling the club and received this email from Peter Pannu on 8 December.

> *"The sale discussion with the group consisting of and led by the owner of HK TVB (Charles Chan), Shanghai Entertainment and Media Group (SEMG) and Shanghai Media Capital (an investment fund) has stalled a bit (possibly dead) following many months of discussions. The figure was at about 40M.*
>
> *'The other interested party in HK is still proceeding with the discussions. Can't mention their names yet.*
>
> *'Please don't mention me as the source regarding the names as I believe the fans deserve to know what has been going on and with whom.*
>
> *'Paladini is paying only 17M out of 13M as guaranteed sums and even that over 4-5 years installments and the 13M contingent is deemed un achievable. If he can*

improve on it, now is a good chance for him,'

Peter

The above came just shortly after saying publicly and saying to me that there were no talks with Gianni Paladini who he consistently said had not made any offers to buy the club.

In 2013 I emailed Peter Pannu;

From: Tom Ross <Tom.Ross@freeradio.co.uk>
To: Peter Pannu
Sent: Wed Jan 09 16:08:22 2013
Subject: Accounts

Hi Peter

Hope you are well.

The release of the half year accounts into the public domain have caused concern amongst the clubs fans who have bombarded me with questions some of which I list below.

1) *Why is one director paid more (around 700k per year) than virtually any other director in professional football when the club is financially in trouble?*

2 *Why are the club paying rent on a property understood to be owned by a director.*

3 *What does it cost to run the club on a monthly basis including everything*

4 *It's understood that the club ended up paying XTEP more money than it received in sponsorship? How was that allowed to happen?*

5 *The accounts make it clear that Mr Yeung and BIHL won't recall their loans for at least 12 months? How does the club intend to find the 21.4 million pounds in January 2014? And what would happen to these debts if and when the club is sold.*

I hope you can give me with answers for the fans.
I hope to hear from you soon
Tom

This is the answer I received

Tom,

Fans are never happy. I give them an inch and they want a mile. I have given the media on my last return a lot of respect but guess this will not stop.

Peter

He was obviously unhappy with my questioning and blamed us in the media for asking questions.

However the following day (10 Jan 2013) I started getting random text messages from him and it was obvious both I and the fans had gotten to him because we wanted answers.

10 January 2013

Vico had been removed. Some more directors will be removed. Actions against Xtep will be taken.
My wage in UK is just 125K after tax. Expatriate terms in all countries cater for housing and allowances.

Tom focus them on what I have achieved. With not a penny for the last two-year, I kept the club and the group afloat.

I have more important things to do. Thanks

I replied saying I don't know how to explain to the fans the difference between the figure of £670k paid to one director when you say you only earned £125k?

His reply!!

'Its all in the accounts...

'Tax is 50 per cent, the total gross up inclusive tax is presented in the account, every single penny and expense is disclosed including the gross up figure for tax purposes. Tom divert the topic to bigger issue and not personal attack. If I resign and go, the whole group will be screwed. Frankly, I am very close to it as I am fed up. Focus them of bigger things. Ask them to come support the team. Remind them in two years,

without finances, under me report profits. Ticket prices instead gone down... give me a break. Got work here. Tom I don't think I will be replying anymore for now.

Its all in the accounts"

21 January 2013

His reply; *"Tom I am really frustrated with this continuous badgering and harassment. How would the accountants know the breakdown and how we accounted. It includes all the fuel, the porsche car , expenses incurred with visiting directors – and the figure are all grossed up to cater for taxes. Tom focus on the damn bigger issues. For F sake, zigic earls 57K a damn week, that managers got us committed to.*

For god sake, what was Karen Brady on, how was she paid bonus, without taxes, overseas and car and fuel and share options. Who is better qualified CEO chairman than me in UK with my achievements.

And don't ask me any more Qs related to published accounts and do what ever u guys want. It does not matter.

What was Gary Cook on, 2.7M a year, his replacement? What are the PL ceo and MD earning? I say I more time, I am on 250K, that includes 50 per cen tax, the contract entitled me to cars, housing and expenses and I report these as P11D expenses and I pay full double up expenses.

Got it...

Other expenses of visiting staff are paid by the club, and to not avoid taxes, they go thro' my name. The accounts show one figure and not break downs. Tom, are the fans and the media so free that u guys don't have anything else to write. No the attach on directors fee, when it is peanuts on our overall turnover. Joke... Good go on, go help me sell the club under these damn circumstances.

I mean now the attack on the directors.'

Peter... I am not attacking anyone. However I am bombarded with questions, but instead of joining in a witchhunt I am asking you the questions, which is what you said you wanted when you first took over...

He replied, *"I can easily resign from UK and HK and can still earn more as barrister and the rest and lead a less stressful life. So CY and the fans and who ever, can sort things out. I kept the place afloat and will keep it afloat until it is sold. Football business is a joke as outsiders may see now and the new parties are asking me what it is like in this business as owners and investors. Can u tell me what I should say to them?*

Ask the fans trust to fork out the money and buy the club or all the fans, say 25K to fork out 1,500 pounds each, and buy the club. Will they do that, they love the club. I lowered their ticket prices, despite all this. Joke

Tom one final thing, do the people understand what is the meaning of "expatriate terms". Like in HK, which hosts multi national overseas companies, expatriate who come with families get expatriate terms.

These are better than their local counterparts. Housing, tax benefits, car, schooling allowances etc. I speak Cantonese and Mandarin and highly qualified and a natural choice by a Chinese owners from HK.

Sometimes, extra compensation is paid for leaving their place of domicile and families behind. I have been in the UK alone since 2009 September. Without perks and benefits, I would not have taken the post. It is simple demand and supply ... And only fools will not understand.

Peter."

On 1 September 2011 I asked him about reports regarding a rich Chinese man who was going to buy the club.

His reply

"Tom,
I have been told that he is a property dealer in China. But that does not mean I am afraid that he will be pumping much into the club as I understand it. The HK80 million loan raised is for the general working capital of the group and some may find its way to bcfc. I guess they want me to run the club in a self sufficient way."

In March 2013 I again asked Peter Pannu about a story that Carson Yeung was trying to sell the club privately.

On 15 March 2013 this reply came from him;

"Tom, a sale agreed privately by CY is a complete nonsense talk in the UK press. CY cannot do so. It has to be done thro' the board of directors. We have a few parties active in the case as potential buyers. Today the group will announce all the outstanding results. It took me a few months to do what the previous board guys took 2 years and cannot do. I will return soon and deal with sales matters now that the group hurdle is sorted, a necessity for any sale to take place. I will copy Coin too."

On 30cMarch 2013 I received the most bizzare txt from PP.

"Tom, Colin – from your sources, is it possible to help me identify the spy who is passing the info out from within BCFC. These are theft of corporate details and causes complete failure of trust and believe and morale issues. He or she is hurting the club and the sale process and is making bad news out of nothing."

On 2 April 2013 I replied;

"Hi Peter. Sorry for delay in replying but I was in Egypt… I have no idea who might be leaking information from the club."

On 1 October I asked PP about his contract with BCFC as I had heard it was close to ending. 1 October 2014.

On 1 October I received this reply;

"Tom my contract was just meant to be for five years. And since Jan, Bihl had paid for it to minimise the UK tax liability. Even if a renewal was offered I would not have taken it up given the dire financial state of the finances at Bihl and Bcfc. The accounts were voted 4-3, with me, Anthony Cheung and Matthew Chan, abstaining as it was felt the account do not truly reflect the proper status quo of the finances. I may stay behind as director and Acting Chairman position with no pay to oversee the operations. I am not motivated by money but the cause and the wishes of the biggest shareholder, that is Carson, still prevails. Panos, his brother in law to be, Ma – his brother in Law, and his son Ryan, are still firmly executing his views and my role is more to watch over the operations on behalf of the fans. So I am not all driven by money.

The novation and then waiver by Bihl of CY's debts means there is a potential tax liability of 1.8M GBP in the UK, 4.5M GBP funding requirement by Bcfc till the end of the season and a creditor in HK seeking 50M HK by 15th October, means Bihl lacks funds. Much depends on the CB to be issued to Vicotr Ma for 120M which he has no money to subscribe to and does not disclose in the accounts that he has been told he won't get the loan of 120M for it from a finance company. The voting directors had chosen to conceal this against the dissenting directors. So the accounts need to be seen in this light and therefore the auditors in the UK and HK has expressed serious concerns. This is borderline fraud and false accounting and false information to the market.

Because of these attempts to conceal the true picture in the accounts, I have fallen out with Ma and Panos, more so the former.

There will be new members joining the board, Ma's wife, and so on.

If the true picture is shown, the finances do not look good, and if 1.8M GBP tax liability accrues, which despite me and the auditor asking for clarifications with the

HMRC, which Ma and Panos refuses, Bcfc runs out of funds in Jan 2015. It means without funding Bcfc is trading whilst insolvent...

The auditors states in the Bcfc and Bihl accounts that there are serious and extreme concerns, as there is no evidence, that Ma can subscribe to the 120M CB, which he told the market about in the announcement on 31.7.2014 and in the accounts, which are seen by some just to beauty up the accounts.

That is covering up the true financial picture.

The sale of club has died as the exchange had sent us a letter which Peter Day has a copy. Exchange does not allow the sale on the basis as SWM wanted it and no one will buy a 25 per cent stake and inject equity with no control of some sort and promise to be sold the balance stake. All these the exchange says will mean Bihl loses the listing status which CY's relatives, including Panos, refuses to give up.

So we are running out of funds, true picture concealed in the accounts, 120M funding is a farce, can't sell the club as the exchange says so, and unless HMRC says 1.8M tax liability is waived, we run out of funds in Jan 2014.

So when the fans says once my contract is over and I don't get paid I will leave, they are wrong, I care about the club."

Thankfully now the receivers are in control of BIHL and of course Birmingham City Football Club. Things are far from perfect financially and of course the club has still not been sold. However the deal done with Trillion Asia has at least keeping the proverbial wolf from the door.

Panos Pavlakis has been looking after the club for the receivers and has done a great job in rebuilding a relationship with the club's supporters that Peter Pannu helped to destroy.

The appointment of Gary Rowett as manager was a masterstroke and without doubt he has done as much as anyone to lift the gloom and doom that surrounded the club. He was my pundit on BRMB for a season or so and I got to know him very well not only as a person but also as a football man. I got to know what sort of manager he would make because he would tell me his coaching philosophies on our long trips. I believe he is destined for big things. I just hope he stays long enough to steer Blues back to the top flight and establish them as a Premier League team and not just a championship side visiting the Premier League.

CHAPTER EIGHT
THE HIT SINGLE

THE BLUENOSE BROTHERS

I had thought about doing a song for the Blues for some time and one day while talking to Ian Danter about it he suddenly said let's do it. I had the tune *Singing the Blues* in my head after hearing it at Ipswich and had already written some of the lyrics.

Dant's is an incredibly talented musician and he set about arranging the music and to be fair we ended up with a fantastic effort that the fans loved.

But Dants had another surprise and that was we were off to Ron Rogers Studio in Monmouth where the former T'Pau man would produce the song. He did a great job and got the best out of me when I was as nervous as hell.

Singing The Blues had a Status Quo feel about it with a middle that was an upbeat chorus of *Keep Right On*. The fans loved it.

I arranged the deal with Cherry Red records and they were brilliant with us and to be fair so was the club. However Karen Brady knew the club made more money selling them through the club shop rather than through the record store HMV. In the end we did both.

It sold extremely well, thousands were shifted and to be honest had they all gone through HMV we would have made the charts.

It was great fun for both of us as we were both passionate Bluenoses.

I went into HMV and on that day we were the number one seller ahead of Michael Jackson. How cool is that. However Jackson sold millions of albums worldwide – but for that one day in Birmingham?

Dants and I were at St Andrew's for a game, me for BRMB and him for TalkSPORT, when it was played over the match day Tannoy at St Andrew's. To see Blues fans singing along with it brought a lump to our throats – sadly neither of our Dads were there to see it.

I spoke to Dants about a second song that I thought we should do. It was a remake of Rod Stewarts 1978 World Cup song *Ole Ola*. Suffice to say it did not do as well as *Singing the Blues*.

The third song came about after Blues had been promoted under Steve Bruce. It was a re-working of ELO's *Don't Bring Me Down* and was Dants idea and what a brilliant one it was. We did not mess about with the arrangement after all it was Jeff Lynne at his best. So we re-wrote the Lyrics and *Can't Keep Us Down* was born.

We got a call from SKY TV's Premier league show to ask if we would perform it as live for the show. Now the pressure was on. We invited the cameras to Roy Davis's Madhouse Studios but we needed an angle. So I asked Blues defenders Stephen Kelly and Mat Sadler to join us.

The idea was they would film us doing the song when I would stop it and say, 'Dants this is not working pal, I am not happy with the bass player and the drummer,' Dants agreed and said, 'what can we do'?

I said I would ring a couple of guys. In walked the two players. Kelly on bass and Sadler on drums and off we went.

SKY loved it. However both Stephen and Matt got loads of stick from the players next time they walked in the dressing room as the manager Steve Bruce played it on the screen.

The song was well liked and sold well, however we made the mistake of having Steve Bruce on the cover with us and when he was sacked it was not a saleable item.

The fourth was double A side to celebrate reaching the Final of the Carling Cup and to be honest was entirely Dants idea. The fans were singing a song on the terraces called, *We're On Our Way*.

So into the studio we went and Dants made it clear he wanted it to be exactly like they sang on the terraces – and it was. The other side was *Keep Right On*, which again we done in terrace style. Great foresight by Dants.

The Bluenose Brothers has been brilliant and a real joy for me to be involved in and I am sure for Dants. It would not have happened but for his unbelievable musical talent

The great news for the fans is that there are no plans for an album, however do we have one last song left in us for Blues? Never say never.

CHAPTER 9
YOU'LL DO FOR ME

I have over the years come up with sayings that have caught on around the area while I also used one liner gags in my Breakfast Show. I have always tried wherever possible to inject a little humour whether in a football commentary or on the Capital Gold breakfast show. Who said football commentary or presenting a breakfast show couldn't be entertaining and include humour? Below are just a few of the ones I have used to give you a flavour of the humour.

The one I am most associated with around the football scene is 'The Game's Gone', I have been saying that for many years, in fact since SKY TV took over running football in the 90s. Changing kick off times, obscene wage levels and the pre-occupation with all things Premier League can be traced back to the formation of the money mad Premier League and so I always said and still do say, 'The Game's Gone'. Football people now greet me with 'The Game's Gone' Tom and to be fair it has. And of course it was a no brainer when it came to a title for this book.

One of my commentary quotes was used in a booked titled *Tell Him he's Pele – and get him back on The Funniest Football Quotes Ever*. By Phil Shaw published in 2009.

During commentary of the Aston Villa v Portsmouth game following Emile Heskey scoring the only goal of the game I said, 'I haven't seen so many men hugging and kissing since I watched **Brokeback Mountain** with the Missus'.

Another saying that has caught on is 'Ding Dong Derby', which I use to describe and local derby match ie Villa v Blues or Baggies v Wolves. However there have been derby games without any ding and not much dong! Interestingly the Birmingham Half Marathon organisers used the saying in their pre 2016 run press releases. They wanted fans to run in their football shirts and used the phrase 'Ding Dong Derby' to promote it. That reminds me I must invoice them!

A phrase that I have used a lot over the last 25 years and already used in this book is 'remember the professionals built the Titanic while the amateurs built the Ark', (I use this when managers insinuate you don't know the game because you haven't played at their level). I was pleased when Ian Danter nicked it and used it on his show on TalkSPORT. By the way he hasn't paid me yet?

When there are draws I have described them by saying 'I don't like draws! Draws are like kissing your sister – which is only just better than kissing your brother.'

'They have that many injuries they could be sponsored by BUPA'.

When Blues beat Arsenal in the Final of the Carling Cup in 2011 I said on the whistle, 'This is better than sex'. My pundit former Northern Ireland international Jon McCarthy replied, 'it is the way you do it lad'.

'He's that slow if he was in a race with a pregnant woman he would come third.'

'He's so negative – the only time he goes forward is at the kick off.'

After Blues striker Nicola Zigic had scored a vital goal I said, 'I love the big man and if I caught him in bed with my missus I would tip toe downstairs and make him a cup of tea.'

'I have seen better centres in a box of Milk Tray.'

After Blues had come from 3–1 down to beat West Ham in the second leg of the Carling Cup semi-final I was so excited and amid the hysteria said, 'You can hear the sound of bubbles bursting all over the East End of London'.

If a caller makes a great point I would always say, 'You'll do for me'.

While talking about a particular or frustrating problem within the game I would say to a caller, 'It drives you barmy.'

At a particularly bad game I said, 'It's the sort of game you would rather watch on teletext', which was pointed out to me by Richard Park that it was the quickest way to get listeners to turn off by telling them the game was not worth listening to. He was spot on – I never used it again.

'If it's got boobs or wheels it will give you trouble.'

'Stop moaning about women drivers – if you don't like women drivers keep off the pavement.'

'Women are always dressing me with their eyes.'

'I had a mate who was driven to drink by a woman – and he didn't have the decency to thank her.'

'Electricity is dangerous. My nephew tried to stick a penny in the plug socket so anyone who says a penny doesn't go far didn't see him shoot across the room.'

'Some good advice – don't bother spending £4 getting your shirt dry-cleaned. Give it to the Oxfam shop they'll wash and Iron it put it on a hanger – and you can buy it back for 50p.'

'Remember love thy neighbour... but don't get caught.'

'I have been going to keep fat classes.'

'Saw a woman with a T-shirt on that said Guesse – so I said about 16 stone – I spent that summer in a wheelchair.'

'I tried dieting once-it was the worst six hours of my life.'

'I went on one of those online computer dating services. They called me today and said they haven't had any replies for six weeks...so did I want to try a week without a photo.'

'I did send my picture to a lonely hearts club...they sent it back and said they weren't that lonely.'

'I went jogging-people thought I was on a sponsored walk.'

'Seriously I have joined joggers anonymous – when I feel like going for a run I dial a number and someone talks me out of it.'

'My dad started jogging in the army – only they called it desertion,'

'I bought this Self Help DVD on how to handle disappointment – when I got home the box was empty.'

'My missus is really serious about her diet – she's using a salad dressing called 600 Islands.'

'It's amazing but true more diets start in dress shops than in Doctors surgeries.'

'Marriage certificate is just another name for a work permit.'

'My wife got undressed in front of the window — the peeping Tom gave himself up.'

'Spent my whole life looking for miss right – didn't realise her first name was always.'

'I am teetotal so I bought my pal a book on the evils of drink – he gave up reading.'

'I lent a bloke £1,000 pounds to get plastic surgery – now I don't know what he looks like.'

'David Beckham's son Romeo just said his first words *Hello*...magazine.'

'Why is it when anyone knocks your door the dog thinks it's for him.'

'After hearing two eyewitness accounts of an accident don't you ever wonder about history?'

'Chicken and egg lying in bed and the egg said, "well that's answered that question".'

'Had an item on the Xtra AM news yesterday about a nutter driving up the M6 motorway the wrong way – so I rang my Mrs and said be careful there's a nutter driving up the motorway the wrong way...She said there isn't there's hundreds of 'em?'

'They were selling tea at £5 a mug...the queue of mugs was 100 yards long.'

I got in late last night and the wife said, "where have you been and I want the truth?" I said make your mind up.'

'Did forum at a rough club last night – they jacked me up and nicked my shoes.'

'Ian Danter is a workaholic – mention work and he gets drunk.'

'I saw him walking down lover's lane holding his own hands?'

'I am fed up – I spent the whole week in a field making a hideout so I could do some bird watching – then she moved to Worcester.'

'I went to see a child psychologist – he was only six.'

'I looked up paranoid in the dictionary – it said what do you want to know for?'

'Have you noticed when you scream in a library everyone says shush – when you scream on a plane everyone joins in?'

'Our school magazine had an obituary column.'

'Love is grand – Divorce is about 100 grand.'

'We used to call my Grandad Spiderman because we couldn't get him out of the bath.'

'The area I live in is rough – if there is a knock at the door after 6pm you hope it's the Jehovah Witnesses.'

CHAPTER TEN
I DON'T TALK ABOUT MY CHARITY WORK... BUT!

As a youngster I had nothing, in fact less than nothing, however I had a fantastic family and great pals all of whom would be there in an instant if needed. Now I have all I want and need both emotionally and financially. I realised, admittedly quite late in life, that life is not just about material things but also putting something back either by actions or deeds.

If I, or any member of my family, needed help I would love to think there were people who would and could help.

However I have also grown to realise just how important health is and that if you have that you really do have everything. This became even clearer after my brush with the 'big C', which I talk about later.

Doing positive things for charity give me a great inner feeling. It's easy to stick a tenner in an envelope but it's much more rewarding to actually do something.

At the end of every football season I am invited to go along to junior football clubs presentation evenings and present the youngsters with their trophies and medals. I love these because we never had anyone to come along to ours when I played non-league. I fully understand I am usually second choice because the junior clubs can't get a pro player from Blues, Villa, Wolves or Baggies to do it. However I am a good second best. It is sad that most professional players won't do these events even though the kids adore them.

And of course you never know who you will meet and what impact they will have on your professional career. I recall doing a presentation night for a local junior football team and one of the kids picking up a medal was a nine-year-old Darren Carter. Who would have thought that night in Solihull that years later I would be interviewing him about his winning penalty that put Blues into the Premier League for the first time? As someone once said, 'It's a funny old game'.

I am privileged and extremely honoured to be an ambassador for the **South & City College** in Birmingham. I just love this organisation, which is brilliantly led by the principal Mike Hopkins. I deal with one of his managers Steve Dourass, who is a likeable caring and understanding man who is tailor made for working in an environment like S&C. They do so much great work in helping those youngsters from a background similar to mine to realise that they can make something of their lives. The success rate of the college is brilliant. I love talking to the kids at their workshops and hopefully inspiring them to believe that hard work can and often does bring success and that just because you didn't go to university doesn't mean you cannot be successful. It is one of the great pleasures in my life along with Help Harry Help Others.

My association with **ACORNS** came about through a personal situation. My nephew Richard sadly died from muscular dystrophy at just 18 years of age in Acorns in Selly Oak. They were not only brilliant with Richard but also my sister Lesley and her family. It was top class and they even turned up at Richard's funeral. I will never be able to thank them enough.

So as a way of saying thank you I made them my chosen charity to such an extent that I became a patron of Acorns. I am so proud to be associated with such a fabulous charity.

One of the first things I did was to get agreement with my BRMB colleagues that half of the admission fee from the BRMB/GOLD football forums would go to Acorns. What happened was that the social club would charge £2 and we would split it 50/50. We would give our 50% to Acorns and the club would give their 50% to their chosen charity.

To further try and raise some money for Acorns I bizarrely and stupidly agreed to participate in a charity boxing match. Nothing wrong with that until I realised that my opponent was to be former World Champion John H. Stracey! I had originally agreed to do it based on going three rounds with a Premier league referee – now that I would have enjoyed.

However Ken Purchase who organised the night told me I was fighting a former world champion in John H. Stracey who had won the WBC world title beating José Nápoles in Mexico in 1974.

Now let's be clear I was conceding ability, technique, weight, reach, and intelligence and anything else you want to throw into the mix. However if nothing else I was game although some would say stupidly kamikaze.

It was held at the Albany Hotel in the city centre (Now the Holiday Inn) and was a posh do – black tie and all. I had a pal and Blues supporter, John White in my corner as Paddy Lynch was forbidden from getting involved by the British Boxing Board of Control. I was also warned about taking part by Dave Roden of the BBBC. This was because the event was not licensed by the sports regulatory body.

I had to have a licence, so on the night I was given a European boxing licence so it could go ahead. All that for two fights – my first and last.

However my already shredded confidence did not improve when Pat Cowdell told me that for me it was probably 'one fight too many'.

My pals Paddy Lynch, Wayne 'Mad Dog' Elcock and Don Aggeson helped my preparation during my training and to be fair I felt good. In the Gym I was doing six two-minute rounds with ease.

I was feeling really good as I climbed into the ring. That is until the bell went for the first round –which, trust me, is better than any laxative! I am being totally honest when I say at that moment I suddenly thought, 'what the hell am I doing here?'

I didn't realise how much nervous energy is expended when you are in front of a crowd and out of your comfort zone. Within 20 seconds I am breathing out of my backside.

I made the mistake of tagging him in the first second and he just looked at me and I realised what a huge mistake that was. I was hammered. I remember going back to my corner looking for an escape route when my second John said, 'brilliant well done, he has not laid a glove on you,' to which I replied. 'well watch the f***ing ref because someone's beating the crap out of me'. Well John collapsed into fits of laughter and that was me on my own for the next two rounds.

I never laid a glove on John H. Stracey (I did not want to upset him again) but the important thing is that we raised £17,000 for Acorns – which I reckon worked out at £1,000 per bruise!

John H. loved it as well and has kept in touch – what a top man.

A few words from GEORGIE MOSELEY

Georgie is the Founder of **Help Harry Help Others Cancer Charity** and Birmingham Drop In Cancer Support Centre. Tom is currently chairman of the trustees and an ambassador for the charity.

'I had the pleasure of first meeting Tom Ross in May 2009. My son Harry used to write anywhere and everywhere to try and tell his story about his journey with Cancer and his Help Harry Help Others campaign. Tom was one of the only people to invite Harry onto his radio show and boy was it a memorable experience.

'Tom had great banter with Harry who at 11 years old gave as good as he got. As soon as he knew Tom was a Blues fan – that was it. Immediately an Aston Villa bracelet was on Harry's wrist. Tom left a lasting impression on Harry as did Harry on Tom. Quite frankly they hit it off and become friends and I will always remember as a mom how Tom was there during our darkest days both visiting Harry after major brain surgery whilst in a coma and sadly after his passing at Acorns Hospice.

'Tom is a genuine guy, a man of his word and if he promises or commits to something its delivered. I am so proud that he become Harry's friend during the last few months of his life and now that Help Harry Help Others is a registered Cancer charity, I am extremely proud that Tom is a valued trustee and one I was proud to appoint Harry's Chairman.

'Whilst I know that Tom has stayed in touch for one reason only – for Harry, he has become a true friend to me, backs me 1million percent, as he knows I am now Harry's voice and for that I am truly blessed by Harry introducing him to me.'

For me to support a charity it needs to 'touch' me on a personal level and to this end I have done coffee mornings for MacMillan, events for Promise Dreams and was at one time a Trustee for the BRMB charity 'Cash for Kids'.

I get hundreds of requests for signed footballs and signed football shirts from people who have organised events for charitable causes. Sadly I just can't get hold of them, as the clubs more often than not say NO to me like they do everyone else. Sadly some people take offence and made it look like I didn't want to help which is definitely never the case. So if I have had to disappoint you or your charity over the last 35 years it was not that I didn't want to help but couldn't through no fault of my own, I apologise.

In May 2011 I met a young man called **Harry Moseley** and this young 11-year-old blew me away and changed my outlook on life forever.

He came into the studio with his mom Georgie and former Villa midfielder Ian Taylor. He explained how he had a brain tumour and that for two years he had been raising money to help find a cure. He had been inspired to do this because his friend in hospital Robert had also had a brain tumour and had passed away. He had raised an amazing half a million pounds from selling beaded bracelets that he made himself. He would sit outside supermarkets selling these bracelets. He went on to explain how he had spoken to an audience of 500 businessmen in London to explain what he was doing and to enlist their help. This amazing boy was 11 and doing these things that would make anyone nervous. Lots of celebrities including David Beckham, John Terry, Ben Sheppard and many more lent their support.

That figure was around £750,000 when he sadly passed away and rose just after his death to 1.2 million pounds.

He was impish and lovable and any man would be proud to have him as a son. In the interview he nailed me so many times with his sense of humour. It was one of the best interviews I have been involved in.

The Prime Minister David Cameron wore one of his bracelets on TV such was the mesmerising personality of Harry.

I kept in touch with him from that day and went along with Ian Taylor, Michael Johnson, Ed James, Oliver and James Phelps (The Weasley twins from the *Harry*

Potter movies) to support him at events at schools etc. He inspired the school children like no adult ever could.

One day his Mom Georgie called me to say he was going into the children's hospital for a major brain operation. She explained that he would go into a coma and the risk was that he wouldn't wake up.

I went a number of times to see him while he was in the coma, just to talk to him and have some banter, hoping that it would help him wake up. Sadly it didn't. I said a lot of prayers at that time.

His Mom called again one night to tell me he had passed away. I was devastated to say the least. He was taken to Acorns where he lay before his funeral. I spent some time there talking to him and explaining how much he had inspired me and more importantly had inspired thousands of people and had made a huge difference in his short life. He had done more good in his 11 years than most of us do in our entire lives.

His wonderful mom Georgie decided that she wanted his legacy to continue and wanted to spread 'Harry Love' as far and wide as was possible. So the charity 'Help Harry Help Others' was founded in his memory with three basic missions. Help Cure, Help Cope, and Help Care.

I was proud to become an ambassador and also chairman of the trustees of Help Harry Help Others. The charity has gone from strength to strength and to date we have raised around 800k since it was formally set up and distributed £600k to causes that come under our Help Cure, Help Cope and Help Care mission statement

Harry Moseley and the HHHOs ambassadors.

Not too long ago we opened a Cancer Drop in Centre at the Meadway in Sheldon. This is where people with cancer can literally drop in and find a warm welcome and a cup of tea. More importantly they can talk to experts about a number of issues to help them deal with their cancer. Lots of times cancer patients or their family just want someone to talk to and that is where Georgie is absolutely brilliant.

Harry's spirit and love lives on in his Mom. I have no doubt whatsoever that she is guided by Harry. Help Harry Help Others has made a massive difference in Harry's memory.

A few words from JAMES PHELPS

James along with his brother Oliver are actors who played the 'Weasley twins' in the hugely successful *Harry Potter* movies. Both are also ambassadors for the Help Harry Help Others charity.

'Tom's voice is as much a part of football for me as the chanting of the crowd, the colours of the shirts and a hot Bovril in the stands during the winter. One of my first memories of football was sitting in the back of my parent's car on a journey somewhere, when the theme music came on for the Goalzone on 1152 Xtra am, and Tom's voice introducing the game. From then on the tradition was set, as well as listening to the phone-in after the game. Tom has the skill to make you feel like you are at the game more than any other commentator I know, not just that, but also making you feel the desire of the players on the pitch or the fans in the crowd.

'Years later I met Tom for the first time and it was clear his passion for football and the Blues wasn't just on the radio. Being a Birmingham fan, I've not had too much to cheer about over the years, though when we have I know Tom has been live on air making everyone know about it. From the 2002 Play-off Final in Cardiff, to the second leg home semi-final versus West Ham in the Carling cup in 2011 and how can we forget the Carling Cup Final itself (Blues won 2–1 for those who have forgotten). He also is able to keep neutral between the Birmingham City, Aston Villa and West Bromwich Albion during any of the games. Though I am sure the only real time he has enjoyed a trip to Villa Park was to see a Bruce Springsteen concert.

'Since then I have got to know Tom and how much he does for the community, through the Help Harry Help Others charity and many others.'

BOXING DAY TSUNAMI

Like millions of others on Boxing Day in 2004 I sat and watched the devastation caused by the Tsunami that followed a huge earthquake in the Indian Ocean. 275,000 people were killed across two continents and 14 countries. The earthquake released energy equivalent to 23,000 Hiroshima bombs.

I sat in tears thinking about the suffering of these people and at a time when we were all enjoying the festive cheer. I rang my boss Andy Turner, The Head of Capital Gold and said I wanted to do a 27 hour 'Radiothon' that would include two breakfast shows to raise money for the Tsunami disaster fund. Within a day it was organised. Not that it took much organising to be fair, just me and my producer Lisa Delaney.

My local manager Adam Bridge was up for it and said start a just giving page with a target of £5,000 pounds, which we did.

I contacted all my business and football pals and recruited a lot to spend half an hour with me during the 27 hours. Astro from UB40, Hayley Evetts who was big at that time in some reality show, and many others.

The idea was that listeners could call in and pledge a sum of money and I would play them a song of their choice.

I was blown away by the way Brummies responded. The lines were red hot, even through the night, with listeners donating £5 or £100 pounds. It was amazing how people had been touched by what had happened.

The business community also responded with West Bromwich Building Society bringing me in a cheque for tens of thousands of pounds and other companies donating various amounts. David Gold and David Sullivan both put in large amounts. The football clubs all donated as well. In fact Steve Bruce turned having been so touched by the disaster and what we were doing. He gave me an envelope with a round £50,000 pounds in it from him and the players–a truly amazing brilliant gesture.

When we finished we were at a massive £140,000 pounds that rose to a final total of £147,000 pounds in 27 hours, which was well over our original target of £5,000.

When the Capital Radio Group finally got round to doing something on air a couple of weeks later they raised around £400,000 pounds country wide from FM and AM stations and yet the generous warm hearted Brummies had raised £147,000 on an AM breakfast Show. Yes I was very proud of my listeners, my friends and my city that day.

REMEMBRANCE DAY

Poppy Day is special to me due to my Dad and my Mom doing their bit and I remember one poppy day taking a call from a 90-year-old listener who was a survivor of The Battle of Arnhem. He was reminiscing about the terrible time he had experienced and the loss of his fellow soldiers – by the time he'd finished both he and I and I am sure thousands of listeners were in tears. I completely lost it when he said to me, 'I can't thank you enough for remembering us'. He was thanking me when the whole of Europe should have been thanking him and others who fought for our freedom.

MG ROVER

The MG Rover Group was the last domestically owned mass-production car manufacturer in the British Motor Industry. The company was formed when BMW sold the car making and engine manufacturing assets of the original Rover Group to the Phoenix Consortium for a nominal sum of £10 in May 2000. The consortium was headed by ex-Rover Chief Executive John Towers.

The first loss for the eight months of 2000 were reported to be around £400m. By 2004 losses had been reduced to around £80m but it never made a profit. The company ceased trading on 8 April 2005, with debts of £1.4 billion, after a proposed alliance with SAIC collapsed. (Shanghai Automotive Industry Corporation).

Over six thousand Longbridge employees lost their jobs and their pensions. They were left with no job, no money, no dignity and no hope

MG Rover were my car sponsors and I was proud to be an ambassador for the brand. Everybody in Brum knew someone who either worked at or knew someone who worked at what was affectionately known as the 'Austin' (Longbridge). The closure was devastating for the city and not only for the workers but for many thousands who relied on MG Rover for a living, such as the bloke who ran the newsagents/sandwich shop opposite the factory gates. He went bust as well as the suppliers to the business who couldn't continue because they solely relied on MG Rover. Some suppliers had been generous in giving MG Rover extra time to pay their bills and so when MG went bust they lost everything as well.

I firmly believe that had BMW not taken the 'Mini' to one of their other plants then perhaps Rover might still be in business to this very day.

I was doing the Breakfast Show on Capital Gold and thanks to Mike Owen, who was at that time a doing consultancy work for BRMB/GOLD, we decided to launch a campaign to help those who had been devastated by the closure losing not only their income but their pensions as well.

I got really angry about the whole thing because we had politicians crying crocodile tears over the closure but they could have helped keep the business going and thousands in full-time employment for years before. Why were the police, council and highways agency to name a few driving around in foreign made cars? Why were the politicians being driven around in non-British vehicles? They had the choice but no, the hypocrisy was there to be seen – they rarely do what they say they are going to do and that still happens today!

We devoted lots of time every morning on the Capital Gold Breakfast show to allow those involved to have their say and to let them know they were not alone. Gemma Cartwright a wife of one of the employees was absolutely brilliant in organising stuff and came into the studio on a few occasions to talk about it.

However while we were getting support locally the message was not getting to people outside of the Midlands. I am convinced that if it had been in Dagenham there would have been more done. I remember the PM Tony Blair driving up Broad Street to the union offices in a foreign car and though 'you hypocrite'.

Every day we would have specialists on who could advise and help employees on what they could do, where they could seek help and we also got on counsellors.

At the time the national media was covering the Pope's funeral, and other big stories and that meant that nationally the news about MG Rover was overshadowed and therefore limited.

I decided that I wanted to do something more positive and a game of football at St Andrew's seemed a great idea to raise funds. After all multi thousands had lost their jobs and many thousands more in subsidiary businesses' were put on short time etc.

Getting celebrities to play would surely not be a problem I thought – how wrong was I?

So I spoke to Blues MD Karren Brady who was already thinking about what the club could do. She was brilliant and was all up for it and wanted it to be a joint venture.

I agreed to sort out the celebrity team and would manage it on the night with Barry Fry. Karren was superb and said the club would deal with the logistics and of course she would speak to their club corporate clients to also help. She made it clear that 'every single penny raised would go to the MG Rover Benefit fund'. Blues were magnificent in their support for the employees of MG Rover.

The idea was that the celebrity team would play against the Blues first team.

However one of the biggest disappointments of my life was the reaction we got from top celebrities.

I and my producer Lisa Delaney contacted the agents of everyone from Cliff Richard to Peter Kay and all we got was, 'He or she would love to do it but...' In the end the only two national names that turned out for the celebrity team were Andrew Whyment (best known for his roles as Darren in *The Royle Family* and Kirk in *Coronation Street*, which he has played since 2000.) and Paddy McGuinness (The comedian, comedy actor, television personality and presenter, best known for his roles in *Max and Paddy* and presenting game shows such as *Take Me Out* and *Benchmark*.)

Lisa and I spent hours every day trying to persuade stars to turn up and to be honest I was not only disappointed, but majorly disgusted at the attitude shown to what was a national employment disaster.

I rang the guy who organised the Arsenal Charity Football Team because I knew they had stars like Spandau Ballets Tony Hadley. He simply said, 'they won't travel to Birmingham.' I explained what had happened to so many people but to no avail.

But after explaining the situation to Karren Brady we both decided that the game was going ahead and to be fair there was certainly no apathy locally. We had loads of ex-professional footballers turning out including Bryan Robson, Tony Morley, Nigel Spink, Tony Daley, Gordon Cowans, Steve Bull, Kevin Francis, Robert Hopkins and a sprinkling of local cricketers. Great support but we desperately needed a big showbiz name-someone who would put bums on seats regardless of the football!

Barry Fry and I managed the celebrities' team and had great fun doing it as well.

The Blues First team won 9–2 in front of a crowd of 7,413 with Morley and Whyment scoring for the Celebrities.

A Trust Fund was set up by Gemma Cartwright and Liz Hanks called 'The Rover Community Action Trust' and the £57,000 raised was paid into the fund which was administered by local solicitors, Shakespeare's.

BLUES ALL STARS

It was former player and assistant manager Ian Atkins who suggested to me about having a regular team after charity game that I organised in 1991–92. The players then included: Terry Cooper, Ian Atkins, Robert Hopkins, Garry Pendrey, Kevan Broadhurst, Malcolm Page, Joe Gallagher and Dave Latchford.

I loved the idea and so did Kevan Broadhurst who got the team going with me and has been with me every step of the way since. He has a great relationship with players, having been in the game all his life and that has contributed greatly to the success we have had.

We have played and continue to play all over the West Midlands and I am delighted to say that unlike other professional charity teams we don't charge a penny and would rather the local cause/charity get all the money. To date we have helped to raise over one million pounds for local charities and worthwhile causes.

It's great to see how the squad has evolved over the years so that today we have a very good squad of ex-players. They include Maik Taylor, Dele Adebola, Paul Devlin, Jeff Kenna, Denis Bailey, Kevin Poole, Stuart Storer, Jae Martin, Dave Barnett, Peter

The Blues All Stars Charity Team 2016.

The first Blues All Stars Charity team in 1992.

Shearer, Martin O'Connor, Ian Clarkson, Geoff Horsfield, Paul Peschisolido, Ian Clarkson, Howard Forinton, Robert Hopkins, Guy Russell and of course Broads to name just a few who regularly turn out on Sunday mornings.

That first ever Blues All Stars team in 1992 included Kevan Broadhurst, Joe Gallagher, Micky Evans, Terry Cooper, Ron Green, Trevor Morgan, Garry Pendrey, Robert Hopkins, Tony Evans, Tony Taylor Keith Bertchin and Steve Lynex and yours truly.

During the last 24 years many players, some great names, have played for the All Stars including Steve Bruce, David Gold, Barry Fry and Noel Blake, Graham Hyde, Paul Peschisolido, Don Givens, Dave Latchford, Phil Sumerhill, Malcolm Page, Brian Roberts, Phil Hawker, Tommy Mooney, Mark Cooper, Tony Rees, Micky Halsall and many more.

Hopefully the All Stars will continue for a long time, but players are less locally-based these days so who knows exactly how long it will. However while we can continue to make a difference to the local communities and earn goodwill for Birmingham City FC then we will.

The formation of the Birmingham City Official Former Players Association is the culmination of a dream that Kevan Broadhurst and myself have had for many years and was a natural evolvement from the Blues All Stars team.

A few years ago Kevan and I discussed the logistics of forming a proper Former

Players Association We enlisted the help of Blues All Star player Dean Holtham who is boss of the Football in the Community at Blues. The club's commercial director Adrian Wright bought into it and we were off and running. The current Commercial Director Ian Dutton has also supported us brilliantly and helped us take the BCFC FPA forward

We now have a members' list of ex-players that includes players from every era from the 1940s to the 2000s.

It is our aim to find as many ex-players as possible. The major reason for the association is to build a bridge between the club, the supporters and its history which as we see it are inextricably linked anyway. It also allows the all ex-players to keep in contact with each other. While by virtue of pitch and hospitality appearances, the ex-players can keep in touch with the club and its fans.

We believe that every single ex-player who has worn the Royal blue shirt should be recognised and made welcome at St. Andrew's.

We are also inviting every ex-manager to join the association with Barry Fry the first to accept membership. The formation of the association is a real positive step in the history of this great club.

We are thriving as an association with Dean Holtham, Mike Wiseman, Keith Dixon, Jeff Kenna, Malcolm Page and Pete Hall along with Kevan and myself forming the committee. We have organised some extremely popular events including back to the 50s–60, back to the 70s, back to the 80s and back to the 90s. This gave the fans a chance to catch up with players they have grown up watching.

We were heavily involved in the very successful 140th Anniversary dinner in front of over 1,100 supporters at the ICC in Birmingham in July 2015. We provided over 65 players and former managers. Some of those came on stage with me and co-host Jasper Carrott to answer questions. The night was topped off by the Bev Bevan Band featuring Jasper Carrott.

One of the highlights was for us to form our own Birmingham City Former Players Association 'Hall of Fame'

To date those in it are:

Trevor Francis

Jeff Hall

Garry Pendrey

Bob Latchford

Malcolm Page

Roger Hynd

Alec Govan

Kevan Broadhurst

Robert Hopkins

Christophe Dugarry

Bob Hatton
Kenny Burns
Gil Merrick
Joe Bradford
Joe Gallagher
Geoff Horsfield
Martin Grainger
Mikel Forsell
Karen Carney

We are currently taking the Former Players Association out on the road with a series of forums at pubs and clubs around Birmingham.

The money raised is used to help those less fortunate. For example we have bought the equipment to turn a wheelchair into a battery operated one. Laptops etc. for children with special needs. Wherever we can help we will try to do so while keeping the former players in touch with the club and the fans.

We also started a newsletter that keeps those ex-players that live elsewhere in the country up to date with all that is happening at St Andrew's.

With some of the first inductees into the BCFC Former Players Association Hall of Fame.

I was also lucky enough to guest for the West Bromwich Albion All-Stars Charity Team for quite a few years, before I formed the Blues All Stars charity team, alongside some great names including:

Garry Pendrey – Tony Brown – Bobby Hope – Derek Statham—John Wile – Brendan Batson– Peter Bonetti – Graham Lovett, who by the way is the funniest man on the planet – John Trewick– Micky Evans – Mick Kearns – John Giles – Ally Robertson – Dave Butler, The late Paddy Grealish – Graham Turner – Joe Mayo – Cyrille Regis, Campbell Crawford – Nicky Cross, Richard O'Kelly, and many more.

I cannot explain how much I enjoyed playing for the Albion All Stars. As a football nutcase it was joy personified.

I remember one time we were playing at the University ground (next door to the West Bromwich Albion current training ground). We only had 11 players and so we persuaded Bomber Brown to be the sub despite him having major problems with his hips at that time. We were losing 2–1 to a team who were, shall we say 'a bit above themselves'.

Midway through the second half Bobby Hope pulled his hamstring and had to limp off and Bomber had to come on despite not wanting to.

To be fair and with all respect Bomber could hardly walk and some of the opposition were laughing and making uncharitable remarks.

But it goes to show that you can't judge a book by its cover (perhaps except this one?) despite hardly moving Bomber scored a hat-trick and we won 4–2.

One thing I learned early on from playing with these guys is that the worst professional is ten times better than a top amateur. I became a better player just by playing with these ex pro's week in and week out. (I know what you are thinking that it didn't take a lot of doing)

A few words from ALAN GEORGE

Alan worked for Birmingham City Football Club and Entertainment and Sports Network Limited before becoming Director and Owner of Gala Events, which specialises in Sports Hospitality and Event Management

> 'Tom Ross is without doubt Birmingham's voice of sport. I have known Tom for over 15 years going back to my days at Birmingham City Football Club and I have always loved his infectious enthusiasm for sport. Since setting up Gala Events almost ten years ago, Tom has hosted many of our sporting dinners and lunches and interviewed some of the top names in sport such as Stuart Pearce, Steve Bruce, Kevin Keegan, Lewis Moody, Carl Froch amongst a number of others. Tom hosts the events in a really professional manner and he is often gutted that he only has 45 minutes to interview these stars, with so many topics for him to discuss! Tom is well

renowned for his football experience, but I will never forget the in depth interview he did with Carl Froch at the Pre-Fight dinner we did before Carl's fight with Mikkel Kessler.

'The customers were really enthralled and Carl even turned round to me afterwards and said "Blimey, that was one of the best interviews I have done; this guy really knows his boxing". It was after this that Tom told me that boxing was his number one passion behind football! It is an absolute pleasure to work with Tom and he is more than a work colleague, he is also a good friend."

Because of what I do I get asked to MC lots of charity events, Q&A sessions and sporting dinners not only for the local football clubs but also for lots of local charitable causes.

I work regularly as a professional MC for GALA Events and host all their Sporting Dinners at Edgbaston for the owner Alan George. These I enjoy immensely with brilliant guests including Steve Bruce, Kevin Keegan, Paul Merson, John Hartson, John Gregory, Gary Rowett, Graham Taylor, and Dean Saunders. Alan gets great guests and does not short change his customers providing good food and a warm friendly atmosphere.

The best gig for him was at Trent Bridge with World Champion boxer Carl Froch. An amazing night as I love my boxing. This was ahead of his fight with Mikel Kessler and during dinner I sat with Nottingham Forest and Newcastle legend Frank Clarke. We got talking about football and Frank asked me who I supported and when I said Birmingham he could not wait to tell me what dirty Bas***ds they were, naming a number of the players. I must say it was a great chat full of banter and believe me I gave as good as I got.

I also hosted a GALA Events dinner at Wembley when Carl fought George Groves. I could not believe it when Carl came into the room at the Wembley Hilton after winning the fight to do a Q&A with me. Such is the respect Alan commands with sporting stars.

Sadly I cannot do every dinner or event I am asked to do as it would be impossible. You would be surprised at how many times I am told that "I don't care" just because I cannot make a dinner or provide a raffle prize. It's not that at all I just cannot physically do every event.

The worst criticism I experienced was at a Blues All Stars charity game at Alvechurch FC. I came in with some of the players and just said to the man on the gate that, 'we are the Blues All Stars team'.

I could not believe it when I found I was being abused on social media sites Facebook and Twitter because I refused to pay an entrance fee.

To say I was upset was an understatement. I was the joint-manager of the All Stars team and had to organise and agree all the games.

Carl Froch joining me for interview just after beating George Groves to retain World WBA & IBF titles.

Over 20 years or running the All Stars and helping raise over a million pounds and I got abuse. Whoever put it on Facebook could have spoken to me face to face because I was at the ground with the team for two hours plus, but obviously didn't have the guts. However they could have had an ulterior motive like supporting another team and thought it would be brave to try and malign me on social media.

CHAPTER ELEVEN
WE ALL HAVE BOSSES

A few words from DAVID LLOYD

David's radio career spans more than thirty years through a series of appointments across programming and management roles across a number of different radio formats. He joined Nottingham's Radio Trent in 1980, where he began a Sony Radio award-winning spell on air. David was headhunted to a senior post in regulation at the Radio Authority (OFCOM's predecessor in radio) Back to the industry in the late 90s; David took on responsibility for the radio stations run by Border TV as Group Programme Director, alongside his Managing Director responsibilities at Century 106. On the sale of that company, David transferred to Chrysalis, where he was initially Managing Director at the Dance station Galaxy 105. David then transferred to manage the two London talk stations, LBC. After a year of working as Programming and Marketing Director at Virgin Radio during its sale process, David crossed to the BBC briefly before being tempted away from the BBC by Orion Media who owned BRMB and now Free Radio.

'Tom is a one-off. A thoroughly honourable, humble character, proudly of the old school – yet someone who has not only lived through, but adapted to the huge changes in his beloved radio medium over the last few decades. A hugely entertaining personality, with an enviable command of the true art of commentary. Turn on Tom and you can smell the game. As he always says, it's about the passion – and Tom has that in spades. His story is a fascinating one – from the tenements to leading sports coverage on huge radio stations and a friend to some of the biggest names in the game. British radio owes a lot to Tom – and he is one of the reasons our Nation's radio commentary sounds the way it does.'

Football on BRMB/XTRA AM/Capital Gold/Free Radio/Free Radio 80s has been an integral and essential part of the lives of Brummies since the 70s. It is now sad to hear NO live football, on Free Radio and I have to say it's not really come as a major shock to me – let me explain.

I have been doing live commentaries on BRMB, now Free Radio, since Capital Radio bought BRMB in 1993. The group programme director Richard Park made it clear that live commentary was the way forward to achieve an audience, as covering local football was an important USP when it came to listeners making a choice as well as attracting advertisers.

Twenty-two years later in June 2015 Free Radio's owners ORION MEDIA LTD decided that the group would no longer be doing live football of any description including live commentary. Did this come as a shock to me? Not really as I said but let me explain further.

We have to go back three years to March 2012 when my Saturday afternoon programme 'The Goalzone' delivered all-time record listener figures of 142,000 for a Saturday afternoon between 2pm and 6pm.

As you will see from the chart below it was the market leader and in fact was the only show on the station to be market leader. Other stations with greater resources could not compete with us. And beating music stations proved that Saturday afternoons was accepted as a time for sport.

My reward for this was to be told that football was being moved to Free Radio 80s on 1152 AM (medium wave).

The official audience survey results in 2012 when I was told football would be taken off BRMB. You can see why I was disappointed.

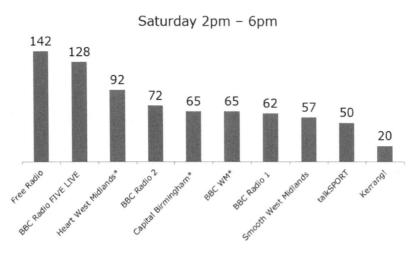

Goalzone

Saturday 2pm – 6pm

Rajar: Union of brmb, Beacon, Gold Birmingham and Gold Wolverhampton TSAs, 6 months ended Mar 2012, stations marked with an asterisk do not cover total survey area

It was no secret that our Programme Director David Lloyd was no lover of football although he repeatedly told and reassured me that he appreciated the importance of it to the radio station.

I was massively disappointed, but once I had my say all I could do was embrace it and get on with it.

It was his decision to move football because as he told me he could get a bigger audience playing music on a Saturday afternoon and also that the differing kick-off times confused the listeners who did not like football.

He also made the point that it interrupted music with midweek games.

My argument was and still is that it was crazy not to appreciate that if the figures were that good for a Saturday afternoon then it's a fair bet that they were having a positive effect on midweeks and Sunday afternoons.

However it was extremely difficult to prove because the RAJAR* audience figures don't allow you to get results for a specific day. So it was difficult to prove whether they had a positive or negative impact, although having said that it was inconceivable in my mind that they would be excellent on Saturday and yet poor in midweek?

Just for information RAJAR stands for Radio Joint Audience Research which is a company set up jointly by the BBC and Independent Radio to survey listeners.

Anyway back to David who assured me that they would get a bigger audience on Saturday afternoons by providing non-football lovers with music. I argued my case but sadly David, who I get on with famously, was having none of it.

We had ticked all the boxes that ORION wanted, such as winning audience and also winning awards, but we were not wanted on FM. So now I had to compete with the local BBC who were on FM while I was broadcasting on a poor AM signal.

However I have to make it clear that ORION always made me feel wanted and valued but it was always loggerheads about where football should sit on the station and on what frequency.

I have no doubt to this day that we would have done even better had David had the foresight and courage to keep The Goalzone programme on FM. Something that I have told him countless times since.

The following season the dumbing down of football on Free Radio continued when I was told that I had to negotiate the football commentary deals with the clubs at a much cheaper price than we had previously been paying. This was difficult but I managed to do it by calling in favours with the clubs and to be fair driving a hard bargain.

To be perfectly honest the football clubs were brilliant and recognised the importance of Free Radio in terms of publicising their club news. I also like to think my 35-year relationships with the clubs also helped.

The following season 2014–15 I was again called in and told there was no money for football but I could do a football 'around the grounds' type of programme similar to BRMB in the 80s. However I managed to be creative with the money they had allowed in my budget and persuade the clubs to do a commentary deal whereby I would do live kick by kick commentary on just 10 games for each club i.e. Villa, Blues, Baggies and Wolves.

At this point I have to say a massive thank you to Jeremy Peace at West Bromwich Albion as they were the only club who refused to accept the deal. I was told that the chairman had said 'no' to our offer. I accepted the decision and was working towards and planning to only do Villa, Blues and Wolves commentaries.

Because of our longstanding and good working relationship dating back to when he ousted Paul Thompson and took over the club I wrote to Jeremy explaining how sad I was with not having a deal after all this time.

I did not expect to hear a word but out of the blue I got a phone call from Jeremy asking me to go and see him.

I did and explained my position to him in a meeting where, by the way, he said in front of his own people that he knew nothing about the situation and had never said 'no' to our offer despite me being told that he had?

A few days later I received another call from Jeremy when he said that because of the excellent relationship and support I had given him in those days of Paul Thompson and also to the football club in many ways he said he was overruling his own people and that we had a deal.

I will always be grateful to Jeremy for that and despite what many think I have always found him to be OK and straightforward.

So we were now all go with the idea being that with 40 weeks in a season I would do one commentary per week, always away and on Saturdays. On any other day I would have my pundit with me and do inserts after each song especially on TV games which is a battle that is very difficult, if not impossible to win.

I was left trying to win an audience with both hands tied behind my back and my legs in shackles.

In June 2015 I again was summoned into David Lloyd's office to discuss what we would be doing the following season. David simply said we will not be doing any live football whatsoever and that included not buying licences from *IRN*, which would have allowed us to broadcast score flashes from the ground. The upshot was that I would only be doing the Monday and Friday night Goalzone Banter Chat and Phone in shows with Ian Taylor and Matt Murray.

I persuaded them to let me do a programme from a selected football ground on Saturday afternoons whereby I would pick up what was happening in games from Twitter sites and from TV etc.

The BBC heard about this and understandably decided to protect their interests and persuaded the Football League that I was not allowed to broadcast from the grounds due to not having being licenced for score flashes.

This meant that I had to sit in the studio and broadcast score flashes taken from TV and various Twitter accounts. It was soul destroying for me as a radio practitioner of 40 years and a commentator who had always been at live games.

After two weeks I went to see David Lloyd and told him it was not for me. I explained that I had to be at games. I told them for 35 years I had broadcast a credible football programme in my own city and had been proud to do so, but what I was doing now was not credible for either the radio station or me personally.

They wanted me to devote a lot of time to the digital side of the business and to be fair this I understood because the way we communicate is so different and from day one I had embraced the social media side. We had around 80,000 followers which in local radio terms was massive and to be fair I enjoyed that side of my daily work routine. Even though some of the personal abuse is unacceptable.

I was still going to Press Conferences and putting the mangers interviews out on social media to satisfy the football fans appetite for information about their club.

TalkSPORT approached me when they heard about what was happening and asked me if I was interested in reporting on games for them? Was I? You bet your boots I was.

It meant I was going to games and hopefully it will lead to doing more for them in the future. I went to London to see the lovely Kay Townsend and Mike Bovil who is in charge of TalkSPORT 2, which is now on air.

That season, I continued at Free Radio running the sports department, even though I was the only one in it, providing stories and sports news for the five radio stations while also hosting the Monday and Friday night Goalzone Banter Chat and Phone in programmes. There was also more than enough to do digitally on the website and on social media sites Facebook and Twitter.

The reaction from the fans to ORION's decision to stop doing football has been heart-warming to say the least. Wherever I have been people come up and ask the same question where have you gone? What has happened to the football? It's been the same on social media and emails. And ex-managers and players have asked what has happened to the football on Free Radio as I turned on and you were not there, just music?

It has been funny as well. I was at my wife Anne's confirmation at St Nicolas's Church in Curdworth. The Bishop Mark Santer was presiding over the ceremony along with his two deputy bishops. One of them in the full regalia including the Mitre on his head and carrying a crook came up to me while I was standing in the church with our deputy Brand Programme Director David Salt. I wondered what he was going to say stood in this historic 850-year-old church! He just said, 'Boing Boing Tom I am a Baggies fan what's happened to the football?' To be honest I just started laughing. The power of football eh?

I thought the future was definitely bright for Free Radio mainly because of the appointment of Adrian Searle to the position of CEO. Adrian is extremely talented in the commercial aspects of radio and he made a significant impact on the financial side of the business.

However in May 2016 Orion Media was sold to the huge Bauer Media Group. They were warm and friendly and have more of an interest in sport although that has not meant the return of live commentaries.

I continued to be frustrated with not doing live football, as the current programme director Mike Newman made it clear to me that such coverage will continue to not form part of the stations plans. I requested a meeting with the group Content Director Owen Ryan and Group MD Graham Bryce, as well as Mike to discuss it. The upshot is that I decided to end my 35 year career at BRMB/Gold/Free Radio and spend what time I have left doing what I think I do best, and that is covering football - rather than sitting looking at a computer screen. To be fair it suits Mike as well, as I was always in his ear about the poor coverage of sport on the station. It is great, however, to leave on good terms - Graham and Owen made it very clear they wanted the door to remain open for me to come back if they decide to change Mike's philosophy. I would be delighted to do so and told them just that in our very grown up and adult conversation. They both made it clear I can walk in and use the studio or facilities at any time I want, and I will continue to help the newsroom with things when needed. All without the daily frustrations! Graham also said Free would be delighted to publicise this book on the station, and for that I thank him. I suppose they believe that is how you should be treated when you have devoted 35 years of your life to a radio station putting it above everything, including at times your family. Sadly it isn't always the case but thanks to Owen and Graham of Bauer for being so understanding.

I really hope it works and they take Free Radio forward because I have spent 35 years of my working life at Free Radio and its predecessor BRMB, so I genuinely want it to do well.

Radio hasn't changed despite all the 'I've dropped the ball' 'I'll take it on board' jargon. Give the listener what he or she wants and they will turn on in their droves. However if you keep re-launching and re-branding without delivering the goods they will turn off in their droves.

They will adopt an 'I've heard it all before' attitude to any more attempts to convince them you have now got it right.

What some people in radio fail to understand is that the only judge that matters is the listener. I remember saying that to Jeremy Kyle when he worked at BRMB. The listener is king – end of story. The minute you forget that and try to force-feed him what he doesn't want you are in trouble.

There is no secret to local radio in my opinion as most people's lives are work-filled, debt laden and they need an escape away from that.

Again in my opinion the radio provides that escape route. Just ensure you deliver an entertaining, humorous, humble, uplifting, engaging and interactive show that is full of the things that matter to them, be it news, sport, weather or music and the listener, or a majority of them, will be happy.

Just after ORION took over BRMB the then CEO Phil Riley called me into his office and asked me if I could recommend someone who could take on the role of Non-executive Chairman of the Orion Media group. I came up with two names- one was the CEO of Cadbury and the other was Geoff Percy the former owner of Simple Soaps whom I had known for a long time and had become great friends with.

I told Phil that Geoff had a vast array of contacts and knowledge of the business fraternity and was incredibly sharp and switched on. I was delighted when Phil asked Geoff who immediately agreed to join as Chairman and had an immediate impact on the business but sadly left when Bauer bought ORION in June 2016.

FOOTBALL RADIO TACTICS

Why is football so important on local radio? Well first and foremost it gives the listener a unique reason to tune in. So at a time when there are so many radio stations and so much choice for listeners, covering their favourite team make it essential listening for them.

However not only to listen to sport, but also to other programmes, there is a loyalty and affinity to a radio station that covers your team. And also covering local football brings in new listeners to the station that might otherwise prefer listening to another radio outside of football. I see this as a wonderful opportunity for the stations programmers and marketing people to come up with a strategy whereby these listeners are persuaded to stay.

I always preferred to do live kick by kick commentary on away games rather than home games even when the home game appears to be more attractive with a higher profile.

Let me explain my reasoning.

For example Villa at home to Manchester United would be a massive game for the media but for me it was far more important to do commentary on West Bromwich Albion away at somewhere like Hull or Blues away at Sheffield Wednesday.

When you are at a home game you are taking people to the game and then keeping them company on their way home. With away games it's the reverse they join you later and generally, but not always, leave you when the game has finished.

In terms of maximising audience for commentary it has to be away games because most people interested in the home game are at the ground watching the game live.

This was something I had many disagreements about with Richard Park in the early days after I had taken over as Head of Sport from George Gavin.

I remember one game where Villa were at home to Manchester United in August 1995. You may remember it was the game Villa won and Alan Hansen came out with the, 'you won't win anything with Kids,' comment on *Match of the Day*.

Against my better judgement and with Ian Crocker constantly being in my ear (remember he had come from Capital Radio where only the big games and big teams mattered) and Richard Park's all things Manchester United are important attitude, I agreed that it would be our live commentary game.

Blues were at Charlton that day and were 0–0 with just 20 minutes to go and Villa winning comfortably 3–1 I switched the commentary to the Valley.

On the Monday I got a call from Richard Park asking why I switched the commentary from Villa Park to the Valley. I explained my thoughts and reasons to which he answered, 'Ross if you believe that then the lunatics really are running the asylum'. I continued to defend my decision when he said, and with not a little menace, 'Tom are you handing in your badge?'

Without doubt someone must have either told Richard Park or someone close to him, such as his London Head of Sport Jonathon Pearce, about us switching commentary. In my view there was no way Richard would have known.

But to this day I believe I did the right thing. Taking the station to number one in the audience ratings confirmed that my way of looking after all clubs and away games getting preference for live commentary was the correct strategy.

From that day though I also realised I was on my own and that every decision would probably end up in Richard's ear. I became very lonely, insular and trusted no one because I had been brought up where loyalty was key.

To be perfectly honest I did not think I would last too long and felt someone was making my life difficult and perhaps trying to get my job by discrediting me with Richard Park.

I have always been strong and never afraid to speak my mind and confront issues head on.

So some time later I spoke to Richard in his office at Leicester Square after asking to see him. On the way there I genuinely believed that I would be gone by the time I was on the train back home.

I explained to Richard that I couldn't do the job if I was continually looking over my shoulder wondering who is telling tales to people in Leicester Square. I also said, 'if I don't get you the audience figures and make you number one then get rid of me,' but inside I was confident that I would do well because I knew what the listeners in Birmingham wanted.

Richard said to me, 'Tom you are part of Park's posse so don't worry about anyone else,' and that was that. From that moment I just got on with it and did not give a toss what was being fed back to London.

Richard never ever gave me a rollicking, but I have to say he did re-focus me on a few occasions which was the same thing in reality. He would say things like, 'if you believe that then the lunatics really are running the asylum,' or 'that's a funny way of handing in your notice Ross,' or 'are you handing in your badge.'

However without any doubt Richard Park is the man whom I owe so much to. He had faith in me and I was determined to work hard for him and repay his faith in me by taking the sport to number one in the city. And that is exactly what I did. He made me successful and taught me so much about the radio business but what was most important for me was that he trusted me to do the job and I repaid him with great RAJAR figures.

One of the keys to our successful audience figures was because we used pundits. They would sit alongside the commentator. It was simple, the commentator would say what has happened and the pundit would say why.

These pundits were former professional players who were instantly recognisable by the listener and whose opinion had credibility.

I have been fortunate to have local football legends on my team of pundits.

Tony 'Bomber' Brown
All time record holder at West Bromwich Albion in appearances and goals and much, much, more. Too many goals and records to list (just google him).

Kevan Broadhurst
Kevan was one of the clubs youngest ever skippers – A tough no nonsense defender who played 167 games scoring 10 goals before he was forced to retire at the age of 27. He was beside me in the commentary box when Blues won promotion to the Premier League for the first time beating Norwich at the Millenium.

Andy Thompson
Andy Thompson a talented defender who played 431 games for Wolves scoring 45 goals.

Pat Heard
Pat was a member of Aston Villas European Cup winning squad and was on the bench for the final in Rotterdam. He played 27 games scoring two goals. Also played for Newcastle, Hull and Sheffield Wednesday.

Dave Bennett
Benno was a member of the SKY BLUES FA Cup winning team of 1987 playing 187 games. He broke his leg four times.

Gary Rowett
A former Blues player who is now their manager who played 114 games for the club. Also played for Derby, Leicester and Charlton.

Tommy Mooney

Tommy played 54 games for Blues and also played for Watford.

Jon McCarthy

Macca was a Northern Ireland International who played 150 games for Blues and was next to me in the commentary box when Blues won the Carling Cup beating Arsenal 2–1 at Wembley in 2011.

Robbie Dennison

A real bargain for Wolves who paid WBA just £20,000 for him. Robbie went on to play 353 games for Wolves scoring 40 goals including a belter at Wembley in the Freight Rover Trophy. He was also a Northern Ireland international.

Matt Murray

Matt Murray was a talented goalkeeper who looked destined to play for England when his career was cruelly cut short by injury in 2010 at the age of 29. However his career was effectively over in 2002, as he only played a handful of games after that due to persistent injuries. He replaced Robbie Dennison as my pundit for Wolves games, but was eventually poached by SKY TV where he now covers games every week. He played 87 games and is now my Monday night co-host on the Goalzone Banter Chat and Phone In show on Free Radio 80s.

Darren Carter

Darren played 58 times for Blues and became a club legend when at the age of 18 he scored the winning penalty at the Millenium that got Blues to the Premier League for the first time. He also played for West Bromwich Albion and is still playing for Forest Green in the National League. Suffered a lot with injuries and that is how he came to do commentaries with me.

Paul Williams

Paul was a central defender who played 169 games for Coventry scoring five goals in a six-year spell from 1995–2001. He also played for Derby and Southampton.

Paul Tait

Paul scored the first ever 'golden goal' in a Final. It was in the Auto Windscreen Shield. It was the time he flashed his infamous T-shirt. Paul was a great player sadly beset with injuries but still played 230 times for Blues.

Ian Taylor

Ian only did a few games as a pundit at live games but was a more than capable stand in for Pat Heard. Tayls was a midfielder who played 290 games for Villa scoring 42 goals including one in the Coca Cola Cup Final win against Leeds at Wembley in the 90s. He is my co-host on the Monday night Goalzone Banter Chat and Phone in on Free Radio 80s

Jody Craddock

Jody played 215 games for Wolves scoring 14 goals before announcing his retirement in 2013. He also played for Sunderland. Jody is also a very talented professional artist and since quitting has devoted more time to it and has exhibited his works.

Steve Daley.

Steve Daley played 244 games for Wolves scoring 43 goals. He was sold to Manchester United for a British record fee of £1,437,500.

Mel Eves

Mel played 180 times for Wolves scoring 44 goals and also played three times for the England B team.

Rob Edwards

Rob was a central defender for Wolves playing 111 times scoring one goal. He also played for Villa and Blackpool. While injured and while looking for a club he would stand in for either Matt or Andy for Wolves games. Rob played 15 times for Wales and is now back at Wolves as first team coach.

A few words from IAN TAYLOR

Ian was a midfielder who had a fifteen-year career making 478 league appearances. He made the move from non-league Moor Green to Port Vale in 1992, after a million pound move to Sheffield Wednesday in June 1994 he was sold on for another million to Aston Villa. He lifted the League Cup and reached the FA Cup Final with the club he had supported as a boy. Later he joined Derby County and Northampton Town before retiring in 2007. Paul Merson said that he could never understand how Ian had never played for England. He currently hosts a Monday night Banter Chat and 'phone in' with Tom on Free Radio 80s.

'I first met Tom when I joined the Villa, it was so memorable I can't remember the event. Working with Tom is great fun, we have a good laugh. There's never a dull moment because I'm never too serious. Regarding football he always wore his Adidas 'Standfinders' and I thought he had a mate in the stands that he was passing to! He knows the banter but not his football! Seriously he's a top guy with a heart of gold. He and I (as an ambassador) do raise money for the Help Harry Help Others charity.'

CHAPTER TWELVE
THE WORST DAY OF MY LIFE

Friday 16 April 16 2004 was one of, if not the blackest day, of my life. I was involved in a fatal car accident. I was leaving a friends in the Bartley Green/ Woodgate Valley area of Birmingham driving my brand new Rover 75 as it was days after being sponsored by MG Rover. It was raining and along with the orange streetlights visibility was poor to say the least. I had only been driving for two minutes maximum when in the space of a split second I saw a man in my headlights and hit him. I got out of the car and went to see what I could do while someone called 999 for an ambulance and the police, although the police were already there. A policewoman came over and tried to make the man comfortable.

The first thing she said to me was, 'don't worry it's not your fault, because we came up the road and saw him staggering up the middle of the road but carried on and turned round to come down and get him out of the road and saw the accident just as we were arriving'.

I was told to sit my car but not to move and wait for the traffic accident police to arrive who would take over the situation.

They arrived with the lead officer PC Mark Crozier interviewing me. He took a statement from me and also breathalysed me and confiscated my phone. They said my car would have to stay there until the specialist accident police arrived who would use their computer equipment to work out what speed I was travelling at when the accident happened. The ambulance came and took the pedestrian Mr Kevin Murphy to hospital. I was then allowed to go home.

I did not sleep much to be honest and was awake at 7.30 the following morning when PC Crozier arrived at my home. He sat me down and told me that Mr Murphy had sadly passed away during the night from his injuries. Despite PC Crozier saying all the initial reports suggested that it was a tragic accident and not my fault, that should have made me feel better but it didn't in any way shape of form.

I was due to go to Charlton to commentate on the Blues game. I desperately tried to find someone to take my place but couldn't so I decided to go, I was all over the place and had to apologise to listeners about the poor quality of the commentary. I could not face doing my XTRA am Breakfast Show for a few days.

On the following Monday I had to go to Bourneville Police Station to be formally interviewed under caution by PC Crozier. I found that a harrowing experience reliving the accident. I had hardly slept since it happened and kept having flashbacks to that moment of impact and still do to this day but not as frequently.

PC Crozier once again said that it all pointed to a tragic accident, yet somehow that did not make me feel any better whatsoever. PC Crozier told me about Mr Murphy and his family and to be honest at that time it made it worse.

I wanted to go to Mr Murphy's funeral but was advised by the police not to as Mr Murphy's family were understandably angry, so instead I sent flowers which I am sure was no comfort to the family whatsoever.

Before the Inquest the *Birmingham Mail* had gotten wind of what had happened and sent reporter Lisa Smith to BRMB to interview me. It was front-page news the following day. I have never wanted less to be the front-page story than I was that day.

I am sure it was the day before the *Mail* called me that PC Crozier contacted me to tell me officially that my phone was being returned as it showed that I was not on phone and that the accident investigators report proved I was not speeding and so I was not to blame.

Despite that I have to say that should have lifted the weight of guilt from my shoulders but it didn't. Why? Because in my mind it was not about who was to blame, but more that a man had lost his life in a tragic accident I was involved in. It was to be the official inquest that would in a bizarre way help lift the burden. .

The *Birmingham Mail* news billboards around the town screamed Radio DJ Ross in death crash? That upset some of my family who saw it and who thought I was the one dead. I have to say there were quite a few times I wished it had been me.

The *Birmingham Mail* reported the accident with facts and in a non-sensational way and for that I was and always will be eternally grateful. I was told by the police that, because of the facts they had accumulated the coroner would formally record a verdict of, 'accidental death' clearing me of any responsibility. PC Crozier also made it clear I did not have to go to the inquest.

However I told him that I wanted to go to the inquest because I had nothing to hide and because I wanted to look the family in the eye and explain how sorry I was. I also said I wanted to answer any questions the family wanted to put to me, however once more PC Crozier said I didn't have to but I had never shirked a tackle in my life and wasn't about to start then.

The clerk of the coroners Court put me in a room to wait for the inquest to start and for me to wait in after it was over so the family could make their way home – she obviously felt there might be a confrontation. I stood in front of the family and said how sorry I was that the accident had happened. They asked me a few questions, which I answered.

The coroner then officially said it was a tragic situation but it was accidental death. It was officially over even if emotionally it wasn't by a long way. I went back into the room to wait for the family to leave when the coroner's clerk came in and said that Mr Murphy's Dad wanted to come in and see me. Now I was a father and thought to myself that he would probably punch me and I decided if he did I would take it because who could blame him?

He entered the room and just looked at me and we were both in tears as he hugged me and I am not ashamed to say I then cried like a baby. It may have been a tough time for me but I have never forgotten that it was a far tougher time for Mr Murphy's family. However it was not quite over for me.

Around two months after the inquest I was set to record one of BRMBs popular football forums with West Bromwich Albion boss Bryan Robson in front of a live audience at the Hampstead Social Club on the border of Great Barr and Handsworth Wood. A week before it was due to take place I received a phone call off my pal Kevan Broadhurst who had heard through contacts and the grapevine that some of the family and friends of Mr Murphy were coming to the forum to 'sort me out'.

BRMBs health and safety officer Bobby Hunt along with the directors and programme controller Adam Bridge wanted to cancel the forum but I said 100% no, as I had done nothing wrong other than turn left instead of right and been involved in a tragic accident.

The police and the coroner's court laid no blame with me. However let me make it clear I was still desperately sad that it had happened and would have done anything to have prevented it. Anyway the forum went ahead although I had advised PC Crozier that the threat had been made.

On the night to say I was nervous was an understatement but thankfully nothing untoward took place, even so walking to and from my car was a scary time.

As I mentioned I still occasionally get flash backs to that night and despite not being to blame I still think If I had turned right instead of left Mr Murphy would still be alive. That is a decision that haunts me to this day.

CHAPTER THIRTEEN
REFLECTIONS

HEALTH

In 2008 I faced my biggest ever fight when I was diagnosed with Cancer of the leg.

The first I noticed was the lump in my right leg, I showed to my friend Dr Sangera who immediately referred me to the Spire private hospital in Solihull. The specialist I saw there completed a biopsy and I had to wait three days for the result. I was as nervous as a kitten. The result confirmed that it was cancer. That moment the specialist said, 'its cancer and malignant,' will forever be etched on my mind. You realise you are not invincible but as vulnerable as anyone else.

Although I joked with the specialist at that time, I felt totally on my own, and was, I didn't tell my family or friends and only confided in my son Jon.

Even though I was told it was not life threatening as it was caught early I still felt isolated and vulnerable.

An appointment was made to have the cancer removed by a top surgeon and graft specialist, Remo Papini at The Spire private hospital in Solihull. Remo was based at the Queen Elizabeth Hospital in Birmingham where he dealt with soldiers who came back from Iraq with serious injuries.

He was amazed that I did not want a general anaesthetic, but agreed to my request for a local anaesthetic. The one he chose was the same as that used by the Army when they need to operate in the field. My son took me to the hospital and stayed with me for the duration.

In the theatre I was given the local anaesthetic after Remo said it would sting a bit – now in the word of understatements that was a belter, it hurt like crazy and I did shout out as Remo said 'just a little prick'. I hope he was on about the injection!

Remo then went to work cutting out and grafting a piece of skin from my thigh. He has a nurse on either side of me and unbelievably one was Villa and one Blues. Remo could not believe the banter that was flying around with me and the nurses arguing about football. The Villa nurse fell about when I asked how many times Villa had won the Leyland Daf Trophy?

After he removed the lump and surrounding tissue he took some skin from my thigh and did the skin graft there and then with what sounded like an industrial stapler. Yes they staple the graft to the area. I could hear it but felt nothing.

When it was over he said, 'make sure you do not knock it as the graft has to take'. He should have told that to the nurse who was due to sit me in a wheelchair and take me back to my ward. He pushed me out of the theatre and bashed straight into the door (it must have been the Villa fan) – that also stung a bit.

As I had never had a day off sick in 30 years I was stupidly back in work the next day despite the boss Adam Bridge telling me how stupid I was, but I had not missed a phone in since 1984 and was not about to start now. The following day I was commentating on West Bromwich Albion at the Hawthorns. The Press officer John Simpson was brilliant and provided a box for me to put my leg on as you have to keep it raised to circulate the blood to help the graft take quickly.

At this time I was super fit and went to the Gym every single day, however after the operation Dr Papini said that I had to stay out of the Gym for around six to nine months. I remember the day he gave me the all clear and said OK you can get back in the Gym, but to be honest I couldn't be arsed and haven't been back since.

I have always been reluctant to talk about this cancer problem because so many people have to deal with much worse things. But, thankfully, despite there being a one in four chance of it returning I have been clear with no hint of it since.

Whilst we are on the subject of anaesthetics I must declare having a morbid fear of dentists in my early life. I never went to the dentist and therefore ended up literally taking my own teeth out as they had become so decayed. Fortunately thanks to my Breakfast producer Lisa I found a dentist in Hall Green who offered a specialist service for patients with my type of phobia. I went and he said no problem all we need to do is x y z. I started to get up and said, 'I will make an appointment knowing full well I would not be back.' But he said no and insisted he dealt with me then. He has since retired but I owe him so much.

I now use Keith Rowe in Solihull who is a massive Baggies fan and can now have fillings etc without any local anaesthetic proving that fear is all in the mind. Unless of course you come face to face with a hungry Lion or Tiger.

Like most men of my age I attend regular health check-ups to make sure everything is fine – my cholesterol level is only 3.1 while my blood pressure is perfect and more what you would expect from a top athlete. I once had a heart check-up and the Heart specialist said, 'You might be a Metro on the outside but inside you're a Rolls-Royce!' I am sure he meant well.

I am not on any medication and have never smoked and I am teetotal, and I believe that my lifestyle coupled with the fact that I have played sport all my life has stood me in good stead healthwise in my later years.

However In 2001 while I was on holiday in Spain I suffered from a severe bout of depression. It resulted in me not eating and when I returned to BRMB six weeks later, I was two stone lighter and very gaunt. Everyone thought I was either ill or had a new woman on the go! Neither was correct but it was a dark time in my life and the only time I have ever suffered with this most debilitating of illnesses.

I remember Karren Brady and Trevor Francis both calling me to see what the problem was, but stupidly I put on a brave face and pretended I was fine when in reality I was far from fine. I was just very depressed but felt ashamed because I was. I was told to get a grip or pull myself together by people who did not know what was wrong. There are no outward signs of depression and to be honest I just did not know what to do.

I was back at work on the breakfast show and my producer Guy Jogo knew there was something wrong because I was not my usual strong, tough, bubbly, cheeky, banter self and kept getting tearful for no apparent reason, although I knew it was personal relationships that were the root of the problem.

I did not want to go on to medication but I did speak to a guy at one of the football clubs who was a psychotherapist. He helped me get all the bricks in my life in order.

From that moment I became obsessed with going to the gym. I went every single day of the year including Christmas day after I had finished my Christmas morning breakfast show on Xtra AM/ Capital Gold. Despite being in my early 50s I was super fit and weighing between 10 stone 11 pounds and 11 stone 2 pounds. However despite being at my fittest and healthiest for years I was told by everyone that it didn't suit me and that I looked ill? Work that one out!

I was doing half marathons, 10k and 6k runs for charity and felt as good as I had ever felt in adult life. My eating habits changed completely. I was on pasta, fish, vegetables and fruit. I stayed fit by going to the gym four times a week and that's the way I stayed until I was diagnosed with cancer in my right leg in 2008.

In 2004 I was, according to headlines in the press and on local TV, mugged and ambushed by bandits in Spain. The reality is I was stupid! I can hear you saying, 'no change there then!'

I was travelling from Marbella and was in the Murcia area on the A7 heading towards Alicante when I stopped to fill up at a service station. The muggers/thieves/bandits must have seen me pull in and put my wallet in the centre console of my car. I had just left the service station when a car with a young Arab looking couple in pulled alongside me and started pointing at my rear tyre. I was suspicious at this time, but pulled over and yes I did have a puncture so I relaxed a little. Now what did not register with me is that he pulled in front of me and not behind as most would. I realised afterwards it was so he could get away quickly.

The young man came and started chatting and offered to help me unload my boot, which had all my luggage inside. So me, the nugget that I am, started passing him my bags and cases etc. for him to put inside my car but he was putting them straight into his own car. I happened to look around my car as I was getting the spare tyre out and saw his girlfriend leaning inside my driver's side door. I immediately clocked all was not well and started shouting at them both and I have to say my language was blue to say the least and I charged at them. However they sped off.

I had not been mugged or ambushed but made to look stupid by a pair of opportunist thieves. She had been leaning in and had taken my wallet with around £200 in and all my credit cards. I immediately cancelled them and to be fair they only used one of my cards on a toll road for around £12.

I continued my journey to Moraira and then went to see the Guardia. They knew all about them and said it was lucky I had not confronted them face to face because the man had a knife, which is what he used to puncture my tyre. They were from Libya and had pulled the same trick a number of times. A few months later I was contacted by the Guardia who informed me that they had both been caught and were being sent to prison. To be honest I hope they rot in jail or worse. It was a valuable lesson and from now on if I have an issue I am ringing the Guardia to come and assist.

MARRIAGE

All of my marriage failures have been my fault, as I have been caught offside more times than Emile Heskey. I consider myself to be a success in all areas other than personal relationships. It probably started when as an 18-year-old at Gothic Electrical. I was seeing three girls, two of which worked in the same building! I am not proud of myself or my behaviour.

My first real girlfriend was Pauline Vernon, she was my first love and therefore an important memory and I'm sure that's true for everyone. I met her at my Brother's wedding and danced away to *Then He Kissed Me* by the Ronnettes.

Even before I was married I was dreadful to girls and would be raging if anyone treated my granddaughters the same way. I am ashamed of my behaviour.

I remember one girl binning me when I was 17 and I thought the world of her so for revenge I took her mom out.

Another time I was at a girl's house in Packington Avenue. The moon was out and so were her parents. Now when I say house it was a prefab, which was a bungalow made out of prefabricated slabs. It backed on to the playing fields beside the River Cole. We heard the door and I had to jump out of the window and leg it over the fields stark naked carrying me clothes. I ended up with getting a rash up and down my both legs from the 'stingers'.

I learned early on it's got boobs or wheels it will give you problems – only joking ladies.

However it was at Gothic Electrical in the mid-sixties where I got the chance to continue and develop my lifelong weakness for women that some would call an illness? I was playing the field as most men of 18ish did, but through ignorance, thoughtlessness and a totally selfish attitude I ended up with two girls pregnant at the same time: Christine (technically my first) and Maureen (the first official Mrs Ross).

I was captivated by Maureen's bubbly attitude. Warmth and smile and we got on great. She took me home to meet her Mom and Dad and they were absolutely brilliant to me and made me welcome in their home and fed me most days.

Another girl at Gothic Electrical was Christine who was gorgeous both inside and out and unfortunately for me and her we started flirting or as it would be called now 'flanter' (flirty banter). To my shame I also started seeing her on the QT.

She fell pregnant at the same time I found out Maureen was also pregnant.

When the news got out, there were huge rows, I remember staying with Maureen at her parent's home in Great Barr when Christine and her Mom turned up. It was a mess and I didn't know what to do, as I loved them both. However I was put under great pressure by Christine's parents because of their strict religious beliefs, so much so that I ended up marrying Maureen at the age of 20 in 1968.

I was not and am still not proud of what I did then, in fact I am ashamed of the way I treated them. I did not show them any respect.

I get on well with my ex-wives, Maureen and Avrill to this day. When we split up we made a pact that we would never say anything bad about each other to the children and also in front of family and friends and we will always provide for the kids. The emotional impact for our families has been minimised because there has never been a war between any of us.

I think it is hard these days to commit to 'until death us do part' – life is so different these days, no longer does Granny Sullivan's 'you've made your own bed so lie in it,' have any relevance.

When I decided to marry Maureen and not Christine I was shunned at every opportunity by most of the women while the rest were not shy in asking me out.

If I got into the lift the females would glare and get out or make some comment – It was one of the toughest times in my life. But not as tough as Christine's who was left to face having a baby on her own. It was not until much later that I realised I deserved all their disgust and much more.

I was 'Jack the Lad' and thought I knew it all but in reality I knew nothing. Christine continued with the pregnancy and my first son Mark was born while I married Maureen.

However I wasn't told anything about the birth despite repeatedly asking. Despite not being with Christine I wanted to be a part of Marks life, but I was not allowed to. I am sure it was her parent's influence that kept me in the dark about my son.

However six months later Christine contacted me saying that if I wanted to I could meet up and see my son and I jumped at the chance. So we met up and just walked along the roads with me pushing my son in the pram. However she made it clear her mom and dad would be furious if they knew.

But then just as suddenly, it ended and I never knew why! They just disappeared. I was now married to Maureen and we had my two lovely kids Thomas and Tracy.

Christine eventually gave birth to Mark and I wasn't even told he was born. They kept him from me although I made repeated requests to see him I was turned down. When Mark was around two Christine contacted me and asked if I wanted to see him. I jumped at the chance and saw him a number of times but then just as suddenly it stopped again.

Christine eventually contacted me to tell me she had married and her husband wanted to adopt Mark and said that she was going to do it and that it was the best for Mark. I agreed somewhat reluctantly but the reality is that it was the best for him if not for me. Christine's husband looked after Mark and brought him up and I will always be grateful to him for that. It was important for me that I did not interfere with that relationship-unless Mark wanted to get in touch.

Around 1999 I got a call out of the blue from Christine saying that Mark listened to me every weekend on BRMB doing the football, but didn't know that I was his dad. She asked if I wanted her to tell him and if I wanted to meet him. I said I would prefer her to tell him who his Dad is but only if he wanted to know. She spoke to him and he said he wanted to know who his biological dad was. She called me and said he did want to know so she had told him and he wanted to meet me. I was overjoyed and couldn't wait to see him. I met him and we got on well and I was hopeful we could develop a relationship no matter how late it was. By this time Christine had separated from her husband so I suppose Mark did not feel he was betraying the man who had brought him up.

I took my daughter Tracy to see him the second time because she wanted to meet her 'brother'. They got on great and met up a few times afterwards and then all of a sudden Mark stopped contact with us. Then just as suddenly he stopped contacting me and my daughter. I asked Christine what the problem was and she simply replied that it was his decision so that was that. I have had no contact with Mark since even though I would love to have a relationship with him but it has to be his decision now – he has to make the first move. Sad though it maybe, it's my fault as I was not there for him in his young developing years.

My marriage to Maureen gave me two wonderful children Thomas and Tracy however we split and divorced in 1979 after I had met and fallen for Avrill who was separated at the time and we clicked immediately. She was blonde vivacious and an extremely nice woman. After splitting with Maureen Avrill and I moved into a new house in Sutton Coldfield while my divorce from Maureen was being finalised.

I then married Avrill and had two beautiful children, Jon and Amy. However things started to go wrong in the 2000s and I was drifting and failing once again in my duties as a husband and friend.

In 2009 Avrill decided she had had enough of virtually living on her own due to my working all hours of the day and night and every weekend. We split up and got divorced and I bought her out of the house I still live in. I am delighted that she met someone who is there all the time and give her the life she deserves

My relationship with women – crikey I've done more for the housing market than David Cameron!

I reconnected with Anne whom I had known years before when she worked at BRMB for a while. Her sister Lisa was my producer on the Xtra am and Capital Gold breakfast shows. Anne had moved to London years before and was working at TV Centre. We caught up on one of her visits home and that was that. She moved back to the BBC in Brum and we eventually moved in together.

She is a very strong person and generous to a fault and as well as being in love we get on together despite having the odd fractious moments that any relationship has.

Having said that she has no sense of humour, which is demonstrated by her not liking *Only Fools and Horses*? She is the only person I have met that doesn't like it.

Most importantly she gets on brilliantly with my extended family and they have accepted her into their lives and for that I cannot thank them enough.

Anne is somewhat younger than me, however we get on great and we tied the knot on 25 June 2015 at the 850-year-old St Nicholas Church in Curdworth, just two miles from our Sutton home. It was the most amazing day.

As I had been married before the Catholic Church would not marry us, which begs the question 'where's the forgiveness and understanding that religion promotes?'

We had to visit the church and meet the vicar Josh to persuade him to agree to marry us. It was a daunting meeting however he was brilliant and eventually said yes. I was delighted because I had fallen in love with the church because it is beautiful and this year celebrated its 850th anniversary.

Our Indian vicar, Josh, after agreeing to marry us said that we would have to attend a Wedding Preparation Course which included a rehearsal of the proceedings together with a meeting with a therapist. Let me tell you what happened:

At the wedding rehearsal there is a line 'With my body I endow...' at which point I said 'hard luck Anne' everyone collapsed with laughter including Josh, who then said, 'If you are going to ad lib on the day, can you let me know?' Clearly religious instruction does not include a clear definition of the term ad lib!

When we first met the therapist at the Wedding Preparation Day she asked us to explain how we felt about being at course to which I replied, 'I think it's a complete waste of time'. She thanked me for my honesty and we moved on. If you don't like the answer don't ask the question.

She gave us a questionnaire to answer and what a farce that was and included questions like:

When you were young who did the ironing – Mom or Dad? Give me strength.

Another was, when you were young and went on holiday who did the driving mom or dad – my answer we didn't have holidays or a car.

Or when you were young who did the decorating mom or dad-my answer, the council.

Anyway we got through it especially as one of the other couples were Wolves fans, so we enjoyed some great banter.

Anne decided she wanted the Nat King Cole song L.O.V.E played as we left the church, but Josh explained they didn't play CD's but the choir would learn it and sing it on the big day?

I had visions of Sister Act with Whoopi Goldberg being played out again.

However the choir was absolutely brilliant and sang it superbly! The whole ceremony was brilliant and Josh was funny as well as serious.

Jasper Carrott jokingly said afterwards he wanted him on tour with him.

Freddie, my grandson was the pageboy whose job it was to walk up the aisle with the wedding rings on a small satin cushion.

When we asked him to be a pageboy he said that he didn't want to walk down the aisle, but would scoot up on his scooter? When I said he would have to wear a suit like Granddad's he made it clear he was only going to do it in his Fireman Sam outfit. I had tears rolling down my face just thinking about it.

My Granddaughters, Jessica, Laura, Mia and Joanna were bridesmaids while Amelia and Sophia were flower girls and all were beautiful. We had my two grandsons Freddie and Zacahry as pageboys and they looked so cute and handsome.

Sian Lloyd was Anne's matron of honour. While Adam Bridge and David Salt were our two ushers with my son Jon as my best man

My stag do was a Jolly Boys outing to Ascot Races and what a time we had from start to finish. Great pals and great fun. However we did not see a horse it was that busy.

We arrived at Ascot and had a reserved parking space in gate number eight. We arrived and our driver turned into gate number one. This was where all the toffs went and we could see them picknicking out of the boot of their Rolls Royce's. The gate steward took one look at our mini coach and waved us away rather dismissively.

We bumped into Alex McLeish as my lot drunk themselves to oblivion in the champagne bar. I was the only sober one. The trip back was one long sing song with two of my best pals Paddy Lynch and Mark Hunt in great form – Paddy entertaining his with his super renditions of some classic songs while Mark Hunt had us all in stiches with his brilliant sense of humour.

We arrived back at Marks house and decided it was time to go for a curry in Knowle. So the festivities continued. Despite all the drink only one person fell over in the restaurant – yes you've guessed it me the teetotaller.

The wedding was magical and brilliant from start to finish. We held the reception at the wonderful Moxhull Hall. They provided a never to be forgotten day in terms of service, food etc. but it was the guests that made the day so special. Anne had worked so hard to ensure everything was spot on and it was.

What was special for me was that every single person there was important to us and had made an impact on our lives. All my family were there apart from my sister Cathy who lives in the USA. My Grandchildren were bridesmaids or pageboys and that also made my day.

The guest list was a veritable who's who with Jasper Carrott, Barry Fry, Glyn Purnell, Tony Brown, David Gold, Ian Taylor, Matt Murray, Oliver and James Phelps, all there with their wives and girlfriends. However they were only there because they are our friends and all have played an important part in our lives and are important to Anne and me.

What was most important was to have all my brothers and sisters celebrating with us as well as my children and grandchildren. However the one downside was that my son Mark was not with us.

What made it extra special was to have my great pals Paddy Lynch and Mark Hunt there to share the day with us. We get on so well as a group including our wives. In fact Paddy walked Anne down the aisle as her Dad is no longer with us.

My oldest friend John Duce was there with Eileen his wife and that brought a lump to my throat. We don't see each other all the time but he is always there for me and I am always there for him. I am sure everyone has a friend like this. There were too many friends to mention individually but again they were there because they are important to Anne and I.

My son Jon was my best man and he was brilliant from organising the stag do to his speech on the day. He was last on speaking and started rather hesitantly and I felt for him but it was all an act. He suddenly said, 'Salty lets go,' and from under the table grabbed a pair of headphones and put them on. They were ones I use for commentating. My programme intro music started and so did he with a parody of me starting a programme with him talking about my past marriages with two defeats it was hilarious. He also played some clips of things that I had said that out of context that were funny. He absolutely nailed it and got a standing ovation after making everyone laugh so much. Just brilliant and so confident. I wonder where he gets that from?

I am as happy as I have been for many years and I am also so happy that Christine, Avrill and Maureen are also content and happy with their respective new partners.

FAMILY

I have four great kids that I am immensely proud of, who have definitely inherited the 'Ross Resilience' as each of them have had to deal with real issues in their lives and they have come through it stronger than ever – each of them is a great person.

They have all had to deal with either health problems within their families or difficult personal relationships

When we were writing this book Keith asked me the question: 'How would your kids describe you?' he was always asking me questions like that – blooming difficult!

Anyway my answer was that I would hope they would consider me to be straight, honest, fair and loving.

My grandchildren are a joy to me and I have plenty of them:

John is married to Emma and they have a daughter Amelia and a baby boy Jackson.

Amy has Mia, Freddie and Zachary.

Tracy is married to Nik and they have two daughters Jessica and Laura.

Thomas has a new partner Samantha and has four children Luke, Thomas, Sophia and Joanna.

So by my reckoning that's a total of 11 and every one of them is fantastic although it did add to the cost of my wedding to Anne while Christmas is a financial nightmare (Only joking).

ME

I would describe myself as a 'Man's Man who much prefers the company of women', by that I mean I am more comfortable in their company. I have never been entirely comfortable with expressing my love for someone. It is just the way I was brought up. Add that to my natural stubbornness, being a Taurean, and you can see why I very rarely said, 'I love you'. However I do show love by deeds and actions. As Big Ron Atkinson says, 'Don't tell me, show me', even though that was football related, it still applies in personal relationships.

If asked to define what love is, I would say it is all about mutual respect and trust. Something I have not been good at as my broken marriages and relationships would testify.

I am now content and happy with my life. I know Anne wants me to be more tactile and that's difficult for her because she knows it is difficult for me but she says I am getting better.

I do send flowers and always remember her birthday and perhaps more importantly bearing in mind the failure of my previous relationships I spend more time at home and I believe we are both content with the way we are.

I am usually a good judge of character and I make that judgement the instant I meet someone. I cannot be two faced with people. If I like you then fine, if I don't I have to keep away. It's the way I am and the only way I can be true to myself. I cannot stand those people who are nice to your face and slag you off behind your back.

I hate hypocrisy. I would do anything for my friends if possible. I don't like falseness in people and won't tolerate it.

I have lots of acquaintances in my life, most that I like a lot but I don't have very many close friends – because I don't let people into my life easily but they know who they are.

I insist on paying my way when out with rich friends. As we say in Brum I will always stand my corner. Thankfully my pals realise this and so we get along brilliantly.

With me what you see is what you get.

CHAPTER FOURTEEN
THE GAME'S GONE

So why in my opinion has the game gone?

I have made and continue to make my living out of football. I love the game with a passion and cannot understand those who say they don't like the game.

Over my 35 years I have witnessed, especially since the birth of the Premier League in 1992, clubs losing touch with their fans.

Fans are now viewed as customers, which in football boardrooms is no more than a revenue stream. The gap between the fans needs and the clubs needs is now a chasm.

The money-mad people involved, either in staying in the Premier League or getting into the Premier League, have forgotten what the game is really all about: the fans.

Just look at the corruption within FIFA and if you wanted a definition of an oxymoron then FIFA ethics committee would be perfect. And it's all caused by the 'love of money'. Whenever money is involved there will be problems and corruption.

But there is also corruption within our own domestic game as players and managers are tapped up to move clubs despite it being illegal.

We have the problem of diving and general cheating during games, as players believe they are above the laws of the game and the laws of the land.

The only answer we get to it all is, 'that's football'.

Without supporters there is no Premier League, no multi-billion pound TV deals and no obscene wages. There is now a massive and growing gap between the needs and wants of a club and those of its loyal fans.

On one side of the gap the clubs and players are in a money-making business, while on the other side the fans are all about history, tradition, glory, passion and winning trophies.

I hope the former West Ham United manager Sam Allardyce had sleepless nights after seeing that young Hammers fan distressed and crying in the stands watching his team get stuffed 5–0 by Nottingham Forest in the FA Cup.

I am sure Sam picked a team he knew would probably be beaten and that is unforgivable because he wanted to concentrate on staying in the Premier League – ironically he ended up getting the sack anyway.

One of the most distressing interviews for me was with Villa boss Paul Lambert, who made it clear to me before the game against Sheffield United, that staying in the Premier League was more important than the FA Cup to him, the owners and players.

I have to admit it was the saddest interview I have ever been involved with in more than 30 years of talking to managers in this area. Paul was sacked not long afterwards.

However, is he to blame or are he and others just victims of this preoccupation with money the Premier League has created?

In my opinion, the formation of the Premier League was the start of the problem, and subsequently created this money monster that has infected and indoctrinated all those involved in it so that 'ker-ching' is all that matters to owners, managers, players and agents alike.

The Premier League does not appear to be interested in the FA Cup or the Capital One Cup because those competitions don't affect their TV negotiations.

I am sick and tired of those who ask 'would you rather win the cup and be relegated or stay in the Premier League?' You don't get a choice!

Blues won the Carling Cup, Wigan won the FA Cup and both went down.

However, they were not relegated because they won the cups but because they were not good enough over 38 games to stay in the Prem.

They could have been relegated and not won the cup.

I bet any manager, including Sam Allardyce and Paul Lambert, would want around 100 tickets for family and friends if they ever reached a Wembley final but not so many for any Premier League game?

It would appear that history, family tradition, Love, emotion, passion no longer come into the clubs equation until it comes to trading on fans affinity to the team. Then all those things become a revenue stream.

Bizarrely the more money the clubs get from TV rights deals the more they want from their supporters when the reality is they could afford to charge lower prices instead of increasing them. This is definitely more prevalent in the Premier League, but some championship clubs have forgotten which side their bread is buttered.

Fans are being asked to pay ridiculous prices for match-day tickets because the owners and chairmen of clubs have paid obscene wages and fees to players and agents. It's not the fans fault.

In 1990 when Greg Dyke met with the top five clubs when he was running London Weekend Television and said he only wanted to show their games and did they not want to share the money between themselves.

Bizarrely Greg Dyke is currently the Chairman of the FA and took great delight in telling us his plans to improve the game when he was one of the men instrumental in starting the problem.

However his meeting with those five clubs was without doubt where the seeds for the birth of the Premier League were sown. By 1992 the top clubs (First Division) had agreed to break away from the Football League and form the Premier League and negotiate their own TV deal. This was football's equivalent of George Orwell's *Animal Farm* because eventually the bigger clubs got more of the money and grew more powerful.

When they started the Premier League it was a two fingers to the remaining 72 clubs.

Since then the Premier Leagues love of money has affected the rest of football and no one seems to give a damn about it.

For example the smaller clubs used to develop players and sell them and that would help to keep them going. However the Academy system has virtually stopped that happening. Now the Tier One academies can go into smaller clubs academies and just steal their best players and only have to pay a nominal amount. Southampton developed Theo Walcott and Gareth Bale and sold them for multi millions of pounds. That could not happen today.

Now if academies have foreign youngsters in from an early age they can class them as home-grown. An example of this is the Manchester City's 19-year-old star youngster Kelechi Iheanacho born in Nigeria moved to Manchester from the Taye Academy in Nigeria in 2014 at the age of 17. However because City registered him as a youngster he is classed as home grown? Utter nonsense in my opinion.

Everything is geared to the Premier League and in particular the bigger, richer clubs. The Premier League will earn around £13 billion from domestic and foreign TV rights deals next season (2016–17).

It has been taken over by greed and the love of money. As fans become nothing more than customers and the game becomes a brand or product whose only use is to produce as much revenue as possible for those in it.

For those managers and clubs that would say I am wrong and that they do care about their fans then why do they continue to disrespect the Football League Cup and the FA Cup? If they really cared about the history and tradition and the fans needs they would always play their strongest team. However the need to amass enough points to stay in the Premier League or reach a Champions League place for the financial benefits far outweighs cup glory for the supporters.

The amount of money in the game has also seen the birth of the football agent who is only in it because of the wealth and abundance of cash. They would be nowhere near the game if there was no money in it. These parasites feed off the game and fuel the player's greed. I believe they are only in it for their own interests and not the clubs or the fans. It is not in their best interest for a player to stay at a club. The more moves a player makes the more money the agents make. I am sure there are some good ones in the game but I would think it's a tough job finding them.

I have had managers tell me of agents who would get everything done in a transfer including the medical and personal terms. However before letting the player sign the contract they would tell the club now you have to sort my fee out and that could be hundreds of thousands of pounds for some big transfers.

The TV money is so large that it could and should be shared more equally across the whole of football from grass roots and also The Championship and Leagues One and Two.

I laugh every time they announce a new multi-billion pound TV rights deal because all that happens is that it goes straight to players and agents. So there is more money than ever coming into the game and yet the clubs have never been poorer. Work that one out?

There is nothing wrong with the 90 minutes, however it's all the rubbish that goes on around the game that is taking football further away from the normal everyday fan.

Therefore, with that in mind, here we go with what I believe would improve the game.

First up. I would line up every player's agent against a wall and shoot the lot of them. Well perhaps that is a bit over the top. OK then, just drop them off on a deserted island with no hope of getting off. In my opinion, these parasites have caused so much trouble in the game; they unsettle players, hold managers to ransom, and have almost single-handedly raised the transfer fees and wages to the ridiculous levels they are now. It's true that chairmen and owners could say no to the obscene demands, however, quite often, they are put in difficult situations by the tactics of the agents. They also take huge amounts out of the game in the shape of their astronomical fees. Fees for what? For touting a player around, and in most cases even when that players is under contract at a club. The only people getting rich are the players and agents and very often with foreign players the money not only goes out of the game but out of the country.

Next I would get rid of the referee's assessors who in my opinion have done more harm to the game and to referees than Joey Barton and his like ever did. NO two games are the same, every single game is a unique event, NO two tackles or fouls are ever the same, so why should we have a situation where referees have to rigidly apply a set of laws and instructions to every individual situation? So get rid of the assessor and allow the referee to use his discretion to judge each situation on its merits. I believe that would make the game better and improve the relationship between the officials and the managers, players and fans. True, the referee would still make mistakes, but he does now anyway.

Eventually goal-line technology was introduced but why stop there. Use video replays to help the referee come to the correct decision but only in game changing incidents such as penalties and violent conduct. This would help the referee to eliminate crucial game influencing mistakes.

I like the idea of a sin bin, as in my opinion it would mean players who have had two yellow cards for minor offences get a 5–10 minute cooling off period. Let's face it, when it's eleven against eleven it's invariably a better game. This would mean that players would only be thrown out of a game for serious violent play or something similar.

I would try and restrict the kick off times to 3pm Saturdays with one on Sunday at 4pm and one Monday at 8pm.

The TV money should be more evenly spread around the game to include all 92 clubs. The way the money is divided now means the fat cats keep on getting fatter, while smaller clubs, who in many cases develop players that the bigger cubs sign, are always living on the breadline and in some cases going out of business. This means that there is a huge gap even within the Premier League between the top teams and the rest. That is not healthy for the game.

I would make the Champions League a straight knock out competition again. Surely, that would make it more exciting for the fans and reduce the number of games played which is one of the biggest complaints from the top managers. Let's face it, it's only a league format because they can play more games for TV and earn more revenue.

I would insist that part of the TV revenue goes to reduce admission prices to an affordable level especially for kids to ensure that we continually create a new generation of fans.

Getting rid of the transfer windows would be high on my agenda, as I believe they favour the bigger clubs and are useful to agents who want transfer fees as inflated as possible

I would drop off ex-Belgian footballer Jean Marc Bosman on the same island as the agents. The Bosman ruling has also contributed to the sorry state of the game where agents can abuse the ruling to persuade players not to sign new contracts. They can then hold the club to financial ransom about a new deal or if they do move, they can demand huge signing on fees as a free agent. That allows the agent to secure himself another huge wedge for doing nothing more that advising a player not to sign a contract. Remember the club may have paid millions for the player and yet he can walk away for free.

I would insist that the Professional Footballers Association become tough on those of their members who seriously bring the game into disrepute. The union in my opinion has been toothless and shown an unwillingness to publicly condemn or take any action against any of its members who transgress. I believe that the union's leader, Gordon Taylor, holds the key to improving behaviour on and off the pitch. The threat of their membership being taken away would have a huge impact on their behaviour.

I might also scrap the financial fair play act as I don't see how it is fair to smaller clubs and really only helps the fat cats get fatter.

Sports scientists also do my head in; having said that they are really nice people and I am talking about the job not the individual. They decide just how long a player can train, how long he can last in a game etc. Who the hell are these people? They would be nowhere near the game if there was no money in it.

I am sure they have a place in the game, but for the life of me I can't see it. But it seems it's fashionable for clubs to have them.

I have known players who were not the best trainers but when it came to Saturday they did the business? Yet sports scientists would be advising managers not to pick them. I am old fashioned I know but if you keep telling a player often enough that he is tired eventually he will be tired.

I understand that players are athletes these days and the demands physically during a game are great but don't try and tell me a player can't play Saturday-Wednesday-Saturday. However if you keep telling him he can't then he will believe you.

It might be controversial but I would scrap the academy system, which only looks like an industry set up to create jobs for college coaches with badges but not necessarily experience at playing professionally. It's geared to helping the bigger tier one academies anyway.

I believe the players that have come through the academy would still come through, but quicker and better prepared for life as a professional were they to work and train with professional players' day in and day out.

Academies take on hundreds of youngsters most of whom don't make it through to the professional level. They need to have so many players to fill teams for academy games. So they also end up disappointing lots of youngsters who think they have made it just by being in an academy

I honestly don't believe academy players are prepared for the step up from academy football to the first team when it matters and you have a responsibility to the team, the fans, and the club and not just to yourself. I can almost hear the academy coaches saying I have no idea what I am talking about

Are they tough enough physically and mentally? I am not sure they are.

My dreams of course, but the reality is the game won't change – in fact I can only see more cottage industries growing within the game, why? Because there is money in it.

I would like to ask every single member of FIFA and UEFA as well as every owner, manager and player to take note of the following words by a genuine football legend, Sir Bobby Robson.

> *'What is a club in any case? Not the buildings or the directors or the people who are paid to represent it.*
> *'It's not the television contracts, get-out clauses, marketing departments or executive boxes.*
> *'It's the noise, the passion, the feeling of belonging, the pride in your city.*
> *'It's a small boy clambering up stadium steps for the very first time,*

gripping his father's hand, gawping at that hallowed stretch of turf beneath him and, without being able to do a thing about it, falling in love.'

We fans want our game back. A game where generations of our families went week in, week out.

A game where the 90 minutes created heroes who we adored from the terraces. A game that created the emotion, excitement and passion that we thrived on and made us fans for life.

A game where the club's directors, managers, players and fans eagerly awaited the FA Cup third-round day.

A game where players and fans had a special relationship and that is why we remember them with a special fondness that is usually reserved for family.

Never has the game been so out of touch with its fans, but the saddest fact of all is that it has all but certainly gone for good and will never return to what it was.

When eventually I pop off this mortal coil (now don't get excited), I want my epitaph to be 'The Game's Gone and Now I Have.'